WOMEN'S WORK AND IDENTITY
IN EIGHTEENTH-CENTURY BRITTANY

Dedicated to William Beik

scholar, mentor and friend

Women's Work and Identity in Eighteenth-Century Brittany

NANCY LOCKLIN
Maryville College, USA

ASHGATE

Published by
Ashgate Publishing Limited
Gower House
Croft Road
Aldershot
Hampshire GU11 3HR
England

Ashgate Publishing Company
Suite 420
101 Cherry Street
Burlington, VT 05401-4405
USA

Ashgate website: http://www.ashgate.com

British Library Cataloguing in Publication Data
Locklin, Nancy
Women's work and identity in eighteenth-century Brittany
    1. Women – France – Brittany – History – 18th century 2. Women – France – Brittany – Social conditions – 18th century 3. Work and family – France – History – 18th century 4. Brittany (France) – History – 18th century 5. Brittany (France) – Social conditions – 18th century
    I. Title
    305.4'89623'09441

Library of Congress Cataloging-in-Publication Data
Locklin, Nancy.
    Women's work and identity in eighteenth-century Brittany / by Nancy Locklin.
        p. cm.
    Includes bibliographical references.
    ISBN 978-0-7546-5819-1 (alk. paper)
    1. Women—France—Brittany—History—18th century—Sources. 2. Women—France—Brittany—Social conditions. 3. Work and family—France—Brittany—History—18th century—Sources. 4. Brittany (France)—History—18th century—Sources. 5. Brittany (France)—Social conditions—18th century. I. Title.

HQ1619.B75L63 2007
305.430944'10933—dc22

2006102511

ISBN: 978-0-7546-5819-1

Printed and bound in Great Britain by Antony Rowe Ltd, Chippenham, Wiltshire.

Contents

List of Maps

List of Tables

Acknowledgments

In the time it has taken me to complete this project I have accumulated a multitude of debts. The most obvious of these have been financial, and I would like to acknowledge the support of the History Department of Emory University, first in their having awarded me a University Fellowship, and for their additional support in the form of a J. Russell Major award in Early Modern History and the offer, which I declined, of a Fifth-Year Fellowship; I would also like to thank the Business Association of my home town of Bellingham, Massachusetts, for the scholarship that helped pay for one of my first excursions to France; and I would like to acknowledge the key support of a Fulbright Research grant which allowed me to live and work in France for a year. In order to prepare the manuscript for publication, I returned to France with the assistance of a Research Travel Award from the Society for French Historical Studies.

The personal debts are the most important and also the most difficult to adequately express. I have been able to complete this project in large part because of the patient and friendly staff members who helped me wade through the municipal and departmental archives of Brittany, especially those at the Archives départmentales d'Ille-et-Vilaine and the Archives départmentales de la Loire-Atlantique. I am especially grateful for the guidance of Professor Jean Tanguy, at the Université de Haute Bretagne in Brest, and for the assistance of James Collins, who shared his extensive knowledge of Breton archives, institutions, and scholarship with me. I would like to thank Julie Hardwick for long brainstorming lunches while we were both working in Nantes. I would like to thank Nina Kushner for her thoughtful questions and infectious enthusiasm. I would like to thank Merry Wiesner-Hanks for her ongoing support and friendship; Sharon Strocchia for her kind and patient insistence on excellence during the dissertation; and William Beik for his attention, care, and guidance. I would like to thank my parents, Muriel Hénault Locklin and Francis G. Locklin, Jr., for their love and encouragement through a long and confusing educational experience. And finally, I would like to thank Doug Sofer for laughs and hugs, comfort when I panicked, long phone calls while we were apart, and black bean soup when we were together.

Introduction

Every morning, I arrived outside the doors of the Archives Dèpartmentale d'Ile-et-Vilaine in Rennes a few minutes before the doors opened to researchers. Most days, a certain genealogist arrived at the same time and, after an appropriate period of nodding acquaintance, we began to pass the time in friendly conversation. One day, he ventured to ask about my research. I told him I studied women's work in the old regime. He was confused. I told him I studied women who had worked for wages or who had had professions. He was interested, and asked for examples. I listed a few of the most common occupations I had encountered in the tax rolls of Brittany—*marchande, tailleuse, fileuse,* and *lingere.*[1] At this, he laughed good-naturedly. "*Lingere is* not a profession," he explained, "My grandmother was a *lingere!*"

My acquaintance at the archive was expressing a fair enough generalization; women in previous generations did not have professions or jobs in the same ways that men did. At the very least, women were not, and perhaps still are not, identified primarily by their work. The elderly genealogist was not denying that his grandmother had regularly worked for wages for most of her life. We have no reason to assume he was negating her importance or questioning her contribution. He was simply stating that she was a grandmother—*his* grandmother—first and foremost. To think of her in any other way, to re-categorize her based primarily upon the work she did, seemed absurd to him. Furthermore, to impart significance to her work was equally absurd. Her primary identity in his view was "grandmother," and so her work and her work identity simply did not matter.

In spite of our best efforts, historians are hard-pressed to escape the same narrow view when thinking about women in the past. After decades of research and scholarly debate, we know much about women. We know about the many legal limitations on women, their economic vulnerability, and the obstacles they encountered under patriarchal authority. We lament that women were defined primarily by their sex and that their lives were shaped by gendered expectations. Thus, we know, their contributions, their multidimensional roles and activities, their own identities, were lost under the artificial categories that scholars used to describe them. And yet, in order to find their lost voices, we also identify women almost exclusively by their sex and by our own assumptions about women and their experiences. In doing so, we risk losing sight of the rich variety of their lives.

This is a study of women in the early modern French province of Brittany, their work, their lives, their rights, their tragedies, and their triumphs. This is a case study of a particular region during a specific time, and yet I hope to join with other regional case studies that challenge the accepted models of women's history. Much scholarship has produced evidence that women were marginalized and wholly defined by the

---

1   The professions are: *marchande* (merchant), *tailleuse* (tailor), *fileuse* (spinner), and *lingere* (a mixture of seamstress, embellisher, and linens merchant).

household, but it is clear now that the picture is much more complicated. Maxine Berg and Pamela Sharpe, studying gender, work, and economics in England, reveal a range of possibilities for women's lives in the seventeenth, eighteenth and nineteenth centuries.[2] Women worked at every level of the economy, serving themselves and their families as opportunities allowed. Judith Coffin and Clare Crowston, describing the seamstresses of Paris in separate and very different studies, illustrate self-awareness, determination, and organization among women in that group.[3] Monica Chojnacka recently explored the lives of women in early modern Venice. Her study shows that even in strongly patriarchal Italian cities, women's lives were richer and more complex than we could have imagined.[4] All of these scholars, and many others, have opened our eyes to the truly rich history of women.

I would like to continue their work on the subject of women by proposing a slightly radical experiment: while studying women, we must try to ignore the fact that our subjects are women. This will help our work in a number of ways. First and foremost, it will expand our available sources. I found I was most successful in the archives when I stopped looking for women. By that, I mean I stopped looking for women workers; instead, I looked for workers and found the women among them. I looked for heirs, for taxpayers, for criminals, for parishioners, and so on. When I went searching for women, I found very little. But, when I chose some other category to frame my research, the sources revealed what I needed to know. I believe that this approach has given me a clear view of what women did and how they fit into the bigger picture.

The second advantage we gain by ignoring that our subjects are women is that by doing so we may be able to shed modern ideas that, unbeknownst to us, are impeding our judgment. It is too easy to let assumptions cloud our vision when it comes to studying the past. Alain Croix, a leading historian of Brittany, once described the "humiliating situation" of out-of-town merchants seeking to sell their wares in the port of Saint-Malo at the turn of the eighteenth century.[5] These outsiders were dependent upon local women who guided them to potential customers and kept them informed of inspection and shipping schedules. Given our knowledge about men and women in the past, it seems reasonable to assume that the men found it humiliating to

---

2   Maxine Berg, *The Age of Manufacture 1700–1820* (New York: Oxford University Press, 1986) and "What Difference Did Women's Work Make to the Industrial Revolution?" *Historical Workshop Journal*, 35 (Spring 1993): 22–44; Pamela Sharpe, "Literally Spinsters: A New Interpretation of Local Economy and Demography in Colyton in the Seventeenth and Eighteenth Centuries," *European History Review*, 44 (1991):. 46–65; and "Gender in the Economy: Female Merchants and Family Business in the British Isles, 1600–1850," *Histoire Sociale/ Social History*, 34:67 (November 2001): 283–306.

3   Judith Coffin, "Gender and the Guild Order: The Garment Trades in Eighteenth-Century Paris," *The Journal of Economic History*, 54:4 (December 1994): 768–93; Clare Haru Crowston, *Fabricating Women: The Seamstresses of Old Regime France, 1675–1791* (Durham: Duke University Press, 2001).

4   Monica Chojnacka, *Working Women of Early Modern Venice* (Baltimore: Johns Hopkins University Press, 2000).

5   Alain Croix, *L'age d'or de la Bretagne, 1532-1675* (Rennes: Éditions Ouest-France, 1993), p. 160.

be so dependent upon women. However, the actual source for this example suggests nothing of the sort. On the contrary, the influential merchant Monsieur La Lande Magon describes the situation in positive terms in a letter to the *Contrôleur Générale* of Finances in 1701.[6] La Lande Magon wrote the letter to protest the imposition of a new fee on outside merchants since the fee, added to what the merchants already paid informally to their intermediaries, would be a financial burden and contrary to "healthy commerce." Historian Andre Lespagnol cited the letter as an example of how outside merchants were at a disadvantage in the marketplace, hence their need for guides.[7] Croix simply read his own interpretation into the example, and described the situation as "humiliating."

Even those of us seeking to restore women's agency would benefit from some distance. Rene Marion raised an excellent question in her comments following a conference panel ostensibly on the subject of "women's networks" in early modern France. Ten years ago, the concept of women's networks held great promise as a way of showing that women recognized their mutual vulnerability and sought to help one another, thwarting the oppressiveness of a patriarchal society. The recent conference panel was an attempt to revisit that theme. However, all of the papers, including my own, offered multiple examples of the ways in which women *did not* operate in networks. Women helped each other in a variety of ways, to be sure. As often as not, though, they competed with one another, exploited one another, even attacked one another, driven by economic, social, and familial motivations that had little or nothing to do with their gender. The networks we found, if we found any, seemed to have as much to do with class and status as with sex. Marion suggested, then, that the very idea of 'women's networks' was less useful than we had originally thought. Our original intention to look specifically for networks of women nearly blinded us to the multiple networks in operation.[8]

We do women a disservice by defining them exclusively by gender. If we studied women as workers and producers, as consumers, as neighbors, as heirs, etc., we could get a much clearer picture of women's complex realities. Identity is a complicated matter. Gender can be a key component of identity, but sometimes other aspects of identity emerge as the most significant, defining characteristics.

I am not proposing that we entirely discard the category of "woman." I am, of course, studying women in early modern Brittany as a group, and I am doing so with awareness that their experiences were likely to have been different from those of men in the same period. I am also not denying what years of scholarship have revealed about women's lives in the past: their generally lower legal status, their economic and sexual vulnerability, and their outright exclusion from a variety of institutions in most western societies since the Roman Empire. I am not denying that

---

6   Letter of 1 May 1701, printed in A.M. Boislisle's *Correspondance des contrôleurs généraux des finances avec les intendants des provinces* (Paris: Imprimerie Nationale, 1883), p. 73.

7   André Lespagnol, *Messieurs de Saint-Malo* (Rennes: Presses Universitaires, 1997), p. 441.

8   The panel, "Urban Women's Communities in the 18th and 19th Centuries," was part of the annual meeting of the Society for French Historical Studies in Milwaukee, Wisconsin (2003).

both men and women in the past used gender as a defining category, and had largely different notions of what that category meant. I am arguing, however, for a more nuanced understanding of what their lives were like. To achieve that, I believe we must put aside much of the baggage we have created for ourselves.

A number of interrelated debates have shaped women's history since its inception. A key feature was the idea that women had once enjoyed a "golden age" of economic equality and had since suffered some kind of cataclysmic decline. This decline has been located by some scholars during the fifteenth and sixteenth centuries, just when male-dominated Europe was undergoing a Renaissance.[9] Multiple studies have outlined the steps taken by guilds, reformers, intellectuals and a variety of authorities in that age to expel women from commerce and industry, quiet their voices, and remove them from public life.[10] Other scholars alternatively located the decline somewhat later, with the advent of capitalism and other economic changes that took work out of the family home and therefore away from women.[11] The overall decline in women's status was credited therefore to a number of changes including economic, philosophical, and political factors. Taken apart or together, these changes led to the downfall of women across Europe. The resulting picture was a bleak one.

An alternative view suggests that there is more continuity than change in women's history; if possible, this is an even bleaker view than the image of an all-encompassing decline in fortunes. According to the "continuity" school of thought, women have been subordinate in every age without relief, consistently at the mercy of the patriarchy. "Within each group of men and women—whether the group is structured by commonalities of race, class, sexuality or whatever—women as a group are disempowered compared to men of their group," writes Judith Bennet.[12]

Both views have been tempered in recent years by a high number of regional case studies that call into question our ability to make sweeping generalizations. It is clear that not all women suffered the same fate, suffered to the same extent, or suffered at

---

9   Joan Kelly denies that the term Renaissance had any meaning for women and that women's history must be periodized according to watersheds in their own spheres. "Did Women Have a Renaissance?" in *Becoming Visible: Women in European History*, Bridenthal and Koonz, eds. (Boston: Houghton-Mifflin, 1977). Most women's historians have also been informed by Alice Clark's classic, *The Working Life of Women in the 17th Century* (London: 1919).

10   Several such studies will be discussed below, among them Martha C. Howell, *Women, Production and Patriarchy in Late Medieval Cities* (Chicago: The University of Chicago Press, 1986); Lyndal Roper, *The Holy Household: Women and Morals in Reformation Augsburg* (London: Clarendon Press, 1989); and Natalie Zemon Davis, "Women in the Crafts in Sixteenth-Century Lyon," in *Women and Work in Preindustrial Europe*, Barbara A. Hanawalt, ed. (Bloomington: Indiana University Press, 1986).

11   Examples of such studies include Caroline Barron, "The 'Golden Age' of Women in Medieval London," *Reading Medieval Studies*, 15 (1990); Susan Cahn, *Industry of Devotion: The Transformation of Women's Work in England, 1500-1660* (New York: Columbia University Press, 1987); and, Ivy Pinchbeck, *Women Workers and the Industrial Revolution, 1750–1850* (London: Virago, 1981).

12   Judith Bennett, "Women's History, a Study in Continuity and Change," *Women's Work: The English Experience 1650-1914*, Pamela Sharpe, ed. (London: Arnold 1998), p. 62.

all. In the early eighteenth century in Breton cities, for example, some women saw their fortunes increase, some suffered a decline, and some seemed as well off as earlier generations. Specifics of class, trade, and family make generalizations nearly impossible. There is continuity and there is change, and we must be very cautious of how we assess the situation.

A couple of other ongoing debates within history deserve mention as they have greatly informed my research. One is the theory of "women's work": how is it that women consistently seem to work at particular trades? Women's work often includes cloth and clothing production and care, food preparation and sales, junk sales, and the care of small children and sick people. Most studies of women's work across Europe during the early modern era reveal the almost universal nature of this pattern. One explanation is that there is a cultural link between women, food, and cloth based in human reproductive biology. Judith Brown proposed a simple key for the establishment of women's work in "Note on the Division of Labor by Sex."[13] In ancient and primitive societies, women could be best relied upon for labor that was compatible with childcare. Women's work had to be easily interrupted, consistent with a safe environment for children, and not require great concentration or much travel. Typically, these requirements translated into preparation of food and clothing. Thus, textiles were the responsibility of women in ancient and classical societies around the world.[14] Women were the cloth-makers of folklore and mythology for ages after textiles had become a commodity on a grand scale, even when commercial production was largely male-dominated. Certain activities, such as spinning and lace making, have never lost their connotations of femininity. The biological-cultural theory of women's work is definitely related to the "continuity" school of thought, claiming as it does that women were relegated to certain tasks since the beginning of human civilization due to reproductive function.

A variation of the continuity theory, offered by Margaret Hunt, is based upon the continuities of political and social patriarchy.[15] Hunt denies that reproductive needs were a constraint on women in the early modern period. Many women had no children, and childcare was often "less of a problem than it is today."[16] The real problem was that patriarchal families channeled funds to serve the needs of male individuals, making the needs of female members secondary. If women dominated a limited range of occupations, it was because their access to resources was cut off by patriarchal family practices.

Judith Bennett supports Hunt's view but places the blame outside of individual families. In her book, *Ale, Beer and Brewsters: Women's Work in a Changing World, 1300–1600*, Bennett denies that women were blatantly forced out of commercial brewing as it became a profitable and prestigious trade. Rather, she tells a story of "remarkable stability," showing that women's work was in "stasis" while the

13 in *American Anthropologist*, 72 (1970): 1075–6.

14 Elizabeth Wayland Barber, *Women's Work: The First 20,000 Years* (New York: W.W. Norton & Co., 1994), pp. 30–31.

15 Margaret Hunt, *The Middling Sort: Commerce, Gender, and the Family in England, 1680–1780* (Berkeley: University of California Press, 1996), pp. 83, 136–7, 146.

16 Hunt, *The Middling Sort*, p. 136.

world around them changed.[17]   Bennett claims that the one constant is women's oppression and shows how women are *always* in low-skilled, low-status, and low-paying jobs. If women brewed ale, it was not due to any biological or cultural link to food production, but due to that trade's low status and profit.

A similar pattern may be found in the history of textile production. Women workers, found in all levels of linen production and sales, were less often found in wool-related trades in any European town after the Middle Ages. By then, wool commanded much higher profits and prestige for producers than other kinds of cloth, and the wool trades were almost always organized into formal, hierarchical, and patriarchal guilds. By the early modern period, "draperie," the prestigious trade in high-end whole cloth, was closed to all women but well-connected widows. This illustrates a process by which "women's work" ceases to belong to women as soon as it becomes profitable.[18]

Worse yet, women were so often relegated to low-skilled and low-status work that women apparently had the power to taint certain tasks just by performing them. Scholars such as Merry Wiesner and Jean Quataert have found that certain women's professions were considered dishonorable by working men specifically because of their identification with the household.[19]   This continuity in women's low status, then, gives lie to the whole notion of "women's work." Since work and its meaning change with the economic and political situation, one would be hard-pressed to insist that women work at "traditional" trades.

Even so, the concept of "women's work" is a useful one for the purposes of this study. It was in the so-called "traditional occupations" that Breton women found the means to support themselves. According to tax records, between 61 and 66 percent of women working in large towns in the eighteenth century were involved with food or clothing trades. In small towns and villages, the percentage of women working with food or textiles was higher, typically around 75 percent, presumably because there were fewer jobs that did not involve these household skills. To be fair, the opportunities for workers in the linen industry are not surprising in Brittany. The Breton linen trade commanded worldwide attention in the seventeenth and eighteenth centuries and offered great opportunities for both men and women. Thus, perhaps the prevalence of women in textiles in Brittany has more to do with the needs of the local industry than with the cultural association of women and textiles. However, the rest of the "traditional" women's occupations are equally well represented.

---

17   Judith Bennett, *Ale, Beer and Brewsters: Women's Work in a Changing World, 1300-1600* (Oxford: Oxford University Press, 1996), p. 7.

18   Martha Howell, "Women, the Family Economy, and the Structure of Market Production in Cities of Northern Europe During the Late Middle Ages," in *Women and Work in Pre-industrial Europe*, Barbara Hanawalt, ed. (Bloomington: Indiana University Press, 1986), p. 204.

19   Merry Wiesner, " 'A Learned Task and Given to Men Alone': The Gendering of Tasks in Early Modern German Cities," *Journal of Medieval and Renaissance Studies*, 25/1 (1995): 89–106; and Jean Quataert, "The Shaping of Women's Work in Manufacturing: Guilds, Households, and the State in Central Europe, 1648–1870," *American Historical Review*, 90:5 (December 1985): 1122–48.

Both the biological-cultural and patriarchal theories are severely limited as explanations for the continuity of women's work and status. The social, legal, and institutional limitations facing women were real, but hardly all-encompassing. While patriarchal institutions and conventions may have hampered some women, other women managed to navigate and even manipulate their situation. In 1746, Marie Jaquette Anquetil wrote to her husband, who was away on a shipping venture in Peru, that the previous owner of her shop in Saint-Malo was pressuring her to sell it back to him. The man harassed her so badly that Anquetil had to file a suit in order to deal with him. "You see the grief a woman gets for not having a man," she wrote, "But God blessed me, for the more I cried, the more was yielded to me." We see, then, not only Anquetil's consciousness of her situation, but her reliance upon the mercy of male authorities and the power, if we may call it that, of her tears.[20]

The idea of women's work, or of "separate spheres" for men and women, is not only useful to historians but was also useful to early modern women. Judith Coffin and Clare Crowston have both demonstrated how the seamstresses of eighteenth-century Paris embraced and utilized the concept of "women's work." It legitimized their claim that they had a right to work in their own way and for their own purposes. Thus, separate spheres, conceptualized as an opposition or a dichotomy, actually served women quite well. As Beatrice Craig has pointed out, most male authorities in the modern era seemed to prefer the idea of the "traditional family economy," a hierarchical model in which women were not separate and definitely not equal. In this model, women took part in economic life as subordinates, to advance the interests of men.[21] Women do not have rights in the family economy, only duties. Thus, women who understood and exploited the notion of separate spheres did quite well for themselves.

This is not to say that the family economy always marginalized women. In certain contexts, the family economy could place women in a position of strength. For example, Darlene Abreu-Ferreira found that women in the northern coastal communities of early modern Portugal were owners or co-owners of ships and highly active in the codfish business.[22] This was because fishing and sales were family owned businesses, and wives, daughters, and widows were crucial to the operation of each company. This situation, plus the existence of inheritance laws that were favorable to women and the fact that men were frequently at sea for extended periods of time, meant that women in these families also did quite well for themselves. Thus, the family economy is not only a valid model for early modern

---

20   Philippe Henwood, "Marie-Jaquette Pignot: une femme de marin à Saint-Malo au XVIIIe siècle," *Memoires de la société d'histoire et d'archeologie de Bretagne*, 71 (1998), p. 336. The title of Henwood's article is another example of how modern assumptions shape historians' representations of the past. Women in France did not take their husbands' names until the revolutionary era. Anquetil used her own name, even in letters to her husband. However, Henwood chose to call her "Marie Jaquette Pignot" after her husband.

21   Craig, "Patrons mauvais genre: femmes et enterprises à Tourcoing au XIXe siècle," *Histoire Sociale/ Social History*, 34:67 (November 2001): 331–54.

22   Darlene Abreu-Ferreira, "Fishmongers and Shipowners: Women in Maritime Communities of Early Modern Portugal," *Sixteenth Century Journal*, 31:1 (Spring 2000): 7–23.

production and trades, but it has room for the success and independence of female participants.

Much early scholarship on women was based upon the acceptance of the family economy model, especially the male-dominated version of it. The problem with such an approach is that it not only misses the promise of separate spheres for women but also treats anyone outside of the traditional household unit as an anomaly. Unattached men and women were categorized as vagrants and troublemakers or burdens on society. Single women and married women with distinct occupations were lost or shoved to the margins. We lost a sense of the wonderful variety of human experience. Current scholarship is changing this view, but there is still a lot of work to be done if we are to get a true picture of early modern society. The first step may be accepting that, while the family economy has certain validity, the model of production must be expanded to accommodate the fluidity of human experience.

Each family in the past had to deal with the needs of its individual members, and could do so in a variety of ways. In the spring of 1687, Janne Hamelin, a cloth merchant in the Breton city of Rennes, set about making her will. She was the widow of Michel Charbonnet and the mother of four children. As she was "in her age," and her husband had been dead ten years, she decided to turn the business over to her children and spend her last days "in peace."[23] The oldest daughter, Thomasse, had already been married and had received her portion of the estate. The only son, Julien, was a monk in the order of Saint Benoise, and, according to Breton custom, was not permitted to inherit anything. That left the two youngest daughters, Perrine and Charlotte, to inherit the shop and its entire inventory. According to the will, the two were to share "the funds, the merchandise, . . . the risk . . . and the profit" of the business and provide for their futures. Perrine had reached the age of majority, being over 25 years of age, and was given the primary rights over the shop. When Charlotte reached majority, she was to be married off and given half of the shop's inventory for a dowry.

This merchant's will demonstrates both the cohesion of the family economy and the flexibility of separate spheres. At least one daughter in that family, and possibly two, could expect to inherit the shop and trade of her mother, and to keep that trade regardless of her future marriage possibilities or the trade of her hypothetical future husband. The family economy model is supported by the parent's act of channeling the children into an appropriate trade that would maintain both status and security. But certainly, in this family, the strictly "patriarchal" motivations are absent. The father and only son have been removed from the economic picture; their needs are meaningless, as are those of the possible future husbands of the young women. The "separate sphere" would seem more significant, as the girls inherit their mother's trade. However, once in control of the resources, either daughter would be free to sell out and use the funds to start anew with a mate. Thus, both models have a place in this analysis.

Brittany offers us a unique portrait of French society in the early modern era. Considered by many, including the Bretons themselves, to be more Breton than French, Brittany provides the opportunity to study early modern French women

---

23   ADIV 4 E 500, records of the notary, Chasse, 24 April 1687.

removed from some of the limitations of the broader French traditions. That is to say, the culture and daily life on the streets, markets, and wharves of Breton cities would have been familiar enough to a visitor from elsewhere in eighteenth-century France. Yet Breton women enjoyed certain legal advantages over their counterparts elsewhere, along with a range of economic opportunities and a reputation for being fiercely independent. Thus, the Breton example will demonstrate the impact of particular legal and economic provisions on the position of women in broader early modern French society.

Brittany was long distinguished by its difference from the rest of France in law, customs, and culture. What is more, visitors and the rest of France often dismissed Brittany as inferior. A chief factor in this phenomenon is the stubborn survival of the Breton language, a Gaelic dialect more similar to Welsh than to French. Bretons, especially those from rural areas, were considered outsiders for their failure to speak "correctly." Above and beyond Breton culture, however, it was the poor state of agriculture and the semblance of isolation from the rest of France that inspired a wide disregard for Brittany. There was little specialization, most people worked with their hands, and the economy was only marginally diversified in the eighteenth century.[24] For example, the linen industry itself, which was the key to Breton prosperity, was late to adopt mechanized spinning and wholly dependent upon women who spun yarn on simple distaffs and wheels.

It is true that Breton peasants were not wealthy; even in the most successful textile regions, many weavers made it through each week by selling enough cloth to buy the next week's bread and yarn.[25] However, in many respects the inhabitants of this countryside were better off than their counterparts elsewhere. Brittany was lightly taxed, as the entire province was exempt from the *taille* and the *gabelle*.[26] Rents were high, but the dominant system of tenure was *domaine congeable*, in which tenants contracted for nine years at a time and owned all buildings and fruit trees on the rented parcel. Lots were often passed down to heirs and a tenant could not be evicted unless the landlord bought out all the property on the land. No improvements could be made to buildings or holdings without the landlord's permission, but farmers effectively enjoyed a permanent tenure.[27] Peasant holdings tended to be quite small and relatively autonomous in Brittany.[28]

Brittany was among the regions of France known to enforce a strict system of partible inheritance, in which all children, regardless of age or gender, inherit an equal portion of their parents' estate.[29] This fragmentation contributes to the image

---

24   Jean Gallet, *Seigneurs et paysans bretons du moyen age à la revolution* (Rennes: Éditions Ouest-France, 1992), p.40.

25   Jean Tanguy, *Quand la toile va: L'industrie toiliére bretonne du 16e au 18e siècle* (Rennes: Éditions Apogée, 1995), p.54.

26   The *taille* was the primary direct tax in France, and the *gabelle* was the salt tax.

27   William Doyle, *The Oxford History of the French Revolution* (New York: Oxford University Press, 1989), p. 11; and James Collins, *Classes, Estates and Order in Early Modern Brittany* (New York: Cambridge University Press, 1994), p. 44.

28   Gallet, *Seigneurs et paysans bretons*, pp. 42–3.

29   Emmanuel LeRoy Ladurie, "A System of Customary Law: Family Structure and Inheritance Customs in 16th-Century France," *Family and Society* (Baltimore: Johns Hopkins University Press, 1976), p. 89.

of Brittany as a "backward" area because it has been assumed by many scholars that only large-scale agriculture can lead to capitalist "progress," and that the dominance of smallholdings impedes economic advancement.[30]   However, for the purposes of this study, the greater importance of partible inheritance is that it gave women access to the resources necessary for maintaining a home or starting a trade. Throughout much of Europe, some form of Roman law dominated, giving most inheritance rights to the oldest son or sons. Only under the most extraordinary circumstances did a woman inherit more than the minimum required dowry to set her up in marriage or a convent. By contrast, the wills and contracts of Brittany reveal how typical it was for a woman to have received all or part of the family home, gardens, or shop inventories.

Breton women had such extensive control over their property that unmarried women were empowered to designate another woman as primary heir. Through the use of a will or "donation," two women could form a legal "perpetual society" with one another and therefore prevent the relatives of either woman from making claims on her estate or goods.[31]   This arrangement was most helpful to the large population of single women in Brittany's urban centers, where women could live by a trade and many found roommates among their peers.

Another Breton custom gave a newly married woman sole control of her assets for the first year and a day after the nuptials. During this period, neither spouse could dispose of the other's property without contractual permission. After the year and a day, husband and wife shared a full "community of property" until separation or death. Many couples filed a contract of "mutual donation," in which they each designated the other as the sole and primary heir. Contrast this with the cases of Italy and England, where it was more common for widows to gain no more than their dowries, while their children inherited the estate.[32]   The case of early modern Brittany is worthy of special attention because it demonstrates the positive impact of a few key rights and customs on the social, legal, and economic position of women in general.

Finally, I want to explain, and perhaps defend, my very traditional organization. This is primarily an economic history, focused as it is on women and their work, but it is by no means limited to economic issues. In fact, I do not believe that either women's or men's work identities can be entirely distinguished from class, age, social status, regional loyalties, or even concepts of honor in the early modern era.

---

30   See the essays in Trevor Aston's *The Brenner Debate: Agrarian Class Structure and Economic Development in Pre-Industrial Europe* (New York: Cambridge University Press, 1985); for a different perspective on peasant entrepreneurialism, see Liana Viardi, *The Land and the Loom: Peasants and Profit in Northern France, 1680–1800* (Durham: Duke University Press, 1993); and, Philip Hoffman, *Growth in a Traditional Society: The French Countryside 1450-1815* (Princeton: Princeton University Press, 1996).

31   Notarial archives ADLA and ADIV. These documents will be discussed at length in Chapter 3.

32   See P. Renee Baernstein, "In Widow's Habit: Women between Convent and Family in Sixteenth-Century Milan," *Sixteenth Century Journal*, 25:4 (Winter 1994): 787–807 for Italy; Amy Louise Erickson, "Common Law versus Common Practice: The Use of Marriage Settlements in Early Modern England," *The Economic History Review*, New Series, 43:1 (February 1990): 21–39, for England.

Furthermore, my intention to approach women from these multiple perspectives rather than viewing them simply by gender means that I must explore a number of demographic, social, and legal, as well as economic, issues. For this reason, I have found it useful to survey women's typical stages of life, their social relationships, and their status under the law. It is only through such a multidimensional approach that we can understand these women on their own terms.

The first chapter will be a portrait of the women of Brittany. The first part of the chapter is a statistical study based upon tax rolls, police records, and parish registers. I break down the population of women from the late seventeenth century to the end of the eighteenth by marital status, occupation (where applicable), and household arrangement in both urban and rural settings. The second part of the chapter is a time line of the typical stages of life and the challenges facing women at each stage. I am able here to establish the complexity of women's lives across the early modern landscape.

The second chapter is an exploration of work issues. I consider women workers in all informal and formal settings in the cities, towns, and villages of Brittany. Breton cities were not as guild-dominated as the larger cities in France, but guilds certainly had a place here. Women were often a part of those organizations in one way or another. In urban areas, however, women slipped in and out of the guilds, or slipped around them altogether, and earned a living in defiance of guild attempts at control. Corporate regulations and police enforcers therefore had an impact on the working lives of women, whether or not they were in the guilds. Work in rural areas was naturally less formal than it was in the cities, and so there are fewer direct sources on women's work in the countryside. Nevertheless, the work of rural women was a key piece of the regional economy and their contributions were very real. Thus, in this chapter, I consider rural women's work with as much attention as I do guilds.

The third chapter is a study of the legal issues faced by women under a complex system of royal French and customary Breton laws. Property, marriage, and commercial laws proscribed women's actions; savvy women understood these laws and took advantage of their protection. Another significant body of law addressed issues of sexual activity, from the illicit to the violent. These laws were designed to both protect and restrict women in terms of their sexuality; some women ignored the laws with impunity while others lost their freedom and their ability to support themselves. Thus, here, too, it would not do to say that women were either helped or hindered by the law.

The fourth and final chapter deals with sociability and honor, and the ways in which a woman's relationships with those around her could define her, support her, and, on occasion, destroy her. In addition to being workers and heirs, women were wives, mothers, neighbors, and friends. Often, those identities were as meaningful to a woman's working life as to her social life; being a protective mother or a sympathetic friend might entail shared work or financial loans. At the same time, work life could lead as easily to rivalry or dishonor as it did to friendship and support networks. Through the community, we see the full complexity of women's lives.

Chapter 1

The Women of Brittany

Before we can delve too deeply into the issues, we need a clear picture of our subject. Often, when we speak of women in the past, we have to rely upon random and fragmentary evidence. In this chapter, I will try to outline the quantitative data available so that we can have some idea of the significance of the sample. I have placed the demographic data, gleaned primarily from tax rolls, in the context of marital status and household arrangements. These categories—daughter, wife, widow, "spinster"—are the ones most often used to describe women, and are an easy place to begin.

Who are these women? What were their living arrangements? How were they identified and counted? What proportion of a given population was made up of single women? Of widows? Only when we have a grasp of the situation can we address the more interesting questions: Who decided how they would be identified, and how did they see themselves? Was their identity grounded in themselves as women—as mothers, daughters, and wives, or as merchants and workers? Or are all these identities too intricately wound to separate? How much of this identity was imposed by others, and how much by the historian?

Demography and the sources

Statistical data is never without complication, and so a few words about my sources and methodology are in order. Demographic studies of the seventeenth century are almost purely based upon parish registers, which record baptisms, marriages, and burials. These sources can only provide enough information to make estimates about the population because they are inconsistent and often incomplete.[1] Furthermore, parish registers do not reflect the numbers of mobile or celibate people. Naturally, widows and unmarried women are invisible in parish registers until they marry or die, and so it is nearly impossible to reconstruct the independent female population based upon parish registers.

Tax rolls are more reliable but introduce their own set of problems. In the seventeenth century, the primary tax in Brittany, and most of France, was the *fouage*, a hearth tax instituted in the fourteenth century. Brittany was exempt from the *taille*, but paid the *fouage* from its inception to the end of the old regime.[2] But the *fouage* rolls are of limited use. As the *fouage* was a hearth tax, the rolls only show the

---

1   For a discussion of the various problems with such sources, see Alain Croix, *La Bretagne aux 16e et 17e siècles: La vie-La mort-La foi* (Paris: Maloine, 1981), pp. 124–33.

2   A. Rébillon, *Les Etats de Bretagne, de 1661 á 1789* (Paris, 1932), p. 522; ADIV C 3370-3371; AMR Liasse 273.

number of households in a town, not individuals, and they include no occupational information. Because clergy, nobles, and the inhabitants of "grandes villes" were exempt from paying the tax, the *fouage* rolls offer no information about city dwellers. Furthermore, the definisle of "hearth" varied from region to region, and the debates over claimed exemptions were constant, making the rolls inconsistent. And lastly, there is a problem of availability because relatively few of the *fouage* rolls have survived and are scattered in the archives; some are with notarial papers, some in family collections, and others with *intendant*'s archives. I have included some data from the *fouage* tax rolls only for comparison of general household information and because there are few other choices of sources for the seventeenth century.

Thus, the primary sources of quantitative data for this study are *capitation* tax rolls, dating from approximately 1710 up to the end of the *ancien régime* in 1789. The *capitation* was a direct and universal head tax instituted in 1695 and collected every year; it was the first tax from which no one, except the clergy, was exempt.[3] Therefore, the *capitation* rolls allow us to see the composition of households in a variety of settings. This means we can get an accurate picture of both independent and married women in cities, towns, and villages during the eighteenth century.

An elaborate system of 22 classifications was created for the implementation of the *capitation*. The nobility were separated from officers and commoners, and paid the tax according to their station and landholdings. Some guilds paid a lump sum on behalf of their members and divided the burden internally. Each taxpayer paid according to status and wealth. A successful wholesale merchant, for example, was expected to pay at least 100 *livres*; town-dwelling rentiers paid an average of 40-60 *livres*. Artisans who owned their own shop paid around 10 *livres*, and soldiers, servants, and day laborers paid one *livre*.[4]

Typical tax roll entries include the name of each head of household, that person's occupation, and the tax levied on each household based on the total income and the number of people living there. The rolls are excellent sources for establishing family and work patterns, and how these patterns change over time. Unfortunately, there are certain inherent limitations in the tax rolls as source material. The first problem, naturally, is one of availability. Though the tax was instituted in 1695, it is rare to find an intact roll book from before 1710. Furthermore, it was impossible to find exactly the same set of rolls for each of the towns in my sample. Thus, my rolls from Morlaix begin in 1709 and those from Saint-Malo begin in 1720. The latest archived old regime tax roll for the majority of my chosen cities dated from 1753, while I have books from Rennes and Nantes finishing in 1777 and 1789, respectively. I have

---

3   See A.M. Boislisle *Correspondance des Contrôleurs Généreaux des Finances avec les Intendants des Provinces* (Paris: Imprimerie Nationale, 1883), pp. 504–508, vol. II for 1701 declaration; see François Bluche and Jean-François Solnon, *La véritable hiérarchies sociale de l'ancienne France* (Geneva: Libraire Droz, 1983) for discussion of social classes and the capitation.

4   The French *livre tournois* was the kingdom's official money of account. The *livre* consisted of 20 *sous*, and each *sous* contained 12 *deniers*. See James Collins, *The State in Early Modern France* (Cambridge: Cambridge University Press, 1995), p. xxvii.

collected similar sets from each town, but the years do not necessarily correspond from one place to another.

Another problem typical of all demographic sources is the uneven recording of information. As noted above, the typical entry had a name, and occupation, and the tax paid. Many logbooks, especially those from the beginning of the eighteenth century, list only a name and the tax paid, providing no occupational information at all. Some list the occupational information for every male head of household, and none for any female head of household. Some provide the names and occupations of every working adult in the home, including the names and occupations of spouses whose work differs from that of the primary entrant. For some years in certain cities, it is impossible to follow work patterns, while other record books provide rich detail about each member of a family.

The inconsistent recording of women's names makes a study of women's work especially difficult. It was not unusual for a married woman or widow to be listed under her own name if she was the head of her household. At times, a woman's name is provided even if her husband is considered the head of the household. Unfortunately, most entries listing married couples consist of the man's name and occupation followed by the phrase, "sa femme" [his wife], and his wife's occupation. Thus, there is no way of being sure if this year's widow was last year's unnamed "femme." In addition, a widow may be identified in one tax roll by her own name, with or without an indication of her status as a widow, and called simply "the widow X" in the next. If she subsequently remarried and returned to her former identity as "femme," then her trail was lost. The difficulty for the researcher is compounded in cases where the town clerk, in the midst of recording hundreds or thousands of names, reverted to shorthand as people familiar to him paid their taxes. Several people in each roll were identified only by a first name, and sometimes only by a nickname.

It is interesting to note the occasional examples of married women identified by name with only a passing reference to their husbands: for example, "Marie X, fileuse, son mari un soldat" [Marie X, spinner, her husband a soldier]. At times, a woman is identified first and her husband is named, but the only profession identified for the home is a feminine one. Alone or as part of a couple, a man would never have been referred to as a "*marchande*," "*tailleuse*," or "*galletiere*," the feminine forms of merchant, tailor, and cake-maker. This suggests that some women were the breadwinners. On occasion, such an entry will offer further explanation: "son mari invalid" [her husband is an invalid], or "son mari absent" [her husband is absent]. As often as not, however, the husbands' unemployment is left unremarked in these cases.

Most occupations in this time period are easily categorized, and I have tried to distinguish between them in order to discuss differences in status and income. A *tailleuse*, a *couturiere*, and a *marchande de mode* all performed the basic service of making, altering, and selling women's clothing.[5] A *lingere* made, embellished,

---

5   Clare Haru Crowston notes that in the garment trades in Paris there was a distinction made between "tailors," or cutters, who were always men, and *couturieres*, or seamstresses, who were women. See her book, *Fabricating Women: The Seamstresses of Old regime*

and sold items like underclothes and household linens, but also performed the basic services of a seamstress. Such occupations are easily identified as comparable clothing trades, and can be considered separate from the lower-paid positions held by spinners and yarn-bleachers. However, the task of distinguishing between women's occupations is not without its problems. The term *blanchisseuse* could equally apply to a textile bleacher or a laundress, and so it was not always possible to gauge the impact of the local textile industry on the employment of women.

Generally speaking, certain occupations were a mark of poverty. The work of a *fileuse* [spinner] or *blanchisseuse* [bleacher] was often poorly paid and offered little hope of stability or upward mobility. It was possible, for example, for a *tailleuse* to move up a tax bracket, join the corporation (assuming female membership was permitted), and avail herself of guild protection. A spinner or a day laborer, by contrast, was likely to remain poor, living hand to mouth for her entire life.

Women who worked in hidden or illicit trades are, out of necessity, largely absent from the statistical portions of this study. Servants are virtually invisible in tax records because they were paid for by their employers and never identified by name. In addition, many servants in urban areas were recent arrivals from the countryside, and they frequently changed employers. Thus, they are even harder to keep track of than married women. Prostitutes, for obvious reasons, did not identify themselves as such for tax purposes. And finally, nuns, like all members of the clergy, were exempt from the *fouage* and the *capitation*, and they were noted only if they had to pay taxes for servants. Women in these three categories—servants, prostitutes, and nuns—were certainly integral parts of the early modern landscape, in a variety of social and economic ways. But, out of necessity, my sources concerning these women are largely anecdotal.

Cities, ports, and towns

The region of Brittany offers a range of populations for study, from tiny villages to huge naval ports and commercial urban centers (see Map 1.1). I have been able to estimate the percentage of female-headed households, and specifically widow-headed households, in all possible settings. From this data, I have been able to extrapolate the percentage of single women.[6] Thus, we can compare the circumstances of women living in a variety of locations (see Table 1.1).

Rennes and Nantes were already large cities by the mid-seventeenth century. Rennes was the administrative center of Brittany and had the region's largest population in 1660, around 30,000 people. The population of Rennes reached a height of 50,000 in the early decades of the eighteenth century, but declined steadily

---

France, 1675-1791 (Durham: Duke University Press, 2002). I have found no such distinction in Breton cities. Women tailors here were regularly identified as *tailleuses*.

6   Judith M. Bennett and Amy M. Froide find single women made up an average of 10–20 percent of the adult female population in any given city during the early modern period, with higher percentages most often found in large urban centers. "A Singular Past," *Singlewomen in the European Past 1250–1800* (Philadelphia: University of Pennsylvania Press, 1999), p. 2.

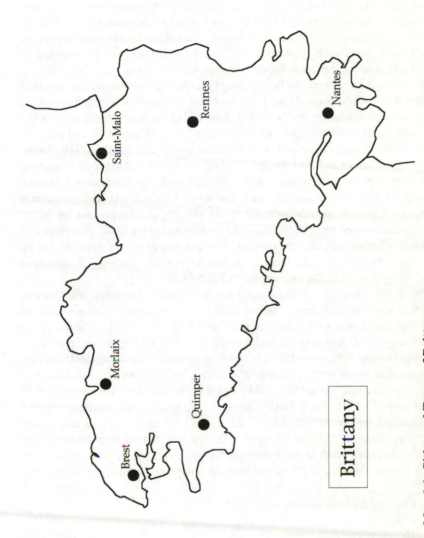

Map 1.1 Cities and Towns of Brittany

and by the eve of the Revolution had leveled off at 42,000.[7] Nantes was a thriving commercial center above all else, serving as a conduit for Brittany and the Loire valley to the Atlantic Ocean. Nantes was smaller than Rennes in the seventeenth century, hovering around 21,000 in 1696, but had grown to 30,000 in 1710 and supported over 80,000 people in 1789.[8] Urban centers by their nature attract a large number of unattached people, and one might expect to find numerous independent women where there was work to be found. Yet, both of these cities had a relatively low percentage of female-headed households, at an average of just under 15 percent. Of those female households, just under half were headed by widows, leaving an average of less than eight percent headed by unattached women.[9]

Saint-Malo and Brest were the two leading ports throughout this era, though they were different in both nature and size. Brest was, and is, a naval port and shipbuilding center. Its population was just under 10,000 at the end of the seventeenth century and had not surpassed 30,000 by 1789. Saint-Malo was more of a commercial port and had twice the population of Brest in 1690, reaching a peak of 25,000 in 1710. But by 1789, the population of Saint-Malo had dropped to 10,000.[10] Ports tend to support a much higher population of widows, self-sufficient wives, and unattached women, due in large part to the frequent absence and loss of men. Brest had the highest percentage of female-headed households in my sample, at 33.6 percent, of which 67 percent were headed by widows. Saint-Malo had a slightly lower percentage of female-headed households, at 22.8 percent, 71.7 percent of which were headed by widows. Thus, single women made up an average of 11 percent of the households of Brest and seven percent of the households in Saint-Malo.

I chose three examples of middle-sized towns: Morlaix, Quimper, and Quintin. Morlaix was a market and textile center of about 7,400 souls in the seventeenth century. The population of Morlaix peaked at 10,000 in the early years of the eighteenth century, but had dropped back to 9,000 by 1789. Quimper was an artisanal and episcopal center with a population of 4,900 at the end of the seventeenth century and no more than 8,000 at the outbreak of the Revolution. Both of these cities had river access to the coast, but neither could support ocean-going vessels, limiting their growth as ports. Quintin was a market center in the heart of the textile-producing region. The cloth bureau, responsible for the supervision of the area's spinners and weavers, was located in Quintin for most of this period, and all local artisans were required to bring their work there. However, the town had no access to either river or coastal transportation, and could not take advantage of commercial traffic. The

7   Croix, *La Bretagne aux 16e et 17e siècles*, p. 135.
8   Ibid., p. 135.
9   The tax rolls used for Nantes were ADLA B 3502, 3519, 3522, and 3530 and ADIV C 4145; for Rennes, ADLA B 3556, 3560, 3583, and ADIV C 3995, and 4043. Nantes had a peak of unattached female heads of household in 1720, at 12 percent of the overall population, and a low in 1753 at 5 percent. It is possible that the discrepancies reflect changing marriage patterns or the movement of single women in and out of domestic service.
10   Croix, *La Bretagne aux 16e et 17e siècles*, p. 135; André Lespagnol, ed., *Histoire de Saint-Malo et du pays malouin* (Toulouse: Privat, 1984) pp. 139–40. The tax rolls for Brest were ADIV C 4117, 4119, 4121 (with two sets in each dossier); for Saint-Malo, ADLA B 3600, 3605, 3614.

population of Quintin was a mere 3,600 at the end of the seventeenth century and 5,000 in 1789.[11]

The percentage of female-headed households in these towns was comparable to those of the large cities. Morlaix had the lowest percentage in my sample, at 13 percent, of which 47.2 percent were headed by widows. Quimper's percentage of female-headed households was identical to that of Saint-Malo, at 22.4 percent, of which 52.2 percent were headed by widows. Quintin's percentage was at 17.5 percent, of which 34.5 percent were headed by widows—the lowest proportion of widows in the sample.[12] In these medium-sized towns, the percentage of households headed by single women were also comparable to the large cities: seven percent in Morlaix, and 11 percent in both Quimper and Quintin.

So far, there are no real surprises. It is no secret that most people in the early modern era did get married, and that households headed by unattached people, especially unattached women, made up a relatively small proportion of the population—between a seventh and a third of the taxed households in this sample. And it is no surprise that at least half, if not most, of the women who served as head of the household were widowed. Thus, we might expect that the situation would be the same in villages, where there tended to be less mobility and fewer opportunities to support oneself outside of a household unit. In fact, we might expect that even more of the female-headed households would be led by widows because it was more difficult for unattached people to support themselves in small towns. And yet, that is not necessarily the case.

Most of the small towns and villages in Brittany participated in the textile industry; the region continued to grow flax and hemp even after the Black Sea became the primary source for raw materials. In addition to the food and fiber crops, most villages supported a small number of crafts and services. Few men or women could afford to devote themselves solely to one economic pursuit. Landernau , in the Léon region near Brest, was roughly the same size as Quintin in the seventeenth century, at 3,500 people. By the end of the eighteenth century, it had not grown beyond 3,600. Dinan, a weaving town near Saint-Malo, supported a population of 5,000–6,000 throughout the entire period. Montcontour, a village near Saint Brieuc, grew from 1,500 in the year 1696 to only 1,800 at the end of the eighteenth century. And Roche-Bernard, near Nantes, hovered between 1,100 and 1,400 people from the seventeenth to eighteenth centuries. In these smaller venues, women headed at least a fifth of the households: in Landernau, 23.9 percent; in Dinan, 29 percent; in Montcontour, 28.5 percent; and in Roche-Bernard, 20 percent. Of the small-town sample, Landernau had the lowest percentage headed by widows, at 40.8 percent. In both Dinan and Montcontour, just under half of the female-headed households were led by widows,

11   Croix, *La Bretagne aux 16e et 17e siècles*, p. 135; "Quimper: Étude de géographie urbaine," *Annales de Bretagne*, 54 (1947): 117–32.

12   The tax rolls for Morlaix were ADLA B 3630, 3631, and 3639; those for Quimper were ADIV C 4126,4128, 4129, and 4130; and those for Quintin were ADLA B 3584, 3596, and ADIV C 4099.

at 48.7 percent and 47.4 percent respectively. And tiny Roche-Bernard had one of the highest showings of widows among female-headed households, at 69 percent.[13]

The *fouage* rolls from the seventeenth century show similar patterns for small towns and villages, the only places in which that tax was imposed. The *fouage* rolls from 1671 to 1695 for Clion, near Nantes, show that in a population of only 300 or so households, at least 20 percent were headed by women.[14] Specifically, 20 percent of the households in Clion were headed by women in 1671, and 31 percent of the households were headed by women in 1696. Of those households, most were headed

Table 1.1 Comparison of Female Heads of Household

Percentage of All Households Headed by Women		Percentage of Female HOH Who Were Widowed	
Brest	33.6	Saint-Malo	71.7
Dinan	29.0	Roche-Bernard	69.0
Montcontour	28.5	Brest	67.0
Landernau	23.9	Quimper	52.2
Saint-Malo	22.8	Nantes	49.2
Quimper	22.4	Dinan	48.7
Roche-Bernard	20.0	Rennes	48.3
Quintin	17.5	Montcontour	47.4
Rennes	14.9	Morlaix	47.2
Nantes	14.7	Landernau	40.8
Morlaix	13.0	Quintin	34.5

by widows (from 80 percent to 85 percent for each year). The same is true of Croisic, also near Nantes, where 24 percent of the 1,120 households were led by women, but by contrast, only 28 percent of those women were widows.[15] In other small towns and villages represented in the *fouage* rolls, the patterns are even more variable. In Blain in 1633, 14.3 percent of the households were headed by women and 88 percent of those women were widows.[16] In Langourla in 1652, a mere 11 percent of the households were headed by women, and only a third of those women were widows.[17] And in Villepot, near Rennes, only 8 percent of the households in 1666 were headed by women, with 83 percent of those being widows; but, that percentage had doubled

---

13   Tax rolls for Landernau: ADIV C 4117, 4119, 4121; for Dinan: ADLA B 3600, 3605, 3614; for Montcontour: ADLA B 3584, 3596, and ADIV C 4099; and for Roche-Bernard: ADLA B 3502, 3522, and ADIV C 4144.

14   ADLA 6 E 31, Commune records for Clion.

15   ADLA E 1452, archives of the Notary, Chessée.

16   ADLA 6 E 6, communal archives of Blain.

17   ADIV 1 F 1640, Fouage rolls for the Côtes-du-Nord.

to 16 percent of the households in 1692, with only 38 percent of those being widows.[18] Clearly, we cannot make assumptions about the population of independent women in small towns and villages. We might expect all village households to be headed by either a man or a widow, but villages often supported a significant population of unattached men and women.

The fact that smaller locales supported a population of unmarried women at all may be linked to the high occurrence of women who inherited property under Breton law.[19] Female property owners, especially those who had an additional source of income, such as sewing or baking, were less likely to need a spouse to survive. It should be noted, of course, that high populations of unmarried women have usually been explained as a result of a gender imbalance that left women without marriage partners. This is one of those assumptions we should challenge. While a lack of marriage partners may have contributed to the phenomenon, I do not believe it is the only possible explanation for the existence of unmarried women. It is entirely possible that some women did not marry because they did not need or want to.[20]

The percentages of households led by women was slightly lower in large cities. Often, as in Nantes and Rennes, the households headed by women were evenly divided between widows and single women. In large urban centers, women were clustered in jobs, earning wages in industrial or servile work, or living off profits earned as tradeswomen, peddlers, and shopkeepers. Perhaps the lower number of female heads of household can be connected to the lack of security and permanence among independent women in cities. Or perhaps their numbers were simply offset by the high number of unattached men who also swelled the ranks of migrant, semi-permanent workers. Such men would have left small towns and villages in search of better opportunities; Claude Nières found significantly higher numbers of migrant men than migrant women among the marriage and mortality records of Breton cities.[21] Whatever the reason, it seems that women were less likely to head households in urban than in rural areas in Brittany, in spite of the greater opportunities to earn a living.

Stages of Life

It has long been accepted that a woman's stage of life has a greater impact on her work life than a man's does. This idea was well established in the work of Natalie Zemon Davis, who noted that women in sixteenth-century France had an "imprecise work

---

18   ADLA 6 E 26, communal archives for the bishopric of Rennes.

19   Breton inheritance law will be discussed in depth in Chapter 3.

20   For a useful discussion of the literature, see Bennett and Froide's "A Singular Past," in *Singlewomen in the European Past*; Pamela Sharpe's "Literally Spinsters: A New Interpretation of Local Economy and Demography in Colyton in the Seventeenth and Eighteenth Centuries," *European History Review*, 44 (1991): 46–65; and Brigitte Maillard, "Les veuves dans la société rurale au XVIIIe siècle," *Annales de Bretagne et des pays de l'ouest*, 106 (1999): 211–30.

21   Claude Nières, *Les villes de Bretagne au XVIIIe siècle* (Rennes: Presses Universitaires de Rennes, 2004), p. 146.

identity" if they had a work identity at all.[22] For many women, work opportunities and obligations changed upon marriage, during childbearing and child-rearing years, and again during old age and possible widowhood. Often, extensive training would have been wasted on girls who grew up to assist husbands in a line of work different from the one they had learned as children. As the bearers of children and the ones most likely to be responsible for raising them, women had to choose work that was flexible, safe, and home-oriented. As a widow, a woman could have remarried into a completely new trade, changing work once again, or she could have taken over a family business. Or, she might have had to scrape by on whatever day-work became available. A woman's work life was forever changing.

Most women married at some point in their lives and had to adapt themselves accordingly, it is true. But there is no justification for our blanket acceptance of this narrow family economy model. This view of women's work lives does not account for those adult, unmarried women who survived for years by their own labor and were not simply between marriages. It also obscures the extent and nature of the work done by married women, whether or not they maintained occupations separate from those of their spouses. We tend to regard a "family business" as a man's business in which his wife was a mere appendage. Yet many couples worked together as partners, both focused on the good of the family as a whole. Their strategies for survival often depended on the life-long work and business abilities of the wife/mother.[23] There is variety in women's experience at every stage of life. Let us explore the possibilities.

Childhood and Training

The first stage of life is childhood, and for the purposes of our discussion I will focus on the kinds of childcare typically available to early modern mothers. Our analysis can then be twofold, as we explore both how girls were treated and how mothers coped with the many demands on their time. At some point, usually by the age of 12, simple childcare gave way to education or professional training. Girls were often at a disadvantage in these areas. As babies and as small children, however, girls and boys shared a common experience.

Margaret Hunt states that childcare was often less of a problem for the early modern woman than it is for the average twentieth-century woman.[24] In many cases, according to Hunt, newborn children were almost immediately sent to a wet nurse; small children were often sent into service or were trained to help around the house; and adolescents were occupied with serious apprenticeships, full-time education,

---

22   Davis, "Women in the Crafts in Sixteenth-Century Lyon," in Barbara Hanawalt (ed.) *Women and Work in Preindustrial Europe* (Bloomington: Indiana University Press, 1986), p. 169.

23   Béatrice Craig explores this issue for the nineteenth century in her article, "Patrons mauvais genre: femmes et enterprises à Tourcoing au XIXe siècle," *Histoire Sociale/ Social History*, 34:67 (November 2001): 331-54.

24   Hunt, *The Middling Sort: Commerce, Gender and the Family in England, 1680-1780* (Berkeley: University of California Press, 1996), p. 138.

or labor. Thus, it would be foolish to judge early modern women's lives by the reproductive obligations one would expect to find in a hunter-gatherer society: women simply did not need to cater every moment to the demands of their helpless children. Elisabeth Badinter takes this theory even further in her book, *L'amour en plus: Histoire de l'amour maternel.*[25] Badinter's thesis is that the "maternal love" of contemporary understanding was an invention of the eighteenth-century *philosophes* and nineteenth-century moralists. Thus, in spite of the high infant mortality rates among children in the care of wet nurses, elite and upper middle-class women alike sent their babies to lower-class wet nurses, who, in turn, sent their own babies to poor, rural wet nurses. Very poor women were known to abandon, neglect, or expose children they were not able to care for.[26]

These scholars may be overstating the case when they claim that motherhood was no problem for early modern women, or even that it was a nuisance, and there is certainly a great deal of debate in this area. Arlette Farge points to the "precarious" nature of life in eighteenth-century cities, and finds that poor women, in need of work and often separated from husbands who were in the army or household service, were ignorant of the dangers their children faced when sent away to a wet nurse.[27] She cites cases of such women becoming desperate or confused by their children's illnesses and the frequency of infant death. Her examples undermine Badinter's notion that pre-modern mothers did not care about their children's lives. We may never know the truth. While we may not be able to understand fully the emotional aspects of childcare in this era, however, we do know that women were able to get away from the demands of motherhood at various points in their lives. The easiest way for them to accomplish this was to send children away, either periodically or permanently.

It is certain that elite and landed families in Brittany sent their children to wet nurses. One need only read a selection of the seventeenth century *livres de raison* to see the regular family expenditures for wet nurses.[28] Sources for the eighteenth century and for the middling classes are less enlightening in this regard, but some poorer people clearly took advantage of this service. In 1768, the servant Petit Pain returned with his wife to Nantes, where they worked for the Juillet family. In the process, they reportedly left their baby with a wet nurse in Paris without having paid the entire bill in advance, a requirement of the wet nurse in question due to the long-distance nature of the contract. Petit Pain was trying to leave servitude and become a merchant, according to the *subdelegué* who interviewed him.[29] He had "an

25   Badinter, *L'amour en plus* (Paris: Flammarion, 1980).

26   Badinter, pp. 92–7.

27   Arlette Farge, *Fragile Lives: Violence, Power and Solidarity in Eighteenth-Century Paris* (Cambridge, MA: Harvard University Press, 1993), p. 53.

28   *Livres de raison* were detailed account books. For examples, see the *livres* of M. De Bouillard de la Rablée, 1632–1652 (ADIV 2 EB 82) and *livre* of M. Deschamps, 1632–1677 (ADIV 2 ED 20); and for contrast see *livre* of M. Couznet, 1661–1682 (ADIV 2 EC 69), as Couznet notes "Madame Jolly, my wife, wants to feed her son, the baby."

29   The *subdelegué* is a local assistant to the *intendant*, or royal commissioner. ADIV C 1286 Complaint of wet nurse, 29 May 1768; interview with *subdelegué*, 17 July 1768; second complaint March 1769 and resolution June 1769.

air of candor," and insisted the wet nurse he hired was financially well off and had agreed to wait a year for her payment. Meanwhile, the wet nurse claimed she was near poverty, that she had other children to care for, and that she intended to send his baby to the poorhouse if she did not get her money. Finally, Petit Pain agreed to send money if the wet nurse would provide an exact accounting of expenses. In a similar case from 1752, the merchant *epicier*, Beaujard, left Paris to return to his native Saint-Malo and left a baby with the wet nurse in Paris. In that case, the *subdelegué* decided that the father in question was so callous that the baby would probably be better off at the poorhouse.[30]

Certainly, the high demand for places in the hospitals and charitable schools attests to a number of displaced children.[31] The rise in illegitimacy during the eighteenth century has been observed elsewhere in France and across Europe. Edward Shorter was among the first to note, "in every city in England and the continent for which data are available, the upsurge in illegitimacy commenced around 1750 or before."[32] James Farr attests to a flurry of edicts against concealed pregnancy and infanticide in France in the late seventeenth and early eighteenth centuries, signaling a rise in official concern over the fate of unwanted babies.[33] Lawrence Stone, in his work on *The Family, Sex and Marriage in England*, attributes the rise in illegitimacy to a shift in social values that made premarital sex, and hence "prenuptial conceptions," more acceptable and more common in the eighteenth century. Laws which forced the fathers of illegitimate children to marry the child's mother or pay for child support, according to Stone, had the unfortunate consequence of making young women more likely to give into sexual advances before marriage.[34] Olwen Hufton, on the other hand, points to a change in the nature of poverty and desperation in the eighteenth century. Crises in the seventeenth century were quick and deadly, creating brief periods of starvation and death. The poorest people were entirely marginalized and rarely procreated. Poverty in the eighteenth century, by contrast, was more likely to be characterized by a continuous cycle of malnourishment and underemployment. "The poor" now tended to be working families, women and children, and people who, in a better economy, would have married and raised a family.[35] When the fine line between malnourishment and starvation started to disappear, babies and small children were the first to suffer. Whatever the reasons for the wave of illegitimacy, whether real or perceived, it is clear that the population was rising, poverty was worsening, and authorities were struggling with how to handle the overflow.

In 1740, the *intendant* of Brittany solicited advice from around the province on the subject of foundlings, and the possibility of keeping them employed or in training until adulthood in order to reduce the number of beggars dependent on

---

30   ADIV 1286, report of 9 February 1752.

31   ADIV C 1286–7 for *intendant*'s correspondence regarding *enfants trouvés*.

32   Shorter, "Illegitimacy, Sexual Revolution, and Social Change in Modern Europe," *Journal of Interdisciplinary History* 2:2 (Autumn 1971): 251.

33   Farr, *Authority and Sexuality in Early Modern Burgundy (1550-1730)* (Oxford University Press, 1995), p. 127.

34   Stone, *The Family, Sex and Marriage in England 1500-1800* (New York: Harper & Row, 1977), pp. 397–8.

35   Hufton, *The Poor in Eighteenth-Century France 1750-1789*, pp. 24, 109, 139.

charity. Obviously, in the cities, abandoned children could be taken to the hospital and trained at some occupation. This was no guarantee of success in life, especially since the dubious parentage of a foundling prevented him or her from ever joining a guild. A skill and steady work did not necessarily secure any kind of honorable status. Nevertheless, training was a push in the right direction: illegitimate or abandoned children who lacked any kind of skill at all were doomed to the most "wretched" servitude.[36] The hospital provided at least the means for survival to numerous urban residents. Rural children, on the other hand, had fewer opportunities.

In the countryside, according to one witness, charity towards the foundling depended upon the local seigneur and at times lasted just long enough to identify the guilty parents and return the unfortunate child to certain desperation.[37] In some parishes, such children were sent to the "lowest" wet nurses and turned out at age seven, at which point they were fit only for begging; "these children are so malnourished for the most part that they do not have the strength to attend to the work that would be asked of them."[38] All agreed that keeping a foundling was an expensive operation since children could not be of proper service until the age of ten. The *intendant*'s correspondents offered various suggestions: one decided that tax breaks and incentives for those who took in orphans were the only solution, an idea that was eventually adopted in a modified form. Le Beau of Ancenis suggested that "robust" children should be sent to the countryside and "delicate" children reserved for urban artisans to ensure efficient service. And M. de la Brettrye of Treguier waxed philosophic about the possible damage done to "natural liberty" by the virtual enslavement of innocent children, only to decide that forced labor was in the end no more contrary to liberty than apprenticeship, school, or the seminary.[39]

It is no easy matter to guess the intentions behind outright abandonment. Mostly, it was a product of poverty. When 30-year-old Charlotte Martin, a worker at a *teinturier's* [dyer's] shop, was asked what would become of the baby she was expecting, she explained that she already had a two-year-old and a five-year-old at the hospital. She planned to "have it received at the hospital because she did not have the means to feed it," and her "shameful" employer-seducer had only offered her enough money to pay the hospital's fee.[40] Other cases are marked by an element of callousness: the midwife, Baudreau, of Nantes complained in 1786 that she had not been paid by the master tailor Des Chateaux for the care of his son. The boy was ten years old by this point, and had just left the care of his wet nurse. His mother, a *lingere* named Jeanne Albert, was nowhere to be found. Like so many others who found themselves burdened with someone else's child, Baudreau said she would have no choice but to bring the boy to the poor house if no one paid for his upkeep.[41]

---

36   Sarah Maza, *Servants and Masters in 18th-century France: the Uses of Loyalty* (Princeton University Press, 1983), p. 32.

37   ADIV C 1286, letter to the *intendant* of 15 August 1740.

38   ADIV C 1286, letter to the *intendant* of 2 October 1740.

39   ADIV 1286, letters of 2 October, 26 July, and 5 August 1740.

40   ADIV 3 B 1447 Declaration de grossesse, 2 January 1716.

41   AMN FF 253 #10, 11 March 1786.

Neither of his natural parents was willing or able to care for him, and the midwife could not take him in without financial assistance.

Dire poverty and the general instability of life in the eighteenth century meant that the abandonment of children was a common problem. The *declarations de grossesse*, in which police across France carefully recorded details from each illegitimate pregnancy, were designed to discourage infanticide and abandonment. Midwives and surgeons risked losing their licenses if they were caught assisting in unreported deliveries. And yet, Didier Riet suggests that these declarations made little or no impact on women who were determined to get rid of their children. In his study of Dinan, Riet found that several women made their declarations, took legal responsibility for the baby and named the father, accepted money from fathers for the baby's upkeep, and then abandoned it anyway. At the same time, some women refused to name the father, refused to accept money, and kept their babies.[42] Thus, abandonment was not a necessary result of either financial need or societal shame.

Similarly, Jean-Luc Bruzulier suggests that many women kept their babies for as long as possible before bringing them to the hospital. Fifty-three percent of the foundlings in Vannes between 1760 and 1789 were over a month old, and 34 percent were over a year old.[43] In 1714, police in Rennes were notified that a three-year-old girl had been left on the church steps; when they found her, they discovered a note sewn to her sleeve identifying her simply as an orphan.[44] The advanced age of some foundlings, and their abandonment at the hospital or church, suggests that someone cared about the children. Perhaps the parents intended to keep the children but found themselves unable to do so, and lacked the funds to pay for their entrance into the poorhouse. Abandonment was not always the solution to unexpected or illegitimate births. Near the century's end, the *subdelegué* at Croisic wrote to the *intendant* with pride that "infants are rarely exposed in this subdelegation. Girls and widows keep and raise their bastards . . . as for legitimate children of the very poor, their neighbors and relatives take care of them. Here, we are born charitable."[45]

It was possible for some parents to make a child's hospital stay a temporary one. Some poor parents sent their children to the hospital because they were going through a rough period, and took them home again later. Others did so because of the availability of inexpensive occupational training there. Even the poor were conscious of opportunities to secure a more stable future for their children. The hospital records of Nantes are especially clear about cases like these. Renée Vincente was presented by her mother for admission into the hospital, with a small sum towards her upkeep, in order to receive some "appropriate" training.[46] Madame Lannay, a *tailleuse*, brought her 12-year-old granddaughter to the hospital in order to learn the same

---

42   Riet, "Les declarations de grossesse dans la région de Dinan à la fin de l'ancien régime," *Annales de Bretagne et des Pays de l'Ouest*, 88: 2 (1981): 186.

43   Bruzulier, "L'illégitimitié et l'abandon à Vannes entre 1760 et 1789," *Annales de Bretagne*, 96:4 (1991): 397.

44   ADIV 3 B 1446, police: street reports, 7 November 1714.

45   ADIV C 1387, letter of 17 December 1777.

46   ADLA H depot 751 E 27, April 1661.

art.[47] Such entries are recorded alongside requests from artisans seeking apprentices. In fact, throughout the seventeenth and eighteenth centuries, the hospital clearly worked as an intermediary between families too poor to keep and train their own children and artisans who sought to gain apprentices, a subsidy from the hospital, and perhaps some religious credit for the charitable act they were performing. Thus, in one move, poor families could temporarily rid themselves of the financial burdens of parenthood while at the same time getting their children practical training.

Among the elite and certain merchants, academic education was of equal importance to occupational training. Elite boys were sent to schools in towns and abroad at young ages, and even elite girls received appropriate schooling away from home. In Rennes, the order of Ursulines educated the "daughters of fine families" in religion and letters.[48] By the end of the seventeenth century, even poorer children had access to this education via the charitable schools in religious houses such as the Dames Budes of Rennes.[49] According to some historians, literacy for both men and women was unusually high in urban Brittany when compared to the rest of France. This was due in particular to the merchant class's high regard for literacy and their access to the numerous schools run by religious institutions.[50] Thus it was no surprise that even the poor merchant Marie-Jacquette Anquetil wrote to her husband in Peru about the cost of school for their two sons and her frustration with the older boy's poor study habits.[51]

At the same time, the complicated nature of convent education is clear in the case of Janne Rose Allix. On the surface, this case looks like any other accusation of kidnapping and possible seduction. Perrine Faquer complained to the police of Rennes on 16 June 16 1747 that her only daughter had been taken away by Monsieur de Villeneuve Cordon. When interrogated, however, Cordon revealed that his wife was Faquer's cousin, and that the young girl had run away from home. Cordon and his wife wanted to keep the girl because of her mother's negligence: "Faquer, the widow Allix, has given her daughter no education whatsoever, and furthermore has abandoned her in a convent. It is not natural for Faquer to have sent the girl to the hospital since they live well on their rents."[52]

Much work in this period was reasonably home-oriented, allowing many parents to see to businesses and trades without making special arrangements for childcare. In one case in 1723, a wig merchant named Duclos did not hesitate to leave his 11-year-old son and 13-year-old daughter in charge of his shop while he visited his sick brother. Unfortunately, his children were attacked and beaten by an unhappy customer. Duclos lamented the violence of the world in his statement to the police,

---

47 ADLA H depot 754, 2 April 1678.

48 AMR Liasse 309, memoire from the sisters, 1649.

49 AMR Liasse 305, lettres patents 31 October 1676.

50 Lespagnol, *Histoire de Saint-Malo,* p. 200; and see also Julie Hardwick, *The Practice of Patriarchy: Gender and the Politics of Household Authority in Early Modern France* (University Park, PA: Pennsylvania State University Press, 1998), p. 97.

51 Phillippe Henwood, "Marie-Jacquette Pignot: une femme de marin à Saint-Malo au XVIIIe siècle," *Memoires de la société d'histoire et d'archeologie de Bretagne,* 76 (1998): 338.

52 ADIV 2 EC 62, 16 and 17 June, 1747, Cordon family papers.

but no one ever suggested that the children should not have been alone.[53] As in many families in which children were kept at home, Duclos' son and daughter were an integral part of the workshop, familiar with both the work and the regular clientele.

In the early modern era, raising children was not considered something distinct from work but merely another component of life. Thus, it is not necessarily true that women's work had to be confined to those trades that are compatible with child rearing. In rural areas, even the requirements of frequent pregnancies and actual childbirth did not always prevent women from working. This was usually more a consequence of economic need rather than a signal of peasant heartiness, but it adds perspective to the issue of whether or not motherhood replaced toil for women.[54] Motherhood represented a change in a woman's life, but it did not mean her occupational activities came to an end.

Marriage, too, did not always mean an end to a woman's own work. Especially in those trades "appropriate" to a woman, such as clothing trades and food preparation, a married woman was able to continue work regardless of her husband's trade. The statutes of the Rennes tailor's guild offered membership to women through the sponsorship of an established member or through work as an apprentice.[55] Such women had a "privileged" status that conferred full benefits, as opposed to the limited membership offered to the widows of guild members. Female tailors only lost their status if they married *within* the guild, since then they would be covered by their husband's privileges. Tailors who married outside the guild were not affected. In such a system, it could be to a woman's advantage to marry outside her own trade and therefore keep her guild status. For some women, then, education and training during their youth would not have been wasted investments. In fact, since women in some trades learned a craft before marriage, kept it during marriage, and continued to work at it in widowhood, we can speculate that some women were able to form a work identity—a self-identification that allowed for pride in and protectiveness of a profession.

Apprenticeship contracts and related work arrangements, such as the acceptance of poorhouse trainees into employment, provide additional evidence of women's training. Carol Loats has studied training contracts from sixteenth-century Paris, and has shown that female apprentices could be accepted to train in a married woman's trade as long as they were under the legal authority of her husband, regardless of his own trade.[56] Such arrangements were common in Brittany in the eighteenth century. For example, Perrine Bonion, of Nantes, was accepted as an apprentice to the midwife Françoise Dufresne in 1769, but she was the legal responsibility of Dufresne's husband, a tailor named François Aubert.[57] In 1689, Françoise Vestu

53   ADIV 2 B 1844(2) 4 June 1723, hearings before the presidial of Rennes. This case also offers us a glimpse of a lone father dealing with issues of childcare.

54   Riet, "Accoucher seule dans l'ancienne France au XVIIIe siècle: motivations et conduites," *Annales de Bretagne et du Pays d'Ouest* 98:1 (1991): 67.

55   AMR Liasse 199, Tailors' statues, 1713; ADIV 5 E 25, Deliberations and receptions, 1733–1786.

56   Loats, "Gender, Guilds, and Work Identity: Perspectives from Sixteenth-Century Paris," *French Historical Studies* 20:1 (Winter 1997).

57   ADLA 4 E 2/72 Notaire Auffray, 12 April 1769.

was placed in apprenticeship at the home of Pierre Liepriere, a *cordonnier* [rope maker], so that his wife could teach her to "sew and tailor in linen."[58] More often than not, contracts for a married woman's apprentice named only her trade and not her husband's. For example, in 1666 Janne Julien, the wife of Jean Loyeau, accepted Françoise Couben and "La petite Baudry" for three years in order to teach them to sew.[59] There is no way to tell if Loyeau would have had any hand in their training.

Unmarried or widowed tradeswomen had total authority over their apprentices. In 1698, Françoise Pasqueceau was accepted at the age of fourteen by the widowed *tailleuse*, Janne Vatrin. Pasqueceau's contract stipulated that she would sleep and live "honestly" with the widow for three years, do her own laundry, and go wherever she was asked to go. In return, Vatrin would teach her the art of tailoring for women, feed her, and allow someone to visit four days a week in order to show the girl how to read.[60] An earlier contract, dated 25 April 1641, placed Allisoun Misagre with the *lingere* Julienne D'Argonne to learn the art and receive room and board for a year in exchange for a simple sum.[61] The terms are almost identical to those of a contract more than a century later, in which a porter named Jacques Poirier put his 13-year-old daughter Perrine into apprenticeship with the *lingere* Jeanne Chesnard.[62] In neither of these two contracts was the marital status of the mistress *lingere* identified, suggesting that they were independent adults or widows. In a slightly more unusual arrangement, the unrelated roommates Anne Chauvigne and Marie Momousseau shared authority over Marie LeTable, their 17-year-old apprentice, as they taught her to be a *lingere*.[63]

A widow quite naturally had authority over her own daughter, and in some cases a woman could very easily pass on her own trade. Anne Hamon was a certified midwife and the widow of a merchant. She wrote that she had personally taught the art to her daughter at the Hotel Dieu at Paris and then returned to Rennes to put the young woman "en maitrise." After only a few years, Anne Nerriere, her daughter, was earning enough as a "matronne jurée" to support them both, and Hamon was able to retire.[64]

Apprenticeship contracts for women are rare, and are overwhelmingly outnumbered by contracts for men. In fact, the low number of contracts for women in any given survey of notarial archives is usually cited as the rational for the belief that women rarely had their own occupations.[65] However, the informal nature of much of women's work would have made such structured arrangements unnecessary.

---

58   ADIV 4 E 501, Notaire Chasse, 3 April 1689.

59   ADLA H dépot 751 II E 27, Hospital records in Nantes, 1661–1666.

60   ADLA 4 E 2/1294 Notaire LeBreton, 18 January 1698.

61   ADLA 4 E 2/212 Notaire Belute, 25 April 1641.

62   ADLA 4 E 2/73 Notaire Auffray, 16 June 1771.

63   ADLA 2 E 3205, Titres de Familles, 1 July 1712.

64   ADIV 3 B 1450, accusations of ill conduct against Nerriere, 2 January 1712. "En maîtrise" and "matronne jurée" status both refer to her having been admitted as a licensed mistress midwife.

65   Such a conclusion was drawn by both Françoise Joyeux, "Les corporations à Nantes au XVIIIe siècle," (1985) and Jean-Yves Kerbois, "Les apprenties Nantais au XVIIIe siècle" (1975) in their respective master's thesis at the University of Nantes.

Certainly, fine tailoring would have been the product of training, but a good deal of the skill necessary to a common *lingere* or *tailleuse* could have been learned at home.

The role of poorhouses and hospitals in the occupational training of young women has already been discussed. But it bears mentioning again simply to point out that typical training mimicked what should have been gained at home and in no way prepared interns for future self-sufficiency. The common nature of the work helped to keep potential earnings low, and made it unlikely that graduates would never again need assistance.[66] On the positive side, the time and money invested by city fathers into the training and employment of professional women at the hospitals may explain why municipal authorities were not always sympathetic to guilds on the warpath against unlicensed workers. On 30 January 1714, the provosts of the tailors' guild of Rennes accepted a request from "Monsieur le premier président" to allow Janne Ruellan to work for the rest of her life as a *tailleuse*, without fear of impediment from the guild. This request was made in recognition of the charity of Ruellan, who had "shared her profession with many girls under the protection of hospital administrators," and now wanted to simply make her living in this "honest fashion."[67]

Marriage

Most people in the pre-modern age would have married at some point, and the members of most households spent time working as part of a family unit. The typical arrangement of a family business is best illustrated through examples from the elite merchant class. André Lespagnol describes the merchant families of Saint-Malo in his book *Messieurs de Saint-Malo: Une élite négociante au temps de Louis XIV.* Marriage in this class usually paired an older man with a younger woman from a wealthy family. As businesses were family affairs, the object was to raise a large family and pass the enterprise from father to son. More often than not, the husband predeceased the wife by several years, and the widow continued to handle commerce until one or more sons were old enough to take over.[68] In order to prepare for this eventuality, merchant wives were involved intimately with commerce, held power of attorney in order to deal with business during their husbands' long absences, and on occasion were noted for their areas of specialization. Jean Des Ages, Sieur Duhoux,[69] reportedly bragged that his wife, Guilemette, was the expert when it came

---

66   According to Hunt, the fact that all women possessed these domestic skills is one of the reasons that women's work was always poorly paid and insecure. *The Middling Sort*, p. 83.

67   ADIV 5 E 26, Tailors' deliberations, 30 January 1714. The guild agreed to grant her privileged status, either for the rest of her life or "until such time as she married a master tailor."

68   Lespagnol, *Messieurs de Saint-Malo*, pp. 121–3 and "Femmes négociantes sous Louis XIV: Les conditions complexes d'une provision provisoire," *Populations et cultures: Études rèuni en l'honneur de François Lebrun* (Rennes: 1989), pp. 463–70.

69   Court records refer to the family simply as Desages, while business records refer to them as the Duhoux merchants. The wife identifies herself as Mme. Duhoux Desages in her own correspondence.

to *toile* [whole linen and hemp cloth] purchases.[70] As her commercial correspondence begins 20 years before his death and spans 40 years altogether, it is clear she was a competent merchant in her own right.[71]

Béatrice Craig has suggested that French women from elite commercial families would not have hesitated to involve themselves at every level of business, in spite of the rising bourgeois ideal of womanhood, because a family business was suitably private. Commerce itself was not a "public" matter if it involved affairs held in trust for future generations.[72] Thus, Mme. Duhoux-Desages wrote to her contact in Cadiz that he should understand "my affairs in Spain are expressly for the establishment of my children," and they were under her personal control even before the death of her husband.[73] Family affairs could also include the work of married daughters, as evidenced by the correspondence of Noel Prigent, of Saint-Malo, with his married daughter in Saint Pierre. Alongside her friendly chitchat about the weather and her babies, she reported on the current price of the cod shipment she had sent, the going rate on herbs and artichokes her father had requested, and shipping timetables to Bordeaux.[74]

For the daughter of a well-established merchant family, marriage indicated a new phase of her life but certainly not a dramatic alteration of her work life. Among the artisans and merchants of the "middling" sort, it was perhaps more likely for a woman to change work upon marriage. Without a doubt, the majority of shopkeepers and craftsmen in early modern France relied upon their wives to help manage a single family business, much as elite merchants did. Unlike elite wives, however, the daughters of middling families would not have necessarily received training in the appropriate trades. Thus, they would have assumed unfamiliar responsibilities upon marriage.

These well-known patterns have helped to create the impression that all pre-modern women served as assistants to the work of their husbands. Much of the scholarship devoted to the important economic contributions of women in the past, and the limitations imposed upon women as workers, has unfortunately reinforced the idea that women's work is always marginal and therefore easily dismissed. It seems evident, however, that a woman played a key role within the family business and took great pains to support her children. It is likely that she viewed her activities as crucial to the family's survival, just as her husband would have viewed his own work. In that case, a wife could have developed a complex identity based upon her part in a joint enterprise. She was a skilled businesswoman, loyal wife, and doting mother through her activities.[75]

70   Lespagnol, *Messieurs de Saint-Malo*, p. 123.

71   ADIV 4 F C 3, Livre de correspondance de Mme Duhoux-Desages, 1703–1746.

72   Craig, "Women and the Family Business: The Case of Tourcoing in the Nineteenth Century," Carleton Conference on the History of the Family, Ottawa, May 1997.

73   ADIV 4 F C 3, letter of 24 December 1708. Unfortunately, her agent in Spain eventually defrauded her of a large sum and hostilities with that country prevented her from pursuing him.

74   ADIV 2 EP 104, Prigent family of Saint-Malo, 1782–1785.

75   See Carolyn Lougee Chappell, " 'The Pains I Took to Save My/His Family": Escape Accounts by a Huguenot Mother and Daughter after the Revocation of the Edict of

At the same time, it is my contention that it was much more common for married women to keep separate trades than has ever been imagined, and that even married women could have maintained a work identity in the more traditional, "masculine" sense. Several of the *capitation* tax rolls from the eighteenth century recorded separate incomes for wives, notably the rolls from Rennes, Brest, and Quimper. For example, 5.8 percent of taxpaying households in Rennes in 1739 reported two incomes, while the smaller town of Quimper in 1763 showed a full 7 percent. Brest, in 1770, reported that 8.9 percent of households had two incomes.[76] These numbers are small, but the presence of any such households is a significant find because they are so unexpected. The number of married couples indicating separate incomes went beyond the expected piecemeal incomes of the very poor. Furthermore, most of our evidence concerning married women's separate occupations has come from scattered anecdotal sources. Rarely have we been able to quantify their existence.

In the tax rolls for these cities, both occupations are listed for households in which the husband and wife have different sources of income. In addition to supplying the number of such households, the records allow us to study the relationship between the occupations and decide, for example, how complementary their working lives were. One might expect to find a weaver married to a cloth merchant or a fisherman married to a food vendor. However, it might be more surprising to find a carpenter married to a baker. In fact, though there are many examples of corresponding occupations in marriage, it appears just as likely that the work of one spouse has nothing to do with that of the other. This is significant because some scholars have assumed that women who did well in a craft or trade during the middle ages and early modern period did so because their husband's work paved the way for them.[77] That is clearly not the case when spouses had dramatically different occupations. A woman baker married to a cabinetmaker probably did not require the assistance of her husband, nor was she likely to have shared workspace with him.

Soldiers and clerks were highly concentrated in Rennes due to the city's position as an administrative center. In Brest, most of the married men in the sample were sailors or fishermen. Many such men, along with domestics and general laborers, were likely to have spent long periods away from home and did not earn high incomes. Sailors, soldiers and migrant laborers were gone for obvious reasons; clerks and domestics were absent if they were part of an entourage or if they were required to live in the homes of their employers. It is not surprising that men in these positions had wives with separate occupations.

Craftsmen, especially *menusiers* and *charpentiers*, both woodworking trades, were also well represented among the households reporting two incomes in the

---

Nantes," *French Historical Studies*, 22:1 (Winter 1999): 1–64, for a fascinating account of how a mother and daughter can construct very different meanings for the identity "mother."

76   ADLA B 3560, Rennes, 1739; ADIV C 4129, Quimper, 1763; ADIV C 4121, Brest, 1770.

77   For example, Margaret Wensky, "Women's Guilds in Cologne in the Later Middle Ages," *Journal of European Economic Studies*, 11:3 (1982): 635. Wensky, studying the silk market in Cologne, suggested that the success of the silk weavers was easily dismissed because most were married to well-off merchants of one sort or another.

sample. Nearly half of the carpenters and cabinetmakers were apprentices or journeymen. Unlike guild members in other European countries, French journeymen were often allowed to marry before becoming masters. Especially in the eighteenth century, when it was becoming more and more unlikely that a journeyman would eventually open his own shop, this meant that many craftsmen could have a home and a family without necessarily involving them in his own work. In Quimper, for example, female bakers and tailors, the largest group of married women with occupations, tended to be married to journeymen cobblers or carpenters. It is likely that these men worked in the shops of their masters, leaving the space at home for the work of their wives. But the lower status of the craftsmen within their respective trades may indicate that their income was insufficient to support the household. The cabinetmaker Nicolas Duverger in Brest was listed with his fellow craftsmen in the artisan tax roll of 1748 with the note, "he was not taxed because his wife paid with the bakers and her commerce is more significant than his."[78] Male domestics were in a similar position. They could marry with their employer's permission, but their work often required them to live apart from their families. That fact and their low income made it necessary for their wives to earn a living without assistance.

Sometimes the low-income or intermittent nature of the husband's income had more to do with the unusual nature of his job rather than his low "status" in the typical sense. Jean Dubois and his wife, Anne Letournoy, were interrogated as witness in a property dispute in Nantes in 1712. In the first interview, Dubois was listed as a musician and his wife stated she was in the process of becoming a junk merchant. Two years later, in a follow-up interview, they are both listed as junk merchants.[79] This would suggest that Anne developed a business and her husband followed her into it, perhaps giving up music in doing so. The same might be true of Marguerite Arnout, a merchant questioned about a neighborhood squabble in 1713. She identified her husband, Bosée, as a *maitre d'ecole* [school master], but it is clear from her testimony that he also worked in her shop.[80]

The rest of the men in the sample who had wives earning a separate income were simple "laborers" of one sort or another. This is to be expected, and merely demonstrates that low-income households required multiple sources of income in order to survive. That is, married men in the lowest paid and lowest skilled positions were more likely to have wives who sought work independently. However, there is no strong correspondence between that fact and their wives choice of occupation (see Table 1.2[81*]). Men who worked as porters and day-workers were not necessarily

78   ADIV C 2145, merchant-artisan *Capitation* for multiple cities, 1748
79   ADLA B 5851 Inquiries for the Prevoté, 11 August 1712; 2 August 1714.
80   ADLA B 5851, Inquiries for the Prevoté, 9 September 1713.
81   I chose these years for the three cities so they would be comparable in time and represent an average count of married women who identified an occupation. In Brest in 1740, there were 79 wives among the 541 women named in the tax rolls. In Rennes in 1739, there were 378 wives among 1,055 women. Both of those were average counts for those cities. In Quimper in 1737, there were only 22 wives among the 350 women named, which was a low count for that city. Later tax rolls, most notably the one from 1763, reported a higher proportion of married women who identified occupations.

married to women in similar work positions. The wives of laborers could be equally found in food trades, textile production, and all levels of retail.

Economic status obviously played a role in determining which households required more than one income and, more specifically, which households were least likely to work as a production "unit." Married women who worked independently were generally married to men who could not support the family alone or to men whose work took them away from the home for extended periods. That is not to say that well-off men never had wives with independent incomes. A lawyer named Sieur LeClerq, living in Rennes in 1739, was married to a wine merchant. Two merchants in the artisan *capitation* roll of 1748 for Rennes were assessed at high rates but were also identified as the wives of court bailiffs.[82] Nor was it strange for a couple to be listed explicitly as partners, such as Guillon and his wife, *marchands du cidre* [cider merchants] in Rennes in the same year.

As important as it is to have numbers, the *capitation* tax rolls by themselves are not a reliable gauge of households with multiple incomes. Recording practices varied from year to year and from town to town, and it is not clear what decided whether or not a woman's own occupation was reported. In fact, supporting qualitative sources demonstrate that not all two-income households were recorded in the tax rolls. Witnesses in the case against Louise Piel in Rennes in 1751, for example, included the clockmaker, Jean Martineau, and his wife, a glovemaker named Jeanne Pennevoise. This couple was not listed among the hundreds of two-income households reported in the *capitation* roll, but they were well-off enough to have each had an apprentice in their respective trades as well as a third servant who took care of the house.[83] Louise Piel, the object of the police inquiry, was herself a *blanchisseuse* who employed a number of young women as embroiderers. Her husband was a domestic in a noble household and was gone for months at a time when his employer went to the countryside. However, the couple was recorded in tax rolls under his name only, with no mention of Piel's work or income.[84] Perhaps the occupations held by Pennevoise and Piel were left out of their respective tax assessments not because their work was economically insignificant, but because it had no effect on the status or tax of their households.

Many additional sources hint at a high number of married women with distinct occupations. Of the 227 women who registered as merchant-artisans with the police of Nantes between 1733 and 1790, 26 were married women with husbands in unrelated trades.[85] This, too, is a deceptively small number, since those who worked informally would not have been listed in *maitrise*, or mastership, registers. Half of the married women in *maitrise* were *tailleuses*, members of one of the few guilds to receive women, and therefore well-off enough to have paid dues. The women named in these registers were not among the few wives identified in the tax rolls of Nantes.

82   ADIV C 2145, merchant-artisan *Capitation* for multiple cities, 1748.
83   AMR Liasse 360, testimony taken 5 March 1751.
84   AMR Liasse 360, inquiry of 1751; ADLA B 3560, *Capitation* of Rennes, 1739.
85   AMN HH 61–86, Bureau of *maîtrise* registration for Nantes.

Table 1.2 Married Women's Occupations

	Brest (1740)		Rennes (1739)		Quimper (1737)	
	% of wives in:	% of those who share work w/ husbands:	% of wives in:	% of those who share work w/ husbands:	% of wives in:	% of those who share work w/ husbands:
Food/Drink Retail	42.8	8.3	21.7	37.9	36.2	0
Miscellaneous Retail	37.5	47.6	17.6	31.2	37.2	0
Cloth/Clothing Retail	7.2	0	19.2	11.4	11.7	9
Health Fields	5.4	0	1.4	0	-	-
Textile Production	3.5	0	20.6	9.3	-	-
Day Labor	1.8	0	19.5	32.3	8.5	12.5
Rent/ Unspecified	1.8	0	-	-	6.4	50

In 1767, the *subdelegué* of Nantes reported the names of all merchants who were not in *maitrise*. Out of 240 junk merchants, 156 were women and 61 of those women were married to someone who was not a merchant. Of linen-cloth merchants and mercers, 117 of the total 130 merchants were women and 25 of those were married.[86] All of this suggests a hidden population of married women, unreported in tax rolls and excluded from formal work institutions.

As did the tax-roll information for Brest, Quimper, and Rennes, the *maitrise* registers for Nantes show that most husbands and wives with separate sources of income had unrelated occupations. Jeanne Maudit, a *toiliere* [whole cloth merchant] in 1750, was married to a surgeon; Marie Texier, a *tailleuse*, was married to a carter;

---

86   ADIV C 1450, *Marchands sans jurande*, 1767.

and, Anne Therese Blais, another *tailleuse*, was married to a "master of writing." This suggests that it was unlikely the pair shared workspace. Food merchants probably could have combined trades, such as the *charcutiere* [sausage maker], Marie Françoise Gié, married to a master baker. But, once again, women with sailors or soldiers for husbands, such as the candle merchant Magdelaine Arnandou or the grain merchant Janne Pavoir, had only to care for themselves and their children.

It is not always easy to tell how extensive a woman's trade was in comparison to her husband's. For just that reason, many historians have dismissed evidence of wives with trades because it has been assumed that the woman's work is part-time or too intermittent to matter. It is therefore important to seek out sources that describe the internal arrangements in a two-income household. Even in cases in which a woman's work was modified to adapt to her husband's, it may have been possible for her to develop skill, contacts, and a sense of possession over her own work. In 1753, in Rennes, a carter named Martin Grassin and his wife, a merchant named Andrée Boursin, were questioned about some debts claimed by another merchant.[87] Grassin simply noted with indignation that he was completely ignorant of his wife's business. Boursin, for her part, explained in detail her system of commerce and showed how she was never in debt to anyone. She always purchased fish from the large-scale dealers in Rennes to fill pre-placed written orders she received from her contacts farther inland or upriver. Those merchants sent payment back with the barge and carriage drivers who had made the deliveries. She never did anything on credit, and kept no books.[88] Boursin angrily denied owing any money to Françoise Flamand, one of her contacts in Angers, and suggested that it was the greed of Flamand's husband, a barrel-maker, which motivated the supposed claim. Boursin produced from memory a list of all her business from the previous six months and a list of character witnesses.[89] It is clear from these documents that Boursin's husband had nothing to do with her activities and that her commerce was significant.

Another example, from a higher-status household, is Marie Guesdon, a cloth merchant and the wife of Nicolas Bennerais, an apothecary in Redon.[90] Guesdon offers an interesting example of the traditional household model because it appears she gave up her business for several years. One of her account books is dated 1721–1760, but it reveals a gap of 25 years, from 1722 to 1747, during which Guesdon did no business in cloth. In a letter written during that period, in 1739, Guesdon identified herself as "La Bennerais, *apothicaire*." During that same period, Guesdon's husband was working for the royal military hospital, service for which he was decorated. However, Guesdon began selling cloth again late in 1747, and by 1759 had initiated the process for separation from her husband. Throughout the 1760s and 1770s, Guesdon lived with her sister and continued her commerce as a cloth merchant. In all, Guesdon maintained a profession for 11 of the 21 years she lived with her husband, and during those years her commerce was regular and unrelated to the apothecary's.

---

87   ADLA 2 E 1091, *Titres de famille,* 13 April 1753.
88   In fact, the *procureur* noted that it would be absurd to expect a fishwife to keep an account book like an elite *négociant*, 31 July 1753.
89   ADLA 2 E 1091, 13 April 1753.
90   ADIV 2 EB 21, Bennerais family papers.

After Guesdon left her husband, she was able to support herself independently. This suggests that she had a measure of independence even within their marriage, and that her profession was a part of that independence.

It is possible that some women relished the opportunity to maintain a separate occupation, or, at the very least, that they did not allow profession to guide all of their choices in life. Renee David, an *aubergiste* [innkeeper], was pursued incessantly by François Berto, another *aubergiste*, for years. He was sure she would marry him. So sure, in fact, that when she married someone else he sued her for breach of contract. In his testimony, he went so far as to say that he thought they were a perfect pair specifically because they were both innkeepers, and therefore in "similar circumstances." However, Renee David had other ideas, and married a locksmith. She kept her business, apparently, and insisted that when Berto gave her money, she assumed it was to pay his tab.[91]

Anecdotes and limited tax roll information can only provide part of the picture. Sometimes, cross-referencing sources makes it possible to find other previously hidden married women. For example, parish registers for Saint-Malo reveal that Françoise Marie Godon, a *couturiere* [seamstress], married a cooper named Jacques Gigou in 1739. In 1753, Godon was listed in tax rolls, still a *couturiere*, now widowed.[92] Her neighbor, Laurance Tournier, also a *couturiere*, married a ship's officer in 1739 and by 1753 was also widowed. In fact, a quick comparison of the marriage acts of 1739 and the tax roll of 1753 revealed six women—four *couturieres*, an *épiciere* [grocer], and a grain merchant—who married in 1739 and were independent widows by 1753. This was likely to have been a typical pattern in port cities, where men were frequently absent and often killed at sea. For these women, maintaining a profession of their own was less a measure of independence and more a matter of survival.

The life of one such wife is touchingly revealed by a series of letters written by Marie-Jacquette Anquetil, a merchant in Saint-Malo, to her husband, Gilles Lavigne Pignot, who had shipped off to Peru in 1745.[93] Marie-Jacquette wrote long letters, worrying as much about her husband's health and safety as about her tenuous financial situation with the shop, their home, and two sons. She repeatedly threatened to sell their silver: "You know how you left me. If I had more money for merchandise, I could be doing much better. I earn only enough to feed us three."[94] She reported having a number of debts, which included the price of sending both of the boys to school, and "jealous rivals" who harassed her at the shop. Sadly, Pignot was among 12 men lost to a fever in late 1746. Marie-Jacquette remained a solitary widow, surviving even her two sons, until her death in 1785.

---

91 ADLA 2 E 155, Titres de familles, 10 December 1759.

92 ADIV 5 mi 1301 R 738, Marriage acts of 1739, Saint-Malo; *Capitation* ADLA B 3614.

93 Henwood, "Marie-Jaquette Pignot," pp. 321–39. All nine letters are printed, unedited, in their entirety.

94 Henwood, "Marie-Jaquette Pignot," letter dated March 1746.

Widowhood

Widowhood was a common stage of life for early modern women and did not always coincide with old age. Women were frequently widowed by their thirties, and many lived until their sixties or later. General demographic studies of the period place the average age of death in the range of 40 years, but that figure includes an extremely high infant mortality rate. Those who survived childhood could expect to make it to their twenties; those who survived their twenties could expect to reach their fifties or sixties.[95] Alain Croix found that 47.7 percent of men and 51.9 percent of women in mid-seventeenth century Brittany died over the age of 50.[96] In the eighteenth century, a widowed man at the age of 35 had a 72 percent chance of remarriage, while widowed women of the same age had a 46 percent chance. At the age of 45, the respective rates drop to 52 percent and 20 percent.[97] Thus many women spent a significant part of their lives alone.

This was not always a negative situation. In fact, Brigette Maillard has suggested that we need to revisit our view of widowhood as something women were "confined to" and unable to "escape."[98] Widows, like women who had never married, had full control of their legal and financial affairs. Many continued to work for years, either in their husbands' trades, their own trades, or something altogether new. Some childless women lived easily on their rents or dowries, or paid for entry into a hospital. Those with children and land or a business were often capable of continuing the family's work with little interruption. And, finally, Maillard points out that widows were found in every level of society and that numerous sources from the seventeenth century suggest common knowledge of happy widows who displayed little interest in remarriage.[99] At the very least, scholars should consider the possibility that many widows consciously chose to remain unmarried.

The widows of wealthy professionals not only maintained a great deal of power for themselves but preserved family fortunes for their children. A series of widows kept the Vatar family in charge of printing through three generations in Nantes and Rennes.[100] The Vatar women, like many such widows, did more than keep shops open and finish up existing contracts. They were relentless in preserving their family's rights and privileges. In the 1770s, the widows of Guillaume and Nicolas Vatar wrote a memoire to the judges of the Chambre Syndicale, who were in the midst of deliberating whether or not a fifth print shop should be allowed to open in Rennes. The women wrote that they recognized they had no right to address the court in person, but that together they were responsible for two of the four licensed

---

95   Alain Bideau, "La mort quantifiée," *Histoire de la population française: tome 2, de la Renaissance à 1789* (Paris: Presses Universitaires de France, 1988), p. 237.

96   Croix, *La Bretagne aux 16e et 17e siècles: La vie—la mort—la foi* (Paris: Maloine, 1981), p. 199.

97   François Lebrun, "Le mariage et la famille," *Histoire de la population française tome 2, de la Renaissance à 1789* (Paris: Presses Universitaires de France, 1988), p. 316.

98   Maillard, "Les veuves dans la société rurale au XVIIIe siècle," p. 214.

99   Maillard, pp. 216–26.

100   Xavier Ferrieu, "Les Vatar ou trois siècles d'imprimerie à Rennes," *Memoires de la société d'histoire et d'archeologie de Bretagne*, 62 (1985): 223–84.

print shops in town. That gave them the right to make their opinions known in writing: "The esteemed deliberants will surely acknowledge the legitimate interests and rights of the widows, for themselves and for their minor children, to be heeded before a fifth shop can be founded which would ruin four ancient and privileged families."[101]

In these cases, the women's determined pursuit of privilege was quite appropriate because they were working for the long-term survival of their families. Examples of such active and influential widows are found throughout France in this period, and they are a natural result of the existence of the family-run business. Andre Lespagnol found that "widow and son" companies were typical among the wealthy merchants of Saint-Malo, for example. Lespagnol denies that the work of such widows carries any significance since these women merely served as bridges from one generation to the next.[102] However, there is ample evidence that well-placed widows, such as the Vatars, did much more than wait for their sons to grow up. Many were active and aggressive in their commercial activities, sometimes in spite of their children's wishes. In 1711, Mme. Marguerite Tasse, the widow of a Saint-Malo merchant named Demaine, approached another widow to share the costs of a commercial venture in Peru. Their correspondence and receipts detail a healthy trade up until 1715, when Tasse died. At that point, Tasse's son attempted to discontinue the trade and confiscate all of the assets of the joint venture. He was sued by his mother's partner, and ended up paying for the remainder of the contract in 1718.[103]

Widows at all levels of society took over their husband's trades to continue to support themselves and their children. On occasion, women took over official posts that were normally closed to them. Gillette Thurmel ran the postal service from Rennes to St. Brieuc with the assistance of her daughter after her husband's death.[104] A widow in Auray continued in her husband's former post as financial officer to the Hôtel Dieu until she was ordered removed by the *Avocat General* of the king in 1720. It is not clear how or why she was reported to the authorities, but the town had apparently tolerated her in the position for years.[105] Widows who took over their husband's crafts were supported by the appropriate guild as long as they had contracts and apprentices to serve. Just about all women who practiced "masculine" trades, such as leather- or woodwork, were widows. Guilmette du Sellier continued in her husband's work as a master painter after his death in 1678; she had to buy his tools back from the daughter of his former employer.[106]

---

101 ADIV 2 EV 2, Vatar family papers. Undated memoire to the Chambre Syndicale, probably 1775; in 1762, Mme. Vatar of Nantes was charged by the *intendant* for having published and distributed an unapproved newspaper (ADIV C 1470); in 1776, the same Mme. Vatar published a catalogue and inventory for her shop's "going out of business sale," and announced the forthcoming grand opening of her son-in-law's print shop in the same location (ADIV 2 EV 2).

102 Lespagnol, "Femmes négociantes sous Louis XIV," pp. 463–70.

103 ADLA 2 E 888, *Titres des Familles*, Demaine 1711–1718.

104 ADIV C 2030, Papers from the archives of the *Fermiers Messageries*, 1747.

105 ADIV 1 BF 1224, remonstrance of 6 August 1720.

106 ADIV 2 EB 53, Bossard family papers, 12 September 1678.

Widows did not always take on the work of their husbands. Those without any specific training or business were left to find work in whatever they could find. The *capitation* tax rolls for Nantes show that 62 percent of textile laborers (spinners and carders, primarily) and 64 percent of food, drink, and hospitality providers were widows in 1749. Forty years later, widows were less prominent in textile industries, but made up 70 percent of food providers.[107] This indicates a certain amount of flux in the demand for workers in textile trades, but also suggest that widows gravitated toward work that could be done in the home and that did not require extensive training or elaborate equipment. These particular widows could have begun their work while married and simply continued it in widowhood. However, it is just as likely that they had worked with their husbands at some trade and had to find a new line of work as widows. More often than not, the sort of work that could be picked up on short notice with little to no training was the same work they would have performed at home for their own families.

Many widows changed work frequently and did not seem attached to a single profession or occupation. Saint-Malo, a port city where widows made up the majority of taxpaying women, offered a variety of work opportunities. Perrine Cleraut, for example, was a 43-year-old widow and wool spinner when she married Jaques Leroy, a porter, in 1739. By 1753, however, she was again a widow and running a boarding house by herself.[108] Her experience was probably typical for early modern widows. Most of the women in each of the *capitation* tax rolls who declined to identify an occupation were widows. This further supports the notion that most widows floundered somewhat when it came to supporting themselves, even if some did quite well.

While some widows could live independently, truly solitary people were rare in the *ancien régime*. It was no easy feat to live for long without the support of a partner or extended family. Elderly widows and celibate women were undoubtedly vulnerable. When possible, they could depend on the support of their children. Tax rolls show numerous women who lived with adult, working children or with roommates. Documents from criminal cases often include pleas from mothers to release their son or daughter from prison because the child is the only source of support. Anne Hamon, for example, was a retired midwife who depended upon her daughter, also a trained and licensed midwife in Rennes; when Hamon's daughter was jailed for alleged prostitution, the old woman was left homeless and penniless.[109] Wills reveal that some women shared costs with roommates or entered into mutually beneficial arrangements for care. Jeanne Celeste Letourneau, for example, left all of her goods to two sisters in Nantes in return for room and board until her death.[110]

---

107   ADLA B 3519 and B3530.

108   ADIV 5 mi 1301 R 738, marriage acts for Saint-Malo, 1739; ADLA B 3614, tax roll for Saint-Malo, 1753.

109   ADIV 3 B 1450, memoire of 25 February 1712. Hardwick has suggested that widows frequently sought to live with adult children in order to avoid the stigma associated with independent women. Women who lived with children or with other relatives pooled financial resources but also maintained an honorable status with regard to the community. *The Practice of Patriarchy*, p. 138.

110   ADLA 4 E 2/72, 31 December 1770.

Widowhood itself did not necessarily bring about drastic changes in a woman's work life, especially if she came from an established trade of her own or a shared family business. However, widowhood and old age combined brought definite crisis to those who did not have sufficient income or support. Those who had been entirely dependent upon a spouse for survival often suffered when forced to live on their own. It should come as no surprise that widows fill up parish charity rolls, or make up the majority of women who reported no specific occupation and paid few taxes. As in all things, the experience varied greatly from one woman to another. For some, the freedom and opportunity afforded in widowhood must have been welcome; for others, who were forced to make painful choices just to survive, life may have been unbearable.

Single women

It is commonly believed that unattached individuals had no hope of survival in the early modern economy. In fact, Hufton makes a strong case for her argument that unmarried women "could only anticipate destitution" in the eighteenth century.[111] In times of economic crisis, only those who could pool their resources could hope for any kind of security, and the work of each family member was crucial to survival. However, cities and towns of all sizes supported a population of unmarried women.[112] Some of these women were undoubtedly preparing for a future marriage, and several survived by pairing up with other women. Nevertheless, whether for a lifetime or on a temporary basis, many women supported themselves independently.

Judith M. Bennett and Amy M. Froide have stated that single women made up an average of 10 to 20 percent of the adult female population in any given city during the early modern period.[113] That percentage might be higher in large urban centers, where one may expect to find numerous migrants from the countryside entering service or seeking work in a particular industry. My estimates for the city of Nantes show that unmarried women actually made up 10 percent of the overall taxable population, and a much higher percentage of the adult female population. Unmarried women in Nantes made up an average of 50.2 percent of the total number of taxed women in *capitation* tax rolls, with a high of 65 percent in 1720 and a low of 34 percent in 1753.

Isolating the unmarried population for study is no easy task. As noted above, names and forms of address were not standardized in the eighteenth century. It is sometimes possible to trace individuals by cross-referencing tax rolls with other sources, such as parish registers and guild registers. But there is no simple way to gauge the number of unmarried women who had never been married or would remain unmarried. In the rolls for Nantes, for example, numerous presumably unmarried women have children, many more than one would attribute to high rates of illegitimacy. Yet we are so accustomed to a woman being identified primarily by

---

111   Hufton, *The Poor in Eighteenth-Century France,* p. 26

112   As widows have been discussed above, this section will deal almost exclusively with never-married women.

113   Bennett and Froide, "A Singular Past," p. 2.

her relationship to a man that the absence of a noted marital status seems to indicate these women were not married.

Seventeenth-century sources are even more difficult when it comes to identifying unmarried individuals. Demographers studying that century are dependent on parish registers, which list only baptism, marriage, and burial. Naturally, unmarried men and women would not be included in such records until death, and would be lost entirely if they left the parish of their birth. Thus, population figures for the unwed are reconstructed based upon the average of unmarried dead in the records. Such figures are often low, based as they are on the assumption that singles were a rarity. Gendered assumptions complicate the picture even more—Croix states categorically that, for women, even the age of 39 was not "definitively celibate," and so his population estimates discount the possibility that a significant number of unmarried women lived anywhere in Brittany.[114]

Based on the *capitation* tax rolls for the eighteenth century, I can estimate that between 7 and 15 percent of Breton households were headed by unmarried women. I come to this number by taking my total number of taxpaying women in a given city and subtracting married women, widows, and roommates.[115] Surprisingly enough, the highest percentages of single female heads of household were found in the smallest towns and villages: Dinan (population 5,500 in mid-century), Landernau (population 3,600), and Montcontour (population 1,600) all had between 14 percent and 15 percent of households headed by unmarried women. The largest cities, Rennes and Nantes, had lower percentages, at 7 percent and 10 percent respectively. Medium-sized cities and ports were also fairly low: Saint-Malo and Morlaix were at the low end at 7 percent; Brest, Quimper, and Quintin all had 11 percent.

In the cities, it is a fairly simple matter to discern how unattached women could have supported themselves. Young women, either born locally or having migrated from the countryside, found work in domestic service or in a local industry. Servants are hard to trace, as they would have been dependent on their employers and absent from the sources. Those who worked in industry paid their own taxes, more often than not, and are easier to locate. Most single women in Rennes or Morlaix worked in some aspect of textile production—carding, spinning, bleaching, or finishing. Unmarried women in Nantes worked primarily in clothing production and sales, as tailors or dress and accessories merchants. Thus, in these places, there is no mystery in the presence and survival of single women.

Small towns and villages, however, offered few opportunities for anyone to live and work independently, and only then in particular circumstances. Most people worked at whatever form of agriculture or manufacturing dominated the area, and the family was the leading economic unit. Young women who did not inherit a home married soon after leaving their natal homes or worked for a few years in order to save up a dowry. Young men who did not inherit did the same or drifted toward big-city opportunities. Widows and widowers remarried as soon as possible or made do with whatever jobs were available, usually for very little money. Skilled workers

---

114   Croix, *La Bretagne aux 16e et 17e siècles*, p. 184.
115   Sisters and unrelated roommate pairs will be discussed below.

served only local needs, and often had to supplement their income with day-labor in the fields.

In this environment, it was a rarity for a woman to have supported herself with a trade for any length of time. And yet, it is precisely in this setting that I have found the highest percentages of unmarried women. It is likely that the high number of female heads of household was linked with inheritance of either property or tenure, and not with access to wage labor or trades. In fact, the majority of single women recorded in these small towns and villages lived alone and, while most declined to identify an occupation, many collected rents. In urban areas, by contrast, unmarried women were often wholly dependent upon their occupations for survival. For that reason, women in urban areas were more likely to name an occupation.

Urban women were also more likely than rural women to create a support network with other women in similar circumstances. In most of the cities in my sample, women were frequently found living together.[116] Hufton has called this phenomenon "spinster clustering," and cites it as an example of how marriage, or at least some kind of partnership, was a requirement for survival in the early modern period.[117] But it is interesting to note the peculiar nature of women's living together in these Breton towns. In every setting, there were a handful of mothers and daughters, aunts and nieces or other relatives, and very poor unmarried women and widows who banded together, and such pairings might not be considered noteworthy by a scholar of this period. But a striking proportion of the "roommates" in this sample were specifically unmarried women in urban areas who worked in clothing or textile production trades. Most were sisters, but many were not. Furthermore, roommates were not necessarily either unskilled or impoverished.

Relatives of a different generation, such as unattached daughters who lived with widowed mothers, usually reported having different occupations. The records for Rennes are most revealing of mixed trades in households occupied by multiple women. The *capitation* roll for 1739 includes eight mother-daughter pairs with different occupations. A mother with children to support was invariably a widow, though not always labeled as such, and she could be found in just about any category of work. The daughters in these cases, following a trend among unmarried, working women, were clothing makers and retailers. Suzanne Bellan, *porteuse d'eau* [water porter], lived with her daughter, a *lingere*. The Veuve Liot, a mill worker, Veuve Blin, a grocer, and La Bouvin, a *gardienne de malades* [caretaker of the sick] also had daughters who worked as *lingeres*. Veuve Challou, a spinner, had two daughters who were *couturieres*. Sebastienne Fresnel, a *vendeuse de denrées* [foodstuff vendor], had two daughters who were secondhand junk dealers. Thus, these children did not

---

116   In other European countries, especially England and Germany, women were actively discouraged from living together and sometimes even prohibited by law from doing so. See Merry Wiesner, "Having Her Own Smoke: Employment and Independence for Singlewomen in Germany, 1400–1750," pp. 192–216, and Margaret Hunt, "The Sapphic Strain: English Lesbians in the long Eighteenth Century," pp. 270–96 in Bennett and Froide, *Singlewomen*. There is no evidence of this happening in Brittany, or even in greater France, in this period.

117   Hufton, "Women Without Men: Widows and Spinsters in Britain and France in the Eighteenth Century," *Journal of Family History*, 9 (Winter 1984); and *The Poor of Eighteenth Century France*, p. 25.

necessarily pick up work from their parents. In at least one entry, it is clear that everyone found work wherever they could: Jean Petit was a porter whose wife was a spinner and whose daughter was a water-carrier.[118]

Sisters, however, and unrelated roommates most often shared an occupation. In the *capitation* roll for Nantes in 1720, for example, there were 16 pairs of sisters among the 100 individual women who made or sold clothing. In 1749 in that same city, there were 24 pairs of sisters and 14 unrelated pairs among 199 clothing providers. By 1789, the rolls included 48 sets of sisters and 3 pairs of unrelated roommates among 350 clothing retailers or tailors.[119] As a textile market, Nantes provided numerous opportunities for workers in cloth- and clothing-related trades. Overall, tailors and clothing retailers made up, on average, 18.7 percent of the total number of taxed women in Nantes, and 44.2 percent of the taxed women in Nantes who identified an occupation. Thus, it is not surprising that most of the unattached women, and by extension a higher proportion of roommates, were in cloth or textile trades. Sometimes these relationships could be quite formal, as in the unrelated pair of mistress *lingeres*, noted above, who contracted together to train an apprentice.[120] Roommates shared a workspace and possibly a clientele, as well. Witnesses in police investigations of alleged immoral behavior among unmarried women include numerous references to work relationships: Catherine Maudit, for example, reported in 1712 that she knew the young, pregnant *boutonniere* [button or buttonhole maker], Françoise Robin because Robin often came to work with her and her roommate, both *tailleuses*.[121] These relationships may indicate a sense of professional survival that went beyond the need to pool resources in an uncertain economy.

There were several factors that influenced the number of roommates in a given population. Certainly, finances played a significant roll, and very poor women in any setting or newly arrived migrants in a large city would have sought each other out for support. These relationships will be discussed in more detail as a question of sociability in Chapter 4. But, here it is interesting to note where there was an absence of roommates. Saint-Malo has a very low incidence of spinster clustering, and it is not clear why that should be the case. True, tax rolls from Saint-Malo report low numbers of unmarried women—an average of 29.3 percent of all taxed women. If single women were the most likely to find roommates, then the low incidence would make sense. However, 71.7 percent of the female heads of household in Saint-Malo were widows, and widows were frequently in need of support. One wonders why more widows did not pool their resources in Saint-Malo. Perhaps widows had stronger family connections that made roommates less necessary. Unmarried women, on the other hand, needed to create their "family" networks.

---

118   ADLA B 3560, Tax roll for Rennes, 1739.
119   ADLA B3502, B 3519, and B 3530: Tax rolls in order.
120   ADLA 2 E 3205, *Titres de Familles*, LeTable family, 1712.
121   ADLA B 5851, *Prevoté* inquiries, 3 March 1712.

Income levels

Vulnerability and poverty were constant companions to the early modern woman. Young women, attracted to the city from small villages, may have hoped to find work in order to build a savings or a dowry. When work was scarce, many turned to prostitution or "dishonorable ways."[122] Those who did find work as servants were often at the mercy of their employers.[123] Women could rarely travel alone any distance in safety, and needed a safe place to sleep at night. Marriage, pregnancy, and other life changes added to the lack of formal training and resources, severely limiting a woman's options when she sought to earn wages. For these reasons, women made up, and still make up, a disproportionate number of poor people.

The majority of the women in Nantes for each *capitation* year studied were in the lowest tax bracket: an average of 51 percent of taxed female heads of household were paying .10 to 1.10 livres a year.[124] In general, those in the next highest bracket (2–4.10 livres) made up an additional 30 percent or more.[125] This means that over 80 percent of the women eighteenth-century Nantes were earning very little. Only one percent of the taxpaying women in that city were assessed at more than 30 livres, and most of those women were living on rents or maintaining family businesses. This pattern creates a pyramid with a very narrow tip; most unattached women were fairly close to poverty.

The situation was much the same in Rennes. There, in 1709, 41 percent of female-headed households were assessed at one livre or less, with an additional 2.5 percent reported as too poor to pay anything. Of the 3.6 percent who paid more than 30 livres, most did not specify an occupation. Two of those women, the widows Kerlean and Monteraut, paid 200 and 300 livres, respectively. As in Nantes, there was a very small population of well-off independent women in Rennes, and many of those women did not report an occupation.

The *capitation* tax records for Morlaix in 1750 reveal an interesting pattern in that 45 percent of independent taxpaying women paid between two and four livres, while only 20 percent were assessed at the lower one livre bracket. In an earlier tax roll for Morlaix, from 1739, 40 percent paid one livre and another 40 percent paid two to four livres. It is true that a majority of the women are still in the two lowest tax brackets. But, compared to the bigger cities, Morlaix supported a greater proportion of women who were probably secure, if not well-off.

In small towns and villages, overall tax levels are quite low. Few people, male or female, ever paid more than 9 or 10 livres in the eighteenth century. However, the income levels for women alone in small towns and villages are fairly comparable to

---

122   Jaques Depauw, "Illicit Sexual Activity and Society in Eighteenth-Century Nantes," in Robert Forster and Orest Ranum (eds), *Family and Society: Selections from the Annales, Economies, Societies, Civilisations* (Baltimore: Johns Hopkins University Press, 1976), p. 150.

123   Cissie Fairchilds, *Domestic Enemies: Servants and their Masters in Old Regime France* (Johns Hopkins University Press, 1984).

124   This would be the lowest level possible, average for servants, spinners, and day-laborers.

125   Average for small shopkeepers and craft workers.

figures for women alone in ports and large cities. In Dinan for 1753, 52 percent of female-headed households paid one livre or less, and 32 percent paid between two and four livres. With 84 percent of taxed women in the two lowest brackets, and only .8 percent paying more than 30 livres, the numbers in Dinan are on par with those for Nantes. Of women in tiny Roche-Bernard in 1753, 63 percent paid one livre or less, and only .5 percent paid more than 30.

Thus, no matter the setting, women in early modern Brittany were consistently assessed at very low levels of income for taxpaying purposes. Women, especially elderly widows, filled the rolls of those too poor to pay in cities where such records were kept. However, the vulnerability and poverty so often associated with independent women in the pre-modern era tell only part of the story. Sometimes, it is a matter of emphasis. Just as I have pointed out that 80 percent of a given population paid less than four livres, I could have just as easily said that 45 percent paid between two and 10 livres. In fact, that is the average figure for Nantes over the course of the eighteenth century. I, like so many other scholars, have focused on the poor and the rich in order to demonstrate the discrepancy between the two. But there is a solid middle group that cannot be forgotten, neither rich nor poor, who made up the bulk of the population of independent or unattached women in Brittany.

Conclusion

It is clear that each stage of life offered unique challenges and choices. There were necessary adaptations for marriage and childcare, but there was room to maneuver. Marriage did not always require a complete abandonment of previous skills and occupations. Married women ran family businesses and sometimes kept a separate source of income. The ability to work independently was crucial to the wife of an absent soldier, sailor, or merchant. Children were often sent away as babies, and again as older children to work or receive training. Children who remained home helped with work when possible, but special arrangements for their care were rarely necessary if parents worked at or near home. Thus, the various stages of a woman's life had an impact, certainly, but did not entirely dictate her work opportunities. There were periods of independence, such as during a husband's absence or after children had gone to work elsewhere. There were periods of economic hardship, when added income was a necessity. And there were occasional opportunities to gain professional status in a formal sense, adding to one's standing in the community.

The household was in many ways the foundation of early modern society, but it did not wholly define each of its members. Men and women connected with others in a multitude of contexts in the community at large, some work-related and others purely social. In the coming chapters, we will cover in detail the work performed by women as well as the ways in which women relied upon personal and professional relationships. There is evidence that some women did identify with each other as workers, making it possible, for example, for fish merchants in Nantes to unite in defense of their market privileges, or for the candle merchants of Saint-Malo to collectively protest fines for those who failed to register their merchandise. These women may have been wives and mothers, but their identities went beyond those roles.

Chapter Two

Work and Identity

Women played an ambiguous and complicated role in the world of work. Work was often a gendered activity, subject to the same patriarchal organization that characterized home life and politics during this period. "Women's work" normally entailed tasks that had long been associated with domestic activity, though most men's work during this period was also home-oriented. Women's work was often necessary for the survival of a household, and yet it frequently has been dismissed as secondary to the work of the primary breadwinner. Since most people did marry and have children, and these changes usually had a more immediate impact on women than they did on men, women were constantly adapting their work to fit their circumstances. From childhood, through marriage, childbirth, and family life, into old age and probable widowhood, women faced a distinct set of challenges. At the same time, they normally had fewer resources and less formal training or support with which to establish themselves. Navigating these waters, surviving, and succeeding within the confines of a clear gender hierarchy often called for ingenuity and persistence.

Yet it would be a mistake to say that work generally had little to do with a woman's identity. Identity is a multilayered and complex phenomenon, and an individual who identifies him- or herself with a particular profession likely does so for a variety of reasons. One might embrace a professional identity for the social status or the financial security it brings. One also might take pride in being a dutiful heir to one's parents, a hard worker, a provider for one's children, and so forth. And so, an early modern woman might have felt pride in her identity as a merchant and guild member, for example, and enjoyed a particular status based upon that identity. But she also might have seen herself as a daughter, a wife, a mother, and a woman, and her work was likely to have been an integral part of each of those identities. In numerous sources, women identified themselves and were identified by others according to their status as heirs, as professionals or laborers, and as members of a family. In most cases, the concepts overlap each other too intimately for the modern scholar to clearly define when a woman was a wife and when she was a worker. The problem is further complicated by the idea of "women's work": the perceived femininity of certain kinds of work. There may be practical considerations that steer women towards certain kinds of work, but a woman also might pursue work that she deems suitable to her identity as a "woman."

Women are associated with work that involves food, clothing, cleaning, or the care of very young, sick, or elderly people. These domestic pursuits are the realm of women workers almost universally in place and time. No one can say with certainty why that is so. In the early modern period, the sexual division of labor was not justified by physical capacity alone; rarely were early modern women prevented from engaging in backbreaking physical labor. Indeed, the peasant woman seemed eminently more suited to fieldwork than a learned, *bourgeois*, or noble man.[1] The restriction of women to certain trades was also not necessarily linked to mental or intellectual capacity. There have always been a select number of educated women, and the average wife of a farmer or merchant efficiently handled household accounts and kept shops in order.

The accepted explanations for the origins of women's work to date usually revolve around two poles: either women have been limited, physically and emotionally, by their reproductive responsibilities (including but not limited to actual childbirth and childcare) or they have been marginalized by the patriarchal practices of their families and larger societies. These interpretations are not mutually exclusive, and, in fact, the former theory is sometimes used to explain the latter. That is to say, a woman's work had to be adaptable to her childcare responsibilities, and therefore had to be performed at home, easily interrupted, and not very complicated. Thus, investment in a girl's education was wasted money; a woman's "training" was limited to what she received at her own mother's knee. At the same time, patriarchal customs dictated that all available resources go to the education and establishment of male children. Thus, girls by necessity made do with less financial support and whatever skills they were able to pick up at home. The main difference between the two theories, if they may be adequately distinguished, is that the reproductive argument ultimately becomes a biological or "natural" justification of women's work, while the patriarchal explanation lays the blame squarely on the culture of male domination over women.

In the association of women with certain work, we find again and again that there is a suggestion of the "appropriateness" of the work. This is true not only in the passive relegation of women to marginalized work, but in the choices women made when given the opportunity. Even when women had access to formal training, for example, and were not limited to whatever skills could be gained for free at home, they still tended to pursue trades that fell within the usual fields: seamstresses, *lingeres*, cooks, and caretakers. That is not to deny that their choices were limited by external forces—it is not at all clear that a woman who wished to become a carpenter could have done so. But it is also not the case that women in early modern Europe were entirely helpless before the whims of their families and their own bodies. Women's work was a product of opportunity and acceptability, skill and inclination.

In this chapter, we will investigate the actual situation of women workers in Brittany, and the extent to which their lives were controlled either by the physical and material needs of their families or by the patriarchal institutions of their society. I will describe market institutions as they pertained to women both inside and outside of the guilds, beginning with the guilds that controlled the workers and the merchants of the cities. I will also cover the commercial and industrial activities of the countryside. Through it all, as I explain the opportunities available to women as well as the limitations they faced, I will demonstrate how women's work was linked to women's identities.

---

1   Lieselotte Steinbrügge, *The Moral Sex: Women's Nature in the French Enlightenment* (New York: Oxford University Press, 1995), p. 14.

Formal work in the marketplace

The guilds in Breton cities were, for the most part, typical of those elsewhere in France. Members of the corps had to be Catholic and of good reputation. Most guild members had to have served an apprenticeship of several years, often beginning their training at a fairly young age. Apprentices eventually served as journeymen and worked to perfect their art or trade. Upon completion of a masterpiece and payment of dues, journeymen were given full guild privileges and the right to operate as guild masters. The stages of guild membership were best suited to the typical male stages of life, and it was common for new masters to marry and set up a household workshop with the assistance of a spouse. Guild masters could then serve as guild officers and oversee inspections of licensed workshops and the policing of unlicensed work. In most guilds, the only female members were the widows of masters, who were allowed to exercise their husbands' privileges until they remarried or until a son took over the workshop. Such widows did not serve as officers and were normally excluded from banquets, assemblies, and other guild functions.

There were no exclusively female guilds in Brittany, such as the *lingeres* of Rouen and Paris. However, a number of guilds in Nantes, Rennes, and Quimper admitted women members on a roughly equal basis with men. Among these were the tailors' and *fripiers'* guilds of Nantes, the tailors and merchants of Rennes, and the tailors of Quimper. These guilds admitted women either as the daughters of masters who maintained guild privileges whether or not they married, or as workers who had served an apprenticeship and paid entrance fees. Women could never serve as officers, and were usually excluded from assemblies and feasts, but in other respects were recognized as licensed mistresses of a craft.

The tailors' guild of Nantes dates back to 1471, and earliest statutes refer to the *"freres et soeurs"* [brothers and sisters] of the confraternity, as well as *"maistres et veuves"* [masters and widows] of the craft. However, the guild did not admit women as full members until 1733.[2] Deliberations on the matter began in 1730, and reveal quite a bit about the reluctance of guild members to admit women. Not surprisingly, the men who specialized in women's clothing were the most upset at the prospect. One unavoidable fact helped make the decision: the large and growing number of women who were working as *tailleuses* already.[3] According to the *capitation* records, 16 percent of taxed women in 1720 identified themselves as *tailleuses*. In 1740, after the guild opened its doors to women, the percentage had risen to 23 percent, and it continued to increase over the course of the century.[4] An increasing number of women sought work as tailors. More importantly, however, women made

---

2   AMN HH 168 #1 Tailors' statutes and deliberations, 1730.

3   In her book, *Fabricating Women: the Seamstresses of Old Regime France*, Clare Haru Crowston describes how the Paris tailors' guild admitted women only as *couturieres*, or seamstresses, and kept the women in second-class status. She goes on to say that the same pattern may be found in Nantes. However, I have not found that to be the case. Women in the tailors' guild of Nantes were called *tailleuses* and were given full privileges over the making of women's and children's clothing.

4   ADLA B 3502 Capitation roll of 1720; ADLA B 3519 Capitation roll of 1740; By 1789, 29 percent of taxed women identified themselves as *tailleuses* (ADLA B 3530.)

up an increasing percentage of working tailors. In 1720, only 25 percent of taxpayers who identified themselves as tailors were women; by 1740, 33 percent of tailors were women. To the guild, these women represented both uncontrolled labor and uncollected revenue. Since it was impossible to eliminate the competition, they decided to regulate it as best they could. The official reason for the admittance of women, however, was the growing population of the city and the growing demand for tailors able to serve the needs of women customers. Decency required that women at least have the option of patronizing a female tailor.[5]

The first official mistresses were few and far between: out of 1213 certificates of *maîtrise* for all trades from the entire period 1733–1791, only 227 survive for women and only 141 of those were for female tailors.[6]   A fee was required, and nearly all of the women certified as mistresses were at least literate enough to sign their own names. Though all applicants required a sponsor, none of the women admitted in their own right seem to have been related to masters of the guild. Master's widows also held the title "mistress," and were allowed to keep it as long as they worked "on their own account." A lengthy investigation and trial in 1763 revealed that a number of widows had rented out their privileges to journeymen tailors. Those who continued to work for themselves were released, while the others were heavily fined.[7]

The *fripiers'* guild of Nantes was a formal organization of junk dealers, and they claimed a monopoly on the sale of all secondhand goods. This guild admitted women as members, possibly for the same reasons that the tailors did. It was relatively easy and inexpensive to establish oneself in the trade of secondhand goods, and numerous women throughout the city were identified as *revendeuses, regrattieres*, and *fripieres*. The trade was also rife with contraband. From the 1740s to the 1780s, the guild did everything in its power to control the various petty merchants around the city who had no guild affiliation. Membership was strict and exclusive, with the added requirement of literacy, since members were expected to maintain a log of the origins of each item in their possession. This was done in order to assuage public fear of commerce in stolen merchandise. However, there was enough flexibility in the guild's operation that even relatively unqualified applicants could join. The widow Clouet, for example, was herself illiterate but was admitted because she had a literate daughter who worked in her shop.[8] In spite of such examples of leniency, guild membership was out of the reach of many of the women who engaged in the

---

5   The Paris corps used same rationale for finally admitting women, according to Martin Saint Leon, *Histoire des corporations de metiers depuis leurs origines jusqu'à leur suppression en 1791* (Paris, 1922). Even so, male tailors throughout France continued to make women's clothing. Indeed, very wealthy women saw it as a mark of distinction to have a male tailor, a fact that inspired mistress tailors of Paris to publicly complain. See Cynthia Truant, "Guildswomen of Paris: Gender, Power, and Sociability in the Old Regime," *Proceedings of the Annual Meeting of the Western Society for French History*, 15 (1988): 50.

6   AMN HH 61-86. Bureau of *maîtrise* registration, 1733–1791. Livre 1757–1763 is missing. The number of mistresses rose over the first half of the century, peaked in the 1750s and then leveled off.

7   AMN HH 168 #11 and #12, Tailors' contraventions, 1762–1768.

8   AMN HH 137 #2 & #15 *Fripiers'* guild inspector's reports, 1740s.

junk trade. In the tax records for Nantes at mid-century, 29 percent of the women who identified an occupation were miscellaneous retailers, but guild records indicate extremely small numbers of women members.[9]

The remaining guilds in Nantes which admitted women on a regular basis were food-related trades. The *maîtrises et jurandes* register for Nantes lists 31 women who were licensed as *lardieres*, *charcutieres*, or *grenieres* [bacon, sausage, and grain merchants].[10] Several more mistresses in such trades are to be found among tax rolls. The majority of these were widows who may have inherited businesses from their late husbands, but there is no way to tell for certain if that was the case. In the *maîtrise* logbooks, those women sworn in as butchers and sausage-makers, with rare exceptions, named a living or deceased spouse. It seems significant that these women were sworn in with a spouse's name while most of the merchants and tailors were not; the practice of recording names in this way links the food makers with their spouses while the tailors and shopkeepers stand alone. In addition, most of the women in food trades were not literate enough to sign their names to their certificates.

In tax rolls, people who identified themselves by a trade usually did not volunteer whether or not they were formally recognized by a guild or some other administrative body. Thus, it is not always easy to demonstrate which workers were official and which were not. However, there is one source that isolates those who were recognized formally as artisans or merchants, and that is the *Capitation des artisans*. Drawn up several times in the mid-eighteenth century, this head-tax roll was organized by trade and was based on official lists rather than on home-by-home counts. This allows us to see which formal trades recognized women members and how many women were registered for each. In the roll for Nantes in 1749, one can see at a glance that 50 of the city's 173 *aubergistes* were women and that each was identified as a widow. Not a single carpenter, mason, or clockmaker was female. But almost a third of the mercers and roughly half of the whole-cloth merchants and fish vendors were women. There were no male *lingeres*, *coiffeuses*, or *marchandes de mode*.[11]

The *capitation des artisans* documents that women were a significant and officially recognized part of the commercial landscape of Nantes, even if they were not necessarily guild members. All sources seem to indicate that such tradeswomen were on par with tradesmen in similar circumstances. They had to register with police, submit to inspections and pay their taxes. Guilds offered a particular kind of protection to their members, however, as well as a privileged status, and most of the guilds in Nantes did not admit women. Among those that did, such as the tailors, one would be hard-pressed to say they were treated as the equals of the male members.

---

9   ADLA B 3519, Tax roll for 1749. Many women identified themselves simply as "marchande," making it difficult to distinguish between petty junk dealers and more established merchants. Such "merchants" were 29 percent of women who identified an occupation.

10   AMN HH 61–HH 86 (1723–1789)

11   ADIV C 2144 *Capitation des artisans*, Nantes 1749. Many of the rolls offer interesting bits of description, such as the report that "all fruit vendors were the daughters of fish sellers or grain porters, and included with their parents there," or that "almost all the *couturieres* were too poor to tax, and that those who sold a little cloth were included among the *marchands de toile*."

In Rennes, the situation for women in the corporations was a little more promising. The first set of *lettres patentes* for the merchants' guild of Rennes is dated 1661, and it is clear that from the beginning, a master's daughter was as welcome as his son.[12] Most French guilds allowed a daughter to pass a certain privilege onto her husband, enabling him to join the guild at a reduced fee. The guild in Rennes went even further and recognized a daughter's privilege in her own right. In fact, the daughters of Rennais master merchants were allowed to run boutiques regardless of marital status. A distinction was made between daughters and widows of masters: according to the statutes in 1674, a widow lost her privileges upon remarriage because "she did not own the rights of her *chef*, as did the daughter of a master."[13] By the end of the century, the guild was prepared to receive the new husbands of masters' widows, provided the women applied for membership in their own names before remarrying.[14] In each of these cases, a woman's guild status was her own and not the provisional coverture of her father.

There were three ways to join the merchant's guild of Rennes: as the child of a master, through service as an apprentice, and by payment of a large fee. Women were apparently received by any of these means. The logbook of guild receptions shows that, in 1761, Jacques Fouche sponsored his apprentice, Françoise le Songeur; Dominique Sanson sponsored his daughter, Michelle Rose Sanson; and Josseline Thommel Desgranges was received for the sum of 80 livres.[15] Renée Le Do, wife of Sieur Landante, was received as a mistress in 1715 based on the membership of her deceased father; apparently, he had been received in 1647, but had never owned a shop or practiced the trade in any way. He had maintained membership solely in order to pass it on to his son and daughter. Thus, Renée and her brother Etienne qualified as soon as they agreed to pay their fees and the back-fees owed by their father.[16] This system of establishing one's children through guild membership complements the Breton custom of partible inheritance, by which all non-noble children inherit equally, regardless of age or sex. Breton law will be discussed at length elsewhere, but it is important to note that families in this region had followed egalitarian inheritance principles for generations. In this context, it seems perfectly reasonable for certain membership benefits to have been extended to daughters as well as sons.

As in the case of Nantes, the tax rolls for Rennes reveal a bit of a discrepancy between the number of women who identified themselves as merchants and the number who held guild status. The struggle between the guild and "unofficial" merchants will be discussed below. Here, I would like to point out the strong presence of women among formally recognized merchants. The merchants' guild's submission to the *capitation des artisans* lists 107 women among its 291 members,

---

12   AMR Liasse 191, Merchants' guild statutes 1660; ADIV 5 E 20, statutes 1674, 1687, and 1735.

13   ADIV 5 E 20, Article XII, statutes 1674.

14   ADIV 5 E 21, merchants' guild deliberations and receptions, 1761–1791.

15   ADIV 5 E 21, deliberations and receptions, 1761–1791.

16   ADIV 3 B 1428, *maîtrise* certificate, 2 January 1715.

making women 37 percent of the guild.[17] General tax rolls reveal that women made up 30 percent of the city's drapers in both 1709 and 1753, while they jumped from 60 percent to 80 percent of the city's *toile* merchants between those same two years.[18] Across the eighteenth century, an average of 20 percent of the women who identified an occupation in tax rolls claimed to be "merchants" of one sort or another, with another 20 percent specifically in cloth or clothing goods.

There seems to have been little technical difference between the memberships of men and women in the merchants' guild. However, in 1735, the statutes explicitly stated for the first time that "widows and daughters" were excluded from assemblies, and it is clear from certain debates at that time that the membership of women in the guild was no simple matter.[19] In 1739, Françoise Perrine Guyonval sued the guild before *Parlement* for having refused her admission, and her lawyers argued that she was "doubly qualified" because both her father and mother were members of the guild. But it is not at all clear that her mother's status carried any weight with the guild or the court.[20]

Guyonval's case is worth considering in some detail because it is in the context of her lawyer's arguments that we find the most explicit statements regarding women's status in the guilds. When Guyonval petitioned the corps of merchant-drapers in Rennes for admission as mistress, she did so not as a widow, nor as a charity case, but as the child of a master and mistress in the guild. She took her case before *Parlement* only after her repeated attempts to join the guild were ignored. In one swift hearing, the guild was ordered to admit Guyonval, and she was formally accepted a few months later. The case was written up by her lawyer in a dramatic pamphlet.

At the heart of this case was the struggle between the formal merchant's guild and the petty merchants of the city. The guild prided itself on being tolerant of petty merchants and other unorganized and informal vendors as long as those people confined themselves to certain goods and small quantities.[21] The guild, concerned that non-members would abuse the generosity of their corporation, kept up a lively schedule of spot inspections and police procedures. Eventually, their attempts to keep control of the local market raised the ire of the numerous non-member merchants who worked in the city. In 1715, the *marchands sans jurande*, a title they embraced for themselves, published a *memoire* against the drapers of Rennes. The official request for separate guild status followed later that year.[22] On the local level,

17 ADIV C 2145, *Capitation des artisans,* Rennes 1748.

18 ADIV C 3995, *Capitation* for Rennes, 1709; ADLA B 3583, *Capitation* for Rennes, 1753; A *Toile* merchant generally sold whole cloth of a hemp or linen fiber, while drapers normally dealt in more luxurious fabrics, such as fine woolens and silk.

19 Regarding assemblies, there is evidence that women in this guild attended at least some assemblies prior to the acceptance of the 1735 statutes. Members in attendance signed in at the end of recorded assembly minutes, and several women's signatures are clear in those records. AMR 11 Z 9, deliberations of guild 1715–1719.

20 ADIV 5 E 20, court papers, pamphlet, and admittance certificate, April–June, 1739.

21 AMR Liasse 191, Guild statutes 1660, 1674; ADLA C 398, guild statutes 1687; ADIV 5 E 20, Statutes 1735.

22 ADLA C 652, *mémoire* and response; ADIV C 1459, petition for guild status. *Marchands sans jurande* translates roughly as "merchants without guild status."

the *Parlement* chose to recommend the *marchands sans jurande* for establishment as a separate guild.[23] The king overruled the confirmation of the *Parlement* and refused the institution of a separate guild. Instead, the king ordered the guilds to be "reunited" with the petty merchants in a single corporation that was entitled to deal in all merchandise.[24]

Petty merchants were ordered to present themselves for membership in the corps within a given time limit or to give up their shops forever. The guild was ordered to admit all reasonable applicants without hesitation. Continued conflict led to a revised set of statutes in 1735 and a renewed royal command for all working merchants to apply for membership in the corps or give up commerce.[25] Several merchants who had applied in 1717 for admission presented themselves a second time. Several did not. A "list war" ensued, as the corps officers attempted to clear up who in the city was running a shop in contravention of the royal dictate, and the petty merchants hurried to protect their peers. Guyonval's case came as the repercussions of the 1735 statute publication were dying down.[26]

On 2 June 1739, she sued the guild's officers before *Parlement* for their refusal to admit her into the guild as a mistress. Guyonval's father had been admitted into the guild in 1717—as a mercer and a *marchand sans jurande,* he had dutifully presented himself for admittance in accordance with the king's order. He had not presented himself a second time in response to the statutes of 1735 because by that time Monsieur Guyonval was very ill. He died early in 1736. According to her lawyer, as soon as her father had been admitted to the corps, Mlle. Guyonval became the "daughter of a master." Secondly, the young woman's mother was a mistress merchant " . . . received on her own merits into the mysteries":

> Therefore, the right of the defendant was proven by the quality of her father. But if it is possible to find the father's status deficient, the status of the mother communicated the rights of the community, the privileges accorded by the statutes, and all the laws imposed on merchants.

Guyonval did not have her own shop at the time of the trial. However, she still worked for her mother, and she claimed as additional support for her cause the 15 years of experience "serving" her parents in their shop.

Guyonval's lawyer explained the specifics of the statutes regarding women's rights in the corporation. "All is common to master merchants and mistress merchants," he pointed out, with the only exception being that "wives and daughters" were excluded from assemblies and incapable of bestowing apprenticeship rights on their employees. In all other things, the rights of mistresses are equal to those of masters.

> This article (19) begins in these terms: "widows and daughters who exercise commerce in the corps and community." Widows are therefore in the corps and community: they

---

23 ADLA C 21, *Parlement's lettres patents,* 1717.

24 ADLA C 652 and ADIV 5 E 20, copies of the *arrêt.*

25 ADIV 5 E 20, later statutes, lists, admission certificates.

26 ADIV 5 E 20—handwritten copies of court proceedings and printed pamphlet. The pamphlet's arguments were taken verbatim from the court proceedings.

therefore transmit to their children the right to the mysteries that the statutes had granted them . . . and by consequence, the defendant has certain right to mastership.

The lawyer here has established the right of the mother to pass her privileges on to her daughter, a premise that was not commonly accepted in early modern corporate law.

Most of the guild's statutes were similar to those found elsewhere in Europe: sons of masters gained admission into the guild without apprenticeship or high dues, as did men who married daughters of masters. Guyonval's lawyer explained that the daughter can give her privileges to her husband "because the daughter of the master has already been received–just as the son of the master and those who have been admitted via service can transmit their privileges to their wives." The pamphlet continues:

> The articles (22, 23, & 24) here express that one accords to daughters what one accords to sons, the words "daughter of master" do not exclude "daughter of mistress merchant"; one does not need to say "community of master merchants and mistress merchants." Thus, a most rudimentary reading of the rules decides in favor of the defendant.

Here they assume that daughters share the rights of their brothers, and that mistress merchants share the rights of master merchants. All are included under the generic terms of "sons" and "masters." On Guyonval's behalf, her lawyer was making a public claim for the equality of women.

By the mid-eighteenth century, a master's daughter only had to present herself for admission before marriage in order to keep her status; she was expected to present her husband for membership, whatever his profession, after the marriage.[27] Here, the timing of her admission was crucial. Guyonval married Gilles De Chateaugiron, a *huissier* in Paris, only a week after her formal admission to the guild.[28] It is likely that she had planned to marry for months but was unwilling to lose her guild status.[29]

---

27   ADIV 5 E 21, guild deliberations and admission entries, 1761–1791.

28   AMR GG 2 mi 72, Marriage acts for Saint-Jean parish, 14 July 1739.

29   When I first read the details of this case, I surmised, as Guyonval's lawyers had, that she had been rejected because of her sex. But the guild's membership logs suggest an alternative interpretation: that Guyonval may have been rejected due to a simple spelling error, and that the guild's struggle was an effort to cover up their own carelessness. The guild recorded the name of every person who petitioned for membership, whether or not he or she was accepted. Guyonval's case clearly refers to numerous rejections from the guild's officers, and yet there is no record of any of her petitions. Earlier records show that Jean Baptiste Guyonval, her father, had been admitted in 1717. Her mother, Yvonne Le Charpentier, was admitted in 1737 as the widow of "Jean Dionvat." On 18 September, 14 and 27 November,, and 6 December, during the months in which Guyonval claimed she had applied for membership, the guild considered and rejected petitions from a woman named Gillone Defour on the grounds that she had no parents in the guild and was not known to have served as an apprentice. On 6 July 1739, the guild officers reported that they had been ordered to receive Françoise Guyonval, but that they had come to a private agreement. She had dropped all charges, and in return they received her as a mistress merchant without further conflict and without paying damages. AMR 11 Z 10, deliberations September 1738–March 1739; admission, 6 July 1739.

Once Guyonval was admitted, guild membership was hers for life. At least in the merchant's guild of Rennes, then, the rhetoric about women's membership was supported by practice.

Some women cloth merchants in Rennes may have been organized as early as the seventeenth century, but they left little evidence of their activities. In 1694, a royal edict was passed that required all corporations and merchant groups to bring in their registers to the *mairie* or renounce the right to do business in the city.[30] At that time in Rennes, the police commissioner listed the names of several representatives who were to take responsibility for the compliance of their peers. Among the names was a "Mlle. DuMont," representing the *marchandes de toile*. Unfortunately, this merely indicates that she was a representative of some group of merchants—we have no way of knowing how large the group was, or how formal. Mlle. DuMont may have represented all of the *marchandes de toile* in Rennes, or merely a select few. In Rennes, *toilers* and more often *toileuses*, or *marchandes de toile*, were free to operate as long as they avoided merchandise that was the exclusive right of the merchants' guild.[31] There is no other evidence of a *toilers'* organization, and no guild was ever established.

Tailors' guilds usually offer some kind of membership to women, and the guild in Rennes is no exception. The tailors' guild in Rennes recognized three classes of membership: masters, masters' widows, and *privilegiones*.[32] This last group consisted of fully licensed mistress tailors who had limited rights over apprentices, were prohibited from making men's clothing of any kind, and were excluded from guild assemblies except to pay dues and register each year. There is an interesting distinction between these women and the masters' widows. As usual, the widows kept their privileges specifically as the widows of masters, and therefore lost these privileges if they remarried outside of the guild. The *privilegiones* held their status personally and only lost it if they married *within* the guild. A mistress tailor who married a master or *compagnon* tailor became party to his license and lost her own; otherwise, the marital status of a mistress tailor had no impact on her license.

The membership lists from 1733 to 1786 show that several women kept their licenses for decades: Olive Biot, for example, was listed in every membership list from 1733 to 1753. In 1753, tax roles show that Olive Biot was training her niece as a mistress tailor, suggesting there was some continuity between generations of tailors. "La Lepine" was received as a tailor in 1738, and maintained her membership in the guild until 1765. There is a *tailleuse* by that name in the tax roll for 1777, though Lepine was no longer listed among the privileged. She may have been unable to pay her dues, and continued to work outside of the guild. The number of women received

---

30 AMR Liasse 191

31 ADLA C 398 #44 Rennes 1711 statutes. *Toilers* generally did not share the elite status of drapers. Other cities, notably Paris, had separate guilds for the different tradesmen, but those were usually groups that had evolved alongside each other. The *toilers* of Nantes attempted to separate in 1696 but were thwarted by the merchant-drapers of that city (AMN HH 175).

32 AMR Liasse 199, Tailors' statutes 1713; ADIV 5 E 25, Deliberations and receptions, 1733–1786.

into the guild peaked in the middle of the century. According to guild registers, in 1739, there were 86 master tailors, plus 10 widows and 35 mistresses; in 1753, there were 73 masters, 15 widows, and 50 mistresses; by 1777, there were only 55 masters, 15 widows, and 27 mistresses.[33] Interestingly enough, the *Capitation des artisans* for 1748 reports only 12 women among 84 tailors.[34]

Other guilds in Rennes gave a clearly inferior status to women members. The *teinturiers*, or dyers, of Rennes did not accept either the widows or the daughters of masters as members, though they did recognize the privileges of men who married them. Women from guild families were not barred from working, however, even if they married outside the guild. The statutes stipulate that such a woman could work as a day-worker of another master but could not open her own shop.[35] General tax rolls from Rennes reveal a small number of women among those identified as *teinturieres*: 3 percent in 1709, 7 percent in 1753, and 12 percent in 1777.[36] Possibly, these women worked for other masters. The *Capitation des artisans* for 1748 reports only 12 women among the 39 *teinturiers*; all of these women were widowed and half were too poor to pay any tax.[37]

Perrine Saudray, the 19-year-old daughter of a master *teinturier*, was probably in a typical situation. Saudray was working as a mill-hand in the shop of Jean Gerart, another master *teinturier*. On May 3, 1712, she and two coworkers set out for home at ten o'clock in the evening, noting that "the work ordinarily finishes at that time." They were accosted by four local women on the bridge and Saudray was badly beaten after quarreling with the other women. In her testimony the following day, Gerart's wife swore that Saudray had been above reproach in the two years she had worked in their shop and added that "the girls who work in the mills ought to be able to go home at night without fear of attack."[38] Here it is clear that certain daughters of masters could work at the same trade but only as hands in the shops of others.

The tailors' guild of Quimper was remarkable in that it appears to have admitted men and women equally on the basis of apprenticeship, masterpiece, and the payment of guild fees. The official name of the guild was the *Tailors, boutoniers, lingeres, bleachers, and couturiers*, and their *lettres patents* were granted in 1659. Women could be admitted as tailors' wives, but women who had met formal requirements were received alone, sponsored by a parent or guardian if they were still minors. In a legal memo written in 1777, guild officers claimed that women tailors had been accepted "since time immemorial in the same rights as master tailors."[39] In fact, figures from tax rolls indicate that women made up a growing percentage of tailors across the eighteenth century. Women were 16 percent of those identified specifically

---

33 ADIV 5 E 25, Receptions, 1733–1786.

34 ADIV C 2145, *Capitation des artisans*, Rennes 1748.

35 ADIV 5 E 28 Teinturiers' statutes, 1647; registers, 1767–1791; and extract of deliberations 1693.

36 ADIV C 3995, *Capitation* for Rennes, 1709; ADLA B 3583, *Capitation* for Rennes, 1753; ADIV C 4043, *Capitation* for Rennes, 1777 .

37 ADIV C 2145, *Capitation des artisans*, Rennes 1748.

38 ADIV 3 B 1450, Inquest of 3 May 1712.

39 ADF 2 E 1520 Tailors of Quimper, various papers and *maîtrise*. Quote taken from case of Marie Françoise Grosille, 7 September 1777.

as "tailors" in 1737, 20 percent in 1748, 26 percent in 1763, and 32 percent in 1772.[40] Other clothing professionals could join the guild for lower entrance fees, lighter obligations, and fewer privileges. *Lingeres*, for example, paid very little to join the guild and tended to work by the day for master and mistress tailors. *Lingeres* were always women, and, according to guild records and tax rolls, there were 20 to 30 *lingeres* working in Quimper at any given time. However, Quimper was unusual for having organized the *lingeres*.

Lingeres were a combination of seamstress and retailer, able to take in clothing for repair or embellishment or to sell household textiles, such as sheets and towels that they had made.[41] Elsewhere in France, notably in Rouen and Paris, the only women to establish exclusively female guilds were *lingeres*, and the designation was a standard category in the *Capitation des artisans*. Here, though numerous and visibly active in the market, they remained unorganized throughout the early modern period. An undated report from the *subdelegué* of Brest to the *intendant* indicated that the *lingeres* in that city "were without fixed number, having neither officers nor mysteries. . . ," whose husbands were sailors or soldiers. They were not organized, but two or three of them were "comfortable."[42] Urban *lingeres* were typically unmarried, and many lived with sisters or roommates. There is little to suggest that *lingeres* kept their trade for decades, as did mistress tailors in Rennes and Quimper. For these women, the work may have been a means toward saving money for marriage. At the same time, a small number of apprenticeship contracts for *lingeres* survive from the period, suggesting that at least some people invested time and money into the appropriate training.[43] In a telling example, the 1749 general *capitation* roll for Nantes reports 109 women who called themselves *lingeres*, while the *capitation des artisans* from that city for the same year reports only 16 women registered as such.

At the end of the eighteenth century, the *Parlement* in Rennes challenged the Quimper tailors for their practice of "admitting" *lingeres* as low-level or partial tailors. At issue was the membership of Marie Françoise Gresille in the Quimper guild. She had trained and worked as a tailor and demanded full privileges in the guild. But she had paid only the low entrance fee required of a *lingere*, and refused to pay more. The guild stood by their refusal to admit her at full privilege: "tailleuses and lingeres are two distinct categories of worker in Quimper, and their rights and privileges are very different. Mistress tailors dress women and have the same rights

---

40   ADIV C 4126, *Capitation* of Quimper, 1737; ADIV C 2146, *Capitation des artisans* of Quimper, 1748; ADIV C 4128, *Capitation* of Quimper, 1763; ADIV C 4130, *Capitation* of Quimper, 1772.

41   AMR 415/2 Police report, 6 March 1703. A police report from Rennes reveals the following inventory of items left by customers with specific orders: a wool skirt and a piece of purple cloth, to use as trim on the hem of the skirt; a white towel and taffeta skirt to be mended; 3½ *aulnes* of white toile and a bit of lace to be made into a shirt and 2 handkerchiefs. The *lingere*, Mlle. Dulorand, had been arrested for an unspecified reason, and these items were goods her customers sought to release from police custody of the shop's merchandise.

42   ADIV C 1448. The *lingeres* were "à l'aise," literally "at ease."

43   See ADLA 4 E 2/212, Julienne D'Argonne, 1641; 4 E 2/70 Elizabeth Giraudais, 1752; and 4 E/73, Perrine Poirier, 1771 for examples of contracts.

as master tailors . . . *lingeres* on the other hand make underwear and linens for either sex, and pay much less for their reception." Lawyers in Rennes failed to see the distinction, saying, "Are not *lingeres*, who work with cloth, the same as *tailleuses*?" At any rate, admitting *lingeres* to any corporation was questionable in the eyes of the court: "*Lingeres* are not *en jurande* in any town of this province, and they can exercise their craft freely and without being subject to any tax."[44] The case was being debated right up to the dissolution of the guilds, and the anti-guild climate may have influenced the language of the court. But the case illustrates the ambiguous status of *lingeres* as professionals in Brittany. Clearly, their work gave them a recognized professional, or at least occupational, identity, even without the status of a formal guild. *Couturieres* and *marchandes de mode*, who sold clothing and accessories, were often in similar circumstances.

Midwives were another group of professional women who suffered from an uncertain status in society. Up to and during the early modern period, midwives were trusted local women who were not organized or regulated in any formal way. The tax rolls for most cities and towns include at least a handful of women who identified themselves as *sages-femmes*, though the designation was not typically officially recognized as a trade. By the early eighteenth century, medical doctors, economists, and moralists were engaged in a steady campaign to train and regulate midwives if not eliminate them altogether. Portrayed as vile and illiterate old women, *sage-femmes* were blamed for seriously diminishing the population through their "murderous routines" and slowly destroying the fiber of the nation.[45] Thus, in mid-century, small programs were established to educate women in the arts and have them certified by surgeons or doctors.[46] Certified midwives were allowed to hang their credentials on their doorposts to advertise their status.[47] Some were protective of this status, as is apparent in the case of the widow Renaud, a certified midwife, who reported La Minier to the police for being a popular, if uncertified, midwife in

---

44 ADF 2 E 1520, Case of Gresille, lawyer's memo August 1778. Gresille's case might be viewed as a woman's attempt to evade the constraints of the guild. At the same time, the support of the *Parlement* ultimately undermined the professional recognition of the more skilled work of the women who had been admitted as *tailleuses*.

45 Gélis, "L'accouchement au XVIIIe siècle: Pratiques traditionelles et contrôle médical," *Ethnologie Française* 6: 3/4 (1976): 325–40. Ironically, midwives were also blamed for the abundance of abandoned babies due to their "indecent and corrupt ways." In any case, surgeons were not above playing dirty. Mme. Ducoudray was a Parisian midwife who went on a royally sponsored national tour in the 1760s and 1770s to promote midwife training and licensing. In 1765, when Ducoudray was holding classes in Rennes, the surgeons there were blamed for a rumor that claimed that all women who responded to the call for students would be shipped out to serve in Cayenne. *Memoire* of 17 February 1765, ADIV C 1326.

46 A. Dupuy, "Les Epidemies en Bretagne au XVIIIe siècle: chapitre III, les medecins-l'administration," *Annales de Bretagne* 2 (1886):195–7; Henri Stofft, "Utilisation de la langue bretonne pour la formation professionelle des sages-femmes au XVIIIe siècle," *Dalc'homp Sonj* 9 (1984) 11–17. Some of these were in advance of Mme. Ducoudray's national tour with her birthing "machine" and classes in *accouchement* (delivery). ADIV C 1326: Ducoudray's Breton tour.

47 AMN FF 253, *Sage-femmes* registry of Nantes, 1771–1779.

Nantes.[48] Mme. Renaud was demonstrating a resentment of her competition, to be sure, but also an awareness of her own special status as a licensed midwife at a time when most practiced informally.

In the right circumstances, the ambiguous position of midwives brought them both recognition and flexibility. The *Capitation des artisans* for Brest in 1748 includes a list of the city's eight midwives, along with this note:

> The midwives should be exempt from this tax. They perform a great service in a city of war such as Brest. For each person they care for who can pay well, they serve 20 by charity, most notably the *filles de joie* of this town.

For most of the cities and towns of Brittany, midwives were not included among the "artisans," but surgeons were always counted. Rennes, for example, listed 13 surgeons in the 1748 *capitation des artisans* and no midwives, while the general *capitation* roll for that city reported 25 women who called themselves *sage-femmes* in both 1739 and 1753. Brest never reported more than ten midwives, but also rarely had more than two or three male surgeons. Brest, ironically had a "feminine" nature about it—as a military port and shipbuilding center, its primary activities were decidedly masculine. But it was precisely those activities that guaranteed a high population of women who were self-sufficient out of necessity: widows, wives of absent husbands, and, of course, the aforementioned *filles de joie*. Midwives in such a city were probably active as the primary healers of women. They were clearly more numerous than male surgeons, and perhaps garnered more respect because of that.

Women were never allowed into medical universities, nor were they formally accepted in the apothecary or surgeons' guilds. Certain widows were known to continue in their husband's practice, especially as a surgeon's wife typically assisted in childbirth and other procedures during her husband's lifetime. But in technical terms, these women were not so different from the numerous uncertified and unregulated women who practiced healing arts in every city and town. Surgeons were often relentless in pursuing unlicensed healers of any kind.

In 1732, master surgeon Francois Vigé issued a declaration in Chateaubriand that prohibited the practice of medicine by anyone who had not been admitted to the guild. He sued Marie Chaben, the wife of a local merchant, for her repeated offenses even after the publication of the new law. In her own defense, Chaben said that she did not actually practice surgery, but had a talent for "the restoration of limbs," and that she had a responsibility to help those in pain. She said she believed Vigé's persecution of her stemmed from her success with wounds he had refused to treat on the grounds that there was nothing to be done. She never charged money, but acted out of charity and thankfulness to God for her gift. Finally, she presented the court with attestations from "distinguished people" who had benefited from her attention, and pointed out in particular the case of the complete cure of a gangrenous leg that Vigé had wanted to amputate. The court decided in her favor and ordered Vigé to pay

---

48   AMN FF 253 15 April 1768.

court costs and leave Chaben in peace.[49] While Chaban may not have been typical of healers, and was not necessarily a "professional" healer, she was clearly a valued member of her community.

Even without a guild to protect them, it was occasionally possible for women to unite when their collective interests were at stake. In 1748, seven women filed a complaint against the police commissioner on behalf of the *marchandes de suifs et chandelles de Saint-Malo.* [50] They had all been condemned to pay certain fines for having sold more than ten *livres* of candles without having filed a declaration with the police clerk. *Suif,* or tallow, was restricted during this time and its use was regulated. One of the women had been fined, though she claimed she had gone to the clerk's office only to find it empty. Having to go to the clerks office was a hardship, she claimed that

> a poor *marchande,* being alone in her shop, is often obliged to leave it entrusted to people she does not know very well in order to go and declare that she intends to sell 10 *livres* of candles; if neither the commissioners nor the director can be found at the office or if neither is disposed to receive declarations when she arrives, the public is in no way served.

The women complained that it was an injustice to take a third of their "feeble fortune" and ask them to put at risk everything they owned. Their pleas fell on deaf ears, and the fines were collected. However, their attempt is significant for the purposes of this study. Such collective action by women, especially in the interests of protecting livelihoods, has been eclipsed by their well-known participation in bread riots and church violence. Rarely, in historical sources, do we see women as agents in economic activity. Here is an example of how some women enjoyed a kind of informal organization for mutual protection.

In Brest, women were prominent in a few formal market organizations, but those organizations were not very powerful. On at least two occasions, the *intendant* intervened to force the merchants' guild of Brest to admit widows who had been refused membership. In 1755, the widow Desnoux petitioned the *intendant* for help, and in 1771 the widow Du Halary followed suit, both claiming unfair practices by the corporation. In response, the guild members claimed that for years their corporation had been meaningless in Brest, and that the growing port city now required some order. The existing shops were mediocre, they said, and chaos reigned among merchants. These women were simply "unqualified" in the eyes of the guild regardless of the fact that both of the widows had operated shops for decades and were well liked by the community.[51] It is interesting to note that the majority of this guild's members were women: 19 of the 35 members in 1748 and 17 of the 31

---

49 *Journal des audiences et arrests du Parlement de Bretagne* (Paris: G. Martin, 1736), chap. 95, book 1, p. 145.

50 ADIV C 1453.

51 ADIV C 1460 Letter to *intendant* re: widow Desneaux, April 1755; enclosed statutes of 1715; letters to *intendant* re: widow du Halary, Oct. 1771–March 1772; undated *memoire* from guild members, referring to both cases.

members in 1771 were women.[52] The *memoire* does not name any officers, and the 31 women and men who make up the corps appear to be equally represented in this affair. Thus, women were strongly represented in the governing body that had rejected both widows.

Another example of women's prominence in Brest, and the lack of formal organization in that city, can be found in the bakers. Modern scholars commonly assert that women in early modern France were never actually bakers, but only ran the shop for their baker-husbands. Widows of bakers supposedly relied on journeymen to do all of the baking.[53] However, the sources for Brest state outright that most bakers were women whose husbands were away at sea or employed at the shipyard. According to general *capitation* tax rolls, in 1740 there were seven men who identified themselves as bakers, three of whom worked at the naval base, and 18 female bakers. The *capitation des artisans* for 1748 reports much higher counts: 81 bakers in all, 79 of them women.[54] The situation was not accepted without question, however, as city leaders tried repeatedly to establish a traditional baker's guild there. Curiously, they phrased their requests throughout the eighteenth century so as to suggest pity for the women who currently baked all the city's bread, even as they sought to eliminate them from the marketplace. In 1748, in a report on the city's arts and crafts, the *subdelegué* wrote,

> The bakers (*boulangeres*) . . . seek to feed their families by their trade, as their husbands in the service of the king do not earn enough to support the household, and are assured that their wives can help by baking or through some other commerce . . . [55]

Among the complaints leveled against these bakers were that they got their flour from random places, instead of from approved vendors, and that they worked inconsistently. Some women abandoned baking from time to time to pursue other activities, making it too difficult for police inspectors to impose quality controls:. "If we had master bakers in a condition appropriate to their craft, the police could operate in Brest as they do in other cities."[56]

A report from 1750 says basically the same thing, but goes into more detail regarding the bakers:

> In Brest, there are neither masters nor the mysteries of baking. There are women who serve in the trade, such as it is here in Brest. These women are the wives of soldiers, sailors, and dock workers, and of men who have entered into service. Most of these women don't even

52   ADIV C 2142, *Capitation des artisans* for Brest, 1748; ADIV C 1460, list of members pertaining to case of widow du Halary, Oct. 1771.
53   See Steven Laurence Kaplan, *The Bakers of Paris and the Bread Question 1700–1775* (Durham, NC: Duke University Press, 1996).
54   ADIV C 4117, *capitation* for 1740; ADIV C 2142, *capitation des artisans* for 1748.
55   ADIV C 1453, *subdelegués* report, 1748.
56   ADIV C 1453, *subdelegués* report, 1748.

have a proper oven, but buy wheat when they have a bit of money, bake it, and sell their bread wherever they can . . .[57]

The *subdelegué* continued by describing the work of the police to find and regulate these women, who had neither weights nor marks to identify themselves as legitimate bakers. Often, bread was confiscated and fines were levied, but many women could not pay the fine "due to their great poverty." The quality of bread was middling, complained the *subdelegué*, and the cost was generally high. The report estimates that over 150 women served as bakers in 1750, but that the total number of itinerant bakers was possibly much higher. The report is followed by a request for the establishment of a proper bakers' guild, with certified masters, an auditor, a *greffier* [court clerk] and police. Presumably, the displaced women would have had to join the guild or find another line of work. At any rate, in spite of repeated requests, Brest was not granted a bakers' guild in the eighteenth century, and the lack of a formal guild was essentially an advantage for women working there.

Other sizeable cities in Brittany, such as the port of Saint-Malo, show little evidence of formalized female labor at any stage. The police and guild records of Saint-Malo do not include the registration of mistresses in any craft, and the general *capitation* rolls do not list occupations for women. However, the roll of the *capitation des artisans* again serves as a record that women were identified as professionals in certain contexts. Many of the women in prestigious trades, such as *draperie*, were widows. Of 74 drapers in 1748, for example, 28 were women and 16 of those were widows.[58] The same is true among the city's butchers, bakers, and secondhand goods dealers. However, unmarried women make up the entirety of the seamstresses [*couturieres* and *lingeres*] in Saint-Malo.

Within the fields generally open to women—selling and sewing—the guilds in Breton cities were no great impediment to the women who could afford to join them. It is true that female members held a second-class status within the guilds, excluded as they were from voting and attending assemblies. And, with few exceptions, women who enjoyed the benefits of membership were brought in as relatives of men members. However, in Breton guilds, especially those in Rennes, the membership of a master's daughter was as secure as that of a master's son. This is unusually generous, even if such status was not as readily available to the children of a "mistress." Furthermore, that membership was not lost automatically upon marriage, as it was in guilds elsewhere. Similarly, it was possible for women to join some Breton guilds through work experience, and not only as extensions of a guild family. These factors suggest the acknowledgment of a work identity that some women kept regardless of their household status. These guilds may have been more or less typical male hierarchies, but they did not seriously prevent women from working at certain trades.

In trades that were traditionally masculine, or that had no connection to the household, women were unlikely to find work. Certain guilds across the region, such

---

57 ADIV C 1447, *subdelegués* report, 1750. The "mysteries" refer to official trade secrets; to be admitted to the mysteries means to be formally recognized as a qualified practitioner.

58 ADIV C 2146, *Capitation des artisans* for Saint-Malo, 1748.

as the *charcutiers* and butchers, admitted the widows of masters in much the same way as all French guilds did. Widows were also admitted, though rarely, in more "masculine" trades like cabinet- or saddle-making. But these widows would have held a limited guild status that left them wholly dependent upon the work of their journeymen and the goodwill of their guild officers. In Breton cities, as in the rest of France, the widows of apothecaries and gold smiths were prohibited from continuing their husbands' work. In these contexts, the gender hierarchy was made particularly clear. Thus, women's experiences from one guild to another varied greatly, and their position as a whole was rather ambiguous. By contrast, non-guild work was less formally structured and offered even more flexibility.

Outside the guilds: Urban work

Most women in Brittany, like most men, had little need of guild membership in order to work. If *lingeres* here were not formally organized, neither were the men who worked as weavers.[59] In fact, for most of the working population of Brittany in this period, guilds operated primarily as an impediment to the economic activities of non-members. Jealous of their privileges, guilds spent much time and energy rooting out contraband and unlicensed workers. But guilds also tolerated and even depended upon this informal sector. Most workers in this circumstance are therefore difficult to define, operating, as they did, at the "margins" of economic life. Women and men were equally well represented among the targets of guild inspectors and police, and among the part-time, itinerant, or invisible work force.

Guilds are, by their very nature and by necessity, exclusive. Using guilds or guild records as a gauge of the extent of the working population will neglect the majority of the population. Most people must work to survive, and the evidence confirms that most early modern women had to and did earn money through their labor. The general *capitation* tax rolls show that female-headed households made up an average of 14 percent of the population in big urban areas such as Nantes and Rennes, and 33 percent of the population of Brest. The other towns and villages are somewhere in between: in tiny Roche-Bernard, where the population never passed 1,400 souls in the eighteenth century, 20 percent of the households were headed by women.[60]

Many of the female heads-of-household identified an occupation, and many more sisters, roommates, and wives also named a trade. Here, the trends are harder to identify. In Nantes, one of the largest cities in France during the early modern era,

---

59   In fact, there was a weaver's guild in Nantes, created by royal ordinance in 1704 in order to maintain standards of production (AMN HH 174). However, it operated more as a control over far-flung workers than as an organization of privileged members. Weavers elsewhere in Brittany did not have a guild but registered with police in exchange for the right to sell (ACN B 3736). Abel Poitrineau makes a distinction between the "métiers en jurande," the guilds with officers and internal regulations, and "métiers statués," or guilds created externally by edicts in order to regulate production. *Ils travaillaient la France: Métiers et mentalités du XVIe au XIXe siècle* (Paris: Armand Colier, 1992), pp. 16–18.

60   These percentages are averages of the figures for each city across the eighteenth-century tax rolls sampled.

57 percent of taxpaying women did not identify an occupation. Yet in Rennes, only slightly smaller than Nantes and serving as the administrative and cultural capital of Brittany, only 26 percent of the women named in *capitation* rolls failed to identify an occupation. Small towns varied just as much. In Montcontour, a village of 1,600 in mid-century, 91 percent of the women listed in the tax rolls stated no occupation or source of income. Landernau, a small town at best with a population of 3,500, reported only 44 percent of taxed women having no trade.

But the tax records only reveal part of the story. Above, in the case of formally recognized work, there were guild records or *maitrise* registers to corroborate the evidence of a significant population of professional women. However, cross-referencing the sources resulted in only a modest overlapping of names between the membership lists, *greffier*'s registers and the names of those who identified a given trade in the tax sources. Therefore, it is quite possible that my estimates, based entirely upon *capitation* tax rolls, are too low. At the same time, there is often a discrepancy in the other direction between the number of artisans recognized officially by each guild and the number of taxpayers who claimed to work in that craft. In the tailors' guild of Rennes in 1777, for example, the guild register lists only 55 masters, 15 widows, and 27 "privileged" women. But the general *capitation* tax roll for that year lists 102 women who called themselves *tailleuses*.

The same cautions apply to the sources for the informal work sector. While an average of 57 percent of the taxpaying women in Nantes identified no occupation, everyone in that vast metropolis had to survive somehow. Police records, among the best sources for "unofficial" workers, describe thriving markets and busy homes that suggest everyone was working at something. If the tax rolls reveal too few of these workers, it may be due to inconsistent recording methods. However, it could also point to inconsistencies in the economy or, more importantly, inconsistencies in how people identified themselves at this level of the economy.

In 1428, the duke of Brittany, Jean I, had issued a *memoire* proclaiming that only the merchants of Nantes had the right to sell outside of open market days within the city limits.[61] This measure was meant to give local merchants precedence over foreign and traveling vendors. However, the drapers and mercers' guild used the document to justify their sole control of all cloth and clothing trade in the city. The guild maintained the right to inspect the goods and premises of every merchant in Nantes. On these outings, a guild officer would accompany city police inspectors to various shops, market stalls, and apartments in search of contraband. In addition, police inspectors were searching for merchandise that had been prohibited; possession of prohibited items, especially foreign-made goods, was a serious offense. A merchant with several contraventions usually suffered complete liquidation of merchandise, with proceeds from the sale split between the offended guild and the *Hôtel Dieu* of the city.

Women are strongly represented in police reports, either as assistants to shopkeepers or as the primary owners of the business. During the day, wives, daughters, and servants tended shops while the master ran errands or oversaw special

---

61   ADLA 5 E corps 52; and AMN HH 132 #1.

projects.[62] Thus, police inspectors usually had to deal with the women of the house. This did not make the job easier. Indeed, the inspector's job was often a dangerous one, inspiring violent reactions from even solitary women.

A proclamation issued in 1750 required all petty merchants in Nantes to register their shops. Over the next 30 years, 58 women approached the *commisaire des policiers des maitrise et jurandes* in order to comply. Sometimes they arrived *en masse*, and were registered as a group, making it impossible to decipher who sold what merchandise. However, of those who did describe their merchandise, the majority sold an interesting hodgepodge of candles, soap, cloth, yarn, butter, and wood.[63] These were women who probably sold whatever they could get their hands on, and while some referred to their "boutiques," there is no way to tell the extent of their inventories or the size of their shops. Of those who mention spouses, most were married to simple laborers or *compagnons* training in a trade.

In 1753, a coalition of the mercers, *marchandes de mode*, *marchands et marchandes de toile*, *fripiers*, and *libraires* formally challenged the rights of the drapers' guild of Nantes to harass them.[64] Several men and women representing each group signed the *memoire*, which was presented to the *mairie* and the police of Nantes. None of these merchants was formally incorporated, though some had petitioned for *lettres patentes*. They demanded that the drapers be made to observe the freedom of commerce that was supposed to be promised to the inhabitants of the city. The police inspector promised to uphold the legal toleration of commerce within Nantes; however, the drapers continued to issue citations for contravention throughout the century, and their victims continued to challenge their sentences.[65]

Other groups resisted the abuses of guild inspectors by pleading for mercy. The *brocanteuses*, or junk dealers, of Nantes wanted to be able to sell one day a week without the *fripiers*' guild running off their customers. In 1781, 58 women formally petitioned for the *maire* to forbid the *fripiers* to run inspections on Saturdays. The *brocanteuses* appealed to the *maire*'s sense of charity, claiming they were merely poor women trying to scrape out a living, unable to join the guild, and beneath the guild's concern.[66] Women seem to have been particularly vulnerable to the *fripiers*' guild: 64 out of 92 citations issued in the 1760s were to women vendors.[67] Unfortunately, their argument failed to move anyone at city hall and their petition was denied.

In Rennes, there was a struggle between the merchants' guild and the city's numerous petty merchants that spanned nearly 60 years. In 1715, the petty merchants tried unsuccessfully to create their own guild.[68] After their request had been rejected by the king, several continued to operate unlicensed shops in spite of a

---

62   This may be seen as a clear advantage for male merchants; female merchants did not have wives to tend the shop in their absence. However, some had apprentices or workers.

63   AMN HH 71, *greffier*'s logbook, 1750–1783.

64   ADLA C 652 #1, *Memoire* and report, 1755. These were cloth, junk, book, and clothing accessories dealers.

65   AMN HH 132, 133, 134 Drapers' statutes and contraventions, 1429–1780.

66   AMN HH 137 # 19 *Memoire*, signed by *brocanteuses*, 1781.

67   AMN HH 138 *Fripiers* contraventions, 1762–1768.

68   ADLA C 652 *Memoire of Marchands sans jurands*, 1715. See the case of Mlle. Guyonval, above.

royal command to join the existing merchants' guild. The guild, in retaliation, drew up a series of lists naming the offending vendors. Women make up at least half of those named in the lists and at least half of those who finally presented themselves for membership.[69]

This is not to say that the merchants' guild and the unlicensed petty merchants were, by nature, distinct groups. In spite of the guild's harsh attitude towards unlicensed merchants, there was a sizable gray area between full membership and contravention. As mentioned above, there were three ways to join the merchants' guild of Rennes: through a father who held the status of master, by working as an apprentice and being sponsored by a master, or by paying a high fee. Several of the unlicensed merchants targeted by the guild were the children or widows of masters, or people who had been members in the past, who had failed to register or pay current dues. More often than not, those cited for operating without a license insisted that they were already members of the guild. In 1736, Mlle. Treguilly, for example, had inherited a profitable *draperie* from her father but had never personally sought membership. Sieur Levesque, a *menuisier* and lawyer, had given his deceased wife's business to his niece, but had never sponsored the girl's membership. And in a rare case of a mother's status being claimed by her son, Jacques Juhel claimed that he had inherited guild membership along with the *epicerie* of his mother.[70]

According to the *capitation des artisans* for Rennes in the year 1748, there were 184 men and 107 women who paid with the *marchands jurés*.[71] However, the *capitation* rolls for the general public listed far higher numbers of people who identified themselves as "merchants." In the rolls for 1739, there were 89 men and 231 women who called themselves simply "marchand" or "marchande," with no indication of their quantity or quality of merchandise. In 1753, there were 128 such men and 268 women. These numbers do not even include those who identified themselves by specific terms: draper, cloth merchant, hat and glove merchant, and so forth. Clearly, there were many more people in retail in Rennes than there were members in the merchants' guild.

Regardless of the machinations of the merchants' guilds in Nantes and Rennes, all French cities tolerated unlicensed vendors who handled only small quantities of merchandise. "Petite" merchants were supposed to be exempt from the harassment of the guild and confiscation of merchandise by the police. That was not the case for unlicensed craftsmen like tailors. The tailors' guild in each city inspected homes for which they had some information that an inhabitant was working as a tailor. If they caught that person in the act, they immediately demanded proof of certification. If no work pieces were visible anywhere in the open, inspectors demanded to see inside of cupboards and even under the bedclothes. Half-finished clothing was proof enough to issue a citation. Charges were also made against women who made men's clothing, whether or not they were in a guild. The rational for admitting women

---

69   ADIV 5 E 20, 5 E 21, and C 1459–corps statutes, logbooks, and lists.

70   ADIV C 1459, List of *marchands sans jurands* in contravention of statutes, 1736.

71   ADIV C 2145, *Capitation des Artisans,* Rennes. There were seven women who identified themselves as married, including the wife of a surgeon and four women married to *Hussiers.*

to the guild was the preservation of modesty, so it was a punishable offense for a women to make men's clothing.[72] However, sometimes the seizures seemed more arbitrary than fair. In 1745, the tailors' guild in Nantes seized the goods of Huer, a *compagnon* tailor working under the auspices of Mistress Bedar. Their rational was that Huer was making men's clothing, as most men tailors did, but that his mistress, a woman, did not have the right to make men's clothing. As an extension of his mistress, Huer was in contravention.[73] In another case, a year later, the tailors of Nantes pursued Claudine Cornu for unregulated work in spite of the fact that she had operated a licensed shop for more than 25 years. They claimed they had discovered she sometimes worked out of a backroom as well as out of her shop, allowing her to avoid guild supervision.[74]

Perhaps most vexing to the tailors' guild were those masters who depended upon unlicensed workers, or who lent their privileges to outside help, in order to get their own work done. Some of these were poor widows who found it easier to sell their privileges than to keep working.[75] Others had given work to members of their households who had not been admitted to the corps, such as the servant of the widow Hervé or the wife and sister of master Duvergez in Nantes in 1753.[76] In 1776, master Hontou, "tailleur pour homme," and his wife, "elle pour femme," were charged with employing unregistered *compagnons*. In his defense, Hontou exclaimed that he had so many clients he could not afford to put limitations on his employees.[77]

As was the case for the merchants' guilds in Nantes and Rennes, the tailors' guilds were faced with a sizeable population of unregulated competition. According to tailors' guild registers for Rennes in 1753, there were 138 members: 73 masters, 15 widows, and 50 mistresses.[78] The *capitation* tax roll for that year listed 188 tailors: 113 men and 75 women.[79] Cross-referencing the two lists shows some overlap, but the vast majority of those who called themselves "tailors" were absent from guild registers. There are few intact guild registers for the tailors of Nantes, but *maîtrise* records for the period 1723–1789 record only 141 women who had ever been admitted into the tailor's guild.[80] Only seven of those were admitted in the 1740s, but *capitation* rolls for the city show 61 women in 1740 and 63 women in 1749 identified themselves as *tailleuses*.[81]

Most of the tailors cited by the guilds of Nantes and Rennes were simply workers who could not afford to join the guild. Just as unlicensed vendors did when faced with a heavy fine and loss of all goods, many tailors insisted they were already members of the guild. Mlle. Rasaux in 1753, who was the daughter of a master,

---

72   AMN HH 170 & 171, for Tailors of Nantes; ADIV 5 E 25 for Tailors of Rennes.
73   AMN HH 170 #7, Tailors' contraventions 1743–1770.
74   ADLA B 5863, 13 July 1746.
75   AMN HH 168 #11, Tailors' contraventions, Nantes, see above.
76   AMN HH 170 #49 and #50, Tailors' contraventions.
77   AMN HH 171 #10, Tailors' contraventions, 1771–1789.
78   ADIV 5 E 25, Receptions, 1733–1786.
79   ADLA B 3583.
80   AMN HH 61-HH 86 (1723–1789).
81   ADIV C 4145 and ADLA B3519. The *capitation des artisans* for Nantes does not include tailors.

assumed that she had held automatic membership. Such was also the case for Mlle. le Breton, who had taken over the apartment and license of her mistress when the latter left for America.[82] Some stated they were about to join, or had always meant to join, like Mlle. Boulay in 1772, or Mlle. Fouché in 1776.[83] Many resolved themselves to the fine and loss of merchandise, and still others decided to fight the inspection physically. Out of desperation or exasperation, numerous people blocked stairways and doors, threw clothing out the window or stuffed it into corners, and finally turned on the inspectors themselves with sticks, stones, and wooden shoes. The Rognan sisters, for example, descended upon the tailors' inspectors "furious like tigers," armed with household implements and yelling threats, after the inspectors had discovered a cabinet full of sewing and clothing. Following that encounter, one inspector filed a complaint but vowed to continue with this "dangerous duty."[84]

There were significant exceptions to the overall intolerance of unregulated work. In fact, some informal workers were recognized for the services they provided. In a letter written to the *Contrôleur Générale* of Finances in 1701, the merchant La Lande Magon of Saint-Malo described the activities of certain women who worked at the cloth bureau. These women were not actually employed by the cloth bureau, but they worked on commissions paid by regional merchants who had come to have their cloth inspected. The women unpacked and repacked the bales of cloth, guided merchants to potential customers, and kept the merchants informed of important port activity and shipping schedules. Their work was so valued that Magon was writing to protest a new fee charged per bale of cloth, since the proposed fee equaled what merchants already paid informally to the women. He suggested that merchants would not be able to pay both the women and the fee, and its establishment would damage the healthy commerce "so desirable" to the kingdom. Some merchants, according to Magon, would entrust entire shipments and sums of money to these women, "in whom they have the greatest confidence."[85]

In some cases, the professional expertise of women was respected enough to warrant their use as legal witnesses. An article by Jean Kerherve describes a late medieval inheritance case that hinged on the testimony of the midwife. A mother and child had both died following an extremely difficult delivery. By Breton law, the woman's property would not go to her husband but to her children, siblings, or parents. At issue was whether or not the newborn girl had died after her mother, in which case the woman's property would have passed through the baby to the baby's father. The priest, on hand to deliver last rites, could only say he was baffled by the "mysteries known to the midwife," leaving the last word up to the midwife

---

82   AMN HH 170 #42 and HH 171 #4.

83   AMN HH 171 #2 and #13.

84   AMN HH 171 #67, 1782.

85   Letter of 1 May 1701, printed in A.M. Boislisle's *Correspondance des contrôleurs généraux des finances avec les intendants des provinces* (Paris: Imprimerie Nationale, 1883), p. 73; see also Andre Lespagnol, *Messieurs de Saint-Malo* (Rennes: Presses Universitaires de Rennes, 1997), p. 441. Lespagnol uses the scenario presented in the letter to show that outside merchants, so dependent on intermediaries, were at a clear disadvantage in the marketplace.

herself.[86] By the eighteenth century, when midwives were so often undermined by the surgeons' guild, an attending midwife's testimony would have still carried such authority. She would have been the only person qualified to judge what had happened during the childbirth she had witnessed.

A more unexpected example of professional testimony comes from Rennes in 1782, where two fish sellers were asked to settle a dispute in the marketplace. Jeanne L'Horne and Louise Guybert, two cod merchants, were sent by police to inspect the merchandise of a woman accused of selling rotten fish. The accused vendor insisted that her fish had arrived from her supplier in poor condition. L'Horne and Guybert declared that the fish was definitely unfit for consumption but that it was unclear how long it had been out on display. Thus, they were not able to decide whether the merchant or her supplier was responsible for the fine due to be paid. The fish was confiscated and the complaint was forwarded to the supplier on the coast.[87] While this sort of conflict was probably commonplace in markets across Europe, it is interesting to note that the police in Rennes called on these women rather than issue a citation themselves. While we cannot be certain of what prompted this decision— did the accused vendor demand a peer's assistance or were police merely unable to visit the market to render their own judgment?—it is another example of the ambiguous position of women in the marketplace. Legally, women had no authority in the market and were often at the mercy of police or inspectors. But their presence and expertise gave them an importance that, from time to time, was recognized in an official capacity.

Much urban work was outside the authority of a formal organization and was open to anyone willing to do it. Among the free trades in a given city, there was little to prevent women from seeking work in any number of areas. Women performed all kinds of services, both as actual servants and as porters, laundresses, and *lingeres*. Women bought and sold a variety of merchandise in the marketplace and in back alleys. And yet women were found primarily in "feminine" trades even when masculine trades, such as weaving and shoemaking, were not under the control of a guild hierarchy. Perhaps this was largely a matter of choice; perhaps part of a woman's identity was choosing work deemed "suitable" for women.

There is little to suggest that women were forbidden to work in certain areas; when informal workers were the targets of police or guild persecution, it was for real or perceived abuses of economic toleration and not for reasons of gender. Thus, the existence of clearly defined "women's work" probably has more to do with cultural norms or circumstance and less with outright prohibition. Most scholars of gender issues would have to agree. Typical explanations for the sexual division of labor rest on the biological, reproductive and pragmatic household demands that occupied so much of a woman's time and energy. Beyond domestic demands, however, historians

---

86 Kerherve, "Un accouchement dramatique à la fin du moyen age," *Annales de Bretagne et du Pays d'Ouest* 89 (1982) 3:391–6. It was decided that the baby had died mere moments after her mother, which was enough to render the father legal inheritor. Kerherve notes with regret that the midwife's testimony had been given in Breton but preserved only in French translation.

87 AMR Liasse 403, Police report of 11 September 1782.

have also noted a complex web of social factors that served to limit women's options as workers. These would include the lack of training and resources available to women, the increasingly political roles that accompanied economic participation but were closed to women, and the cultural stereotypes that influenced what a woman could reasonably do and still be perceived as respectable.[88] In spite of the limitations, however, the gendered nature of work did not lock women into rigid roles. There was still room to maneuver, and, indeed, such flexibility was often a necessary component of survival in the early modern economy.

Rural Brittany

As in other parts of rural France, peasant families in Brittany generally followed a family economy model. That is, the family worked as a unit under the male head of household. The specifics of the division of labor may have varied from region to region, but the importance of the contributions of every member of the household was undeniable. That is often given as the explanation for the quick remarriage of widows and widowers—no home could operate efficiently without the work of a husband and a wife.[89] Among Breton peasants, the man of the house farmed the land for cereal and fiber crops and cared for cows and horses. Rural wives ran their homes and made extra income by bringing yarn, butter, and eggs to the market. Both probably worked in the fields at harvest time, but Breton peasant women were as likely to be feeding field hands as they were to be cutting grain stalks or pulling flax.[90]

Peasant women, working as part of a family unit, are largely invisible in early modern sources. But it would be unfair to characterize the work of rural women as merely supplemental to that of rural men. According to the account books of Sieur Bouillard de la Rablée, several of his tenants traded spun yarn for seed, which they in turn planted, harvested, and used to pay rent. On 2 April 1640, for example, the farmer Voulldan was given 20 pounds of raw wool with the understanding that he would receive a bushel of buckwheat when he returned the wool spun and bleached. It was clearly stated that his wife would do this work.[91] In such circumstances, it would be difficult to claim that the work of one spouse was essential and the work of the other supplemental.

Unattached young women often found work as a servant in another peasant household, caring for children and livestock or bringing meals out to laborers in the fields. Such a girl would have been part of the household until her own marriage,

---

88   See, for example, Natalie Zemon Davis, "Women in the Crafts in Sixteenth-Century Lyon," in *Women and Work in Preindustrial Europe*, ed. Barbara Hanawalt (Bloomington: Indiana University Press, 1986); Martha Howell, *Women, Production and Patriarchy in Late Medieval Cities* (Chicago: University of Chicago Press, 1986); and Judith Bennett, *Ale, Beer and Brewsters in England: Women's Work in a Changing World, 1300–1600* (Oxford: Oxford University Press, 1996).

89   Poitrineau, *Ils travaillaeint la France*, p. 45.

90   Yann Brekilien, *Les paysans bretons au XIXe siècle* (Paris: Hachette, 1966), p. 40.

91   ADIV 2 EB 82, *Livre de raison de Bouillard de la Rablée*, 1634–1652.

and she may not have been paid a wage for her efforts, especially in hard times.[92] Without the protection of a household, a young woman had no choice but to turn to charity to survive. The *Contrôleur Général* wrote in 1709 to the *intendant* at Rennes, troubled by reports that rich peasants in Tréguier, in northern Brittany, were responding to the bad economy by firing their domestics, especially their spinners.[93] As a result, the women became beggars, and a burden. The *Contrôleur Général* wanted the *intendant* to pressure wealthy peasants to keep their spinners employed, to uphold the cloth industry and keep young women off the streets.

Opportunities for individuals were fewer in the countryside, but hardly non-existent. Peasants in the early modern period were far from self-sufficient, and some villagers fulfilled local needs as millers, butchers, and tailors. Merchants, sometimes with small shops, operated in village centers and the occasional notary served whole regions. Thus, even in very small towns and villages, there were opportunities for enterprising spirits to engage in some activity beside the local industry or farming. However, those with such a small customer base were especially vulnerable to every economic downturn. Mid-eighteenth century reports to the *intendant* on the state of local artisans are particularly revealing, like this from the village Tredias in 1767:

> There are 4 tailors, one boy and others who have wives and children, none of whom keep a shop, but sell door-to-door by the day and most of the time work for laborers at whatever is needed . . . one Jacques Moison used to be a cabinet-maker, working by day in people's homes but it's been a long time since he has abandoned his craft in order to work at other jobs.[94]

Other villages had similar reports. Village women who did manage to live by their own occupations were generally not well-off; in Saint Pern, *lingeres* worked by the day, earning "three or four *sols*, and not always that much." At Broons, "all the petty *marchands et marchandes* do not live by their commerce, but by odd jobs." Commerce was so bad that local merchants worked as day laborers on the side in order to survive. The report from Saint Lary summed it up the best:

> One has the honor to observe to Monsieur the *subdelegué* that there are neither routes nor a market in the parish of Saint Lary, that the day-workers are miserable and that even the merchants are no longer at ease; in a word, misery is general to the entire parish.[95]

These general comments had few references to women workers in particular, but each village reported two or three *lingeres* and *tailleuses*, all of whom worked "à la journée" for extremely low wages.

The few women who identified occupations in these tax records were likely to have been working temporarily before finding husbands. In Redon, the *subdelegué* reported that "the lingere's trade is not an enduring profession." *Lingeres* were "girls without any kind of fortune who work at the trade until marriage, when they abandon

---

92 Brekilian, *Les paysans bretons*, p. 79
93 Letter of 3 June 1709, in Boislisle's *Correspondance des contrôleurs généraux des finances*, p. 163.
94 ADIV C 1449.
95 ADIV C 1449.

it. They are not incorporated or in any kind of community, nor are they licensed."[96] Presumably, this was the case in most places, including some of the larger cities. Without any training or licensing issues to overcome, women would have been able to pick up some kind of domestic or home-based work as needed. Especially in rural areas, where there was not much of a customer base and where all hands were needed to keep a farm running, there would have been little reason for a woman to continue working independently after marriage.

In central Brittany, villagers did not have to go all the way to Rennes for markets. Small and middling towns, such as Quintin, supported commerce for the surrounding areas. Cloth merchants in Quintin registered their seals with the police.[97] Roughly 13.8 percent or 20 out of the 145 merchants registered at Quintin in 1738 were women, and only three out of those 20 (15 percent) were identified as widows. None of the merchants were registered with other family members, either fathers or husbands. Many of these merchants did not hail from within Quintin, but came from one of the local villages. Though they may have been rare, independent women merchants were not unheard of, even in rural areas.

The occupations identified for women in the *capitation* tax rolls of small towns and villages were similar to those listed for women in larger towns. In Landernau, for example, a textile-producing town with a mid-eighteenth-century population of only 3,000, the taxpaying women were identified as textile laborers (13.7 percent of all taxed women), food providers (12.2 percent), and retailers (14.2 percent). A few female weavers were counted among the textile workers of Landernau, in contrast to Quintin, where no women weavers at all were listed in the tax rolls. The number of clothing producers and retailers in Landernau was quite low, however—not as low as in Brest (6 percent) or in Quintin (5 percent), but only half as many as in Nantes (19 percent) or Rennes (21 percent).

Compare these figures to those for Dinan, a slightly larger textile town with a mid-century population of 5,500. Far fewer women in Dinan reported occupations, and those who did were most likely to be spinners or bleachers rather than retailers of any sort. The number of women in Dinan who do not identify an occupation is high at 72 percent, while a fairly low percentage of taxed women in Landernau named no source of income (44 percent).[98]

Landernau and Dinan were larger than most villages, however, and may be more appropriately called small towns. Montcontour, a small village near Saint-Brieuc, had fewer than 500 households by the mid-eighteenth century. The *subdelegué's* report for 1750 noted that whole cloth retailers in the village were not well off and that *lingeres* "do not sell linens, have no shops, and only live off their work door-to-door for 3 *sous* a day and food."[99] The *capitation* rolls for Montcontour list very few heads of household, and most of those (91 percent) report no source of income.

---

96   ADIV C 1447.

97   ADCA B 3736.

98   As compared to eighteenth-century averages of taxed women identifying no source of income; 57 percent in Nantes, 59 percent in Saint-Malo, and 62 percent in Brest.

99   ADIV C 1447.

However, Roche-Bernard, a village where the population never topped 300 households in the eighteenth century, tells a different story. In spite of its tiny population, more women named an occupation here than in Landernau or Montcontour; most of those who named an occupation worked with food or clothing or in retail. The records also reflect a surprising level of consistency from one year to the next. Twenty-two of the women named in 1738 are listed again in 1753; most of these women maintained a particular occupation during those years. Perrine Huguet, a midwife, was listed for both of those years, as was the *lingere* Marie Loyer and the baker Jaquette Tremont. None of these women was identified as a widow, and possibly had never married. In larger cities and towns, the percentage of women named in successive rolls is far lower. The repetition in Roche-Bernard may be a consequence of the small size of the town and the low number of years between tax rolls, or it may simply be a case of better reporting.

Textile production occupied much of rural Brittany, but the division of labor by sexes within the household varied slightly from one area to the next. Jean Tanguy figures that in 1755, only 6.7 percent of the weavers in Quintin, and one percent of the weavers in surrounding villages, were women. In Quintin, in central Brittany, most of the artisans were full-time weavers by the late seventeenth and eighteenth centuries. Certain families lived well off of that trade and did not need to do anything else. Thus, it was less likely that women would have become weavers. Men could stay at the looms all day long while women cared for the house, the children, and the hens and cows, often spinning with a distaff at the same time. By contrast, farther west, the weavers of Léon were also farm-workers, meaning that no single member of the household did all of the weaving since the loom would have been idle when that person went to the fields. There, in Léon, 30 percent of the weavers were women.[100] This would seem to indicate that the extent of women's participation in weaving was dependent on the activities of the men in their households.

Tanguy's figures for Quintin are supported by the logbooks of the cloth office in the city from 1720 to 1788.[101] Along with the usual collection of police reports dealing with contraventions against cloth standards, the registries of weavers' marks from 1738 have survived. Each weaver, whether from the countryside or from the town itself, had to have registered a personal seal with the cloth bureau in order to sell cloth in town. Approved cloth eventually carried the seal of the weaver, the inspector, and the merchant who brought it to market. About 4 percent of the registered seals in these records belonged to women. Many of the seals contain the weavers' names, though most of them, male or female, could not sign the registry. Only 18 percent of the registered women were widows, 5 percent noted a spouse, and the rest were women of unspecified marital status. Often, weavers from the same family registered together, such as the sisters Anne and Charlotte Coute, or Françoise Le Vaccon and five Le Vaccon men, who could have been brothers or cousins. Several area villages registered whole families at once, with a seal for each weaving member. This suggests that every member of a weaving household was

---

100 Tanguy, *Quand la toile va; L'industrie toilière bretonne du 16e au 18e siècle* (Rennes: Editions Apogee, 1995), p. 50.

101 ADCA B 3736.

Table 2.1 Sexual Division of Textile-related Work in Rennes and Region

	1709		1753		1777	
Retail Trades	Total Workers	% female	Total Workers	% female	Total Workers	% female
Lingere	35	100	75	100	71	100
Boutonier	8	100	0	-	4	100
Lace Merchant	6	100	6	100	3	100
Couture	47	96	51	100	30	100
Hat Merchant	35	80	18	77	25	72
Embroiderer	9	78	90	99	57	100
Yarn Merchant	8	75	4	0	5	40
Toile Merchant	35	57	38	82	12	58
Glove Merchant	26	38	6	33	17	17
Tapissier	15	33	8	25	16	31
Draper	43	28	20	30	4	0
Tailor	129	9	188	32	250	41
Production Trades						
Bleacher	60	100	93	100	89	98
Knitter	5	100	33	100	5	100
Spinner	169	95	82	98	28	75
Dyer	123	3	99	7	82	12
Weaver	42	0	61	0	81	0
Comber	15	0	36	0	32	9
Divider	0	-	2	100	4	100
Dresser	0	-	8	100	22	100

required to register. If all weavers had to identify their products separately, they may have had separate looms. This supports Tanguy's notion that Quintin weavers were full-time weavers. Children did not merely help out or pick up the slack for the primary weaver—they eventually registered their own seals.

The sexual division of labor in textile-related work can be illustrated based on *capitation* tax data from the textile region surrounding Rennes:

In the table above, note that, while men "tailors" easily outnumber women, there are rarely men who work as "*lingeres*" or in "*couture*." Women in these categories often performed the same functions as a tailor for women: making, embellishing, or altering clothing. Note also that the number and percentage of female tailors rises slowly but steadily over the course of the century, while the number and percentage of female *couturieres* and *lingeres* remains relatively stable. There is a slight growth in raw numbers in all three of these categories. It is possible that more women were performing this kind of work for wages at the end of the period or that more women were conceiving of their work in a more formal way.

Among whole cloth merchants, *toile*, or linen cloth merchants were more likely to be women, while drapers, luxury cloth merchants, were more likely to be men. Even so, there is usually not a significant difference between the two categories in terms of real numbers, and both saw a decline over the eighteenth century. There is a similar decline among overall workers in textile production. Here, however, the sexual division of labor is made quite clear and remains fairly steady from one year to the next. Women make up the overwhelming majority of spinners, and men are the primary dyers and weavers, though 1777 reveals a rise in both male spinners and female dyers. As all of these trades offered similar benefits in terms of status and pay, it is not clear why the division of labor was so strictly maintained or why it might have started to shift at the end of the century.

In most European countries by the early modern period, just about all weavers were men and all spinners were women. Rural women from the period are portrayed as constantly spinning in paintings, folk tales, and other sources. There were occasional examples of women weavers and men spinners, but these were in the minority. The distinction between weaving and spinning is a mysterious one from a cultural standpoint. Tanguy and other scholars explain this distinction as a result of economic necessity; several spinners were needed to keep one weaver busy.[102] Women were not prevented in any way from being weavers. But women were needed to do the spinning, and so they generally did not weave.

This explanation does not go far enough, however. It leads us to question why spinning was women's work. The simplest explanation is that spinning could be learned at an early age and performed easily alongside household chores. Thus, women of every age, little boys, and elderly men could spin because they were not fully occupied with field work or other demanding activities. Another explanation is economic: spinning was a common skill and was therefore low-paying and demeaning work that few men would stoop to perform.[103] Finally, there is a cultural explanation. By custom, in song and folk tales, women are spinners.[104]

There is an almost universal quality to the linkage between spinning and femininity. In societies as disparate as ancient Egypt, India, and Greece, as well as in medieval and early modern European cultures, spinning was women's work and

---

102 Tanguy, *Quand la toile va*, p. 50; and Gay Gullickson, "The Sexual Division of Labor in Cottage Industry and Agriculture in the Pays de Caux," *French Historical Studies* 12:2 (1981): 177–99.

103 Margaret Hunt, *The Middling Sort: Commerce, Gender, and the Family in England, 1680–1780* (Berkeley: University of California Press, 1996), p. 83.

104 Jane Schneider, "Rumpelstiltskin's Bargain," *Cloth and Human Experience* (Washington, DC: Smithsonian Press, 1991), p. 191.

women were spinners.[105] However it began, the association of women with spinning was widespread and the work was loaded with feminine connotations. Women in Brittany may have spun because that is what women were supposed to do.[106] And, in fact, the ageless quality of spinning was preserved in Breton culture as it was in few others. The earliest spinning wheels were too rough and ill suited to working with the stiff hemp and flax fiber common to Breton textiles. That fact, plus the low-capital and low-tech nature of home work in this province, meant that many women were spinning with a distaff and spindle well into the nineteenth century.[107] Thus, throughout the early modern period, Breton women were consistently portrayed with a distaff, whether they were at the market, in the fields tending cows, or relaxing by the fire late at night.

The *fileuses* of Brittany may have been anonymous, but they were hardly insignificant to the eighteenth-century economy. Wanting to keep French cloth manufacture competitive with that of England, the *intendant* Orry sent inquiries to his *subdelegués* across the province in 1731 to determine how best to get a fine quality of cloth at the lowest price.[108] The foundation of a good cloth industry was high quality yarn, and the *intendant* targeted spinners for the first phase of advancement. Breton yarn supplied both local weavers and those in Rouen, so the work of the spinners was of utmost importance for French industry. Most *subdelegués* report back that they would simply have merchants tell spinners to pay attention to their work. Others provide more detail on the local work force. Benoit from Nantes wrote that local spinners worked exclusively with flax and would not see the point in trying to get a finer yarn out of hemp, which was harder to work with.[109] Mr. de la Ville wrote from Dinan that spinners there worked with hemp but did not make fine yarn of it. When asked why, the spinners said that

> they found that they could spin 4 *livres* of common yarn in less time than it took to spin 1 *livre* of fine yarn; that out in the countryside they finished their own raw hemp but they could not find enough material to finish and dress a fine yarn; and furthermore, no one spins in this season: women and girls are entirely occupied with the house.[110]

De la Ville went on to say that a local *blanchisseuse* told him finer yarn and cloth was more expensive to bleach anyway; it had to stay in the bleach three days instead of the one day required by common yarn.

---

105 Elizabeth Wayland Barber, *Women's Work: The First 20,000 Years* (New York: W.W. Norton and Co., 1994), pp. 30–31.

106 Julie Hardwick points to a potential disadvantage for spinners: while serving as a source of income, spinning "ultimately helped keep women within the spatial confines of the household" and contributed to the "narrowing of opportunities for women" See *The Practice of Patriarchy: Gender and the Politics of Household Authority in Early Modern France* (Pennsylvania State University Press, 1998), p. 100.

107 The persistence of manual spinning was a key element of to the "quaintness" of Brittany celebrated in the romantic painting of the "Pont-Aven" school of the mid-nineteenth century.

108 ADIV C 1554, Filatures.

109 ADIV C 1554, letter dated 11 August 1731.

110 ADIV C 1554, letter dated 3 September 1731.

The issue came up again in the 1750s, as the *intendant* considered starting a number of spinning centers and making the new winding reels required equipment for spinners. Gille de Bremion warned from Nantes:

> If we make new rules and worry spinners in the least way, we will surely see a decrease in their numbers when nothing is more important than increasing the number of spinners. No doubt, it is always better to have them spin better; but it is better that they spin badly than not at all. High prices and compensation would best encourage this sector so useful to industry.[111]

By the end of the century, there were a small number of spinning centers, usually attached to schools or poorhouses, and raw hemp and wool were distributed among poor women for spinning. In this way, several cities found a way to simultaneously increase industry and charity.

Measures to improve Breton spinning did not stop there. In 1760, the *Société d'agriculture, de commerce, et des arts*, a creation of the Estates of Brittany, issued as part of its core observations a plan to encourage rural spinners through the awarding of prizes for examples of fine spinning.

> The linen and hemp yarns and the cloth made from them could more or less increase our prosperity in proportion to the attention of our spinners. Their perfected art will give birth to two new industries: that of cotton from our colonies and that of fine hemp textiles . . . the Society therefore regards spinning as one of the principal arts in every way.[112]

Following this report, the Estates voted on November 13, 1760, to approve 2,700 livres to be divided among the nine parishes of Brittany and distributed in the form of cash prizes to the top three spinners of each district.[113] Thus, on this occasion, the importance of women's work was noted at even the highest levels. Furthermore, while there are no records of recipients of these prizes, the recognition of their accomplishments surely would have been a source of pride for the top producers.[114]

Conclusion

Tax roll data provides a snapshot of women's working opportunities in eighteenth-century Brittany. Of the taxpaying women who named an occupation, most were involved with work that has historically been identified as "women's work." Overall, miscellaneous retail, food provision, and cloth or clothing production were typical feminine occupations. Yet there were still differences in the work opportunities from

---

111 ADIV C 1554, letter dated 9 August 1759.

112 "Corps d'observations de la société d'agriculture, de commerce et des arts, établie par les états de Bretagne" (Rennes: Jacques Vatar, 1760), p. 196.

113 ADLA C 444, deliberations of the estates, 1760.

114 For the early nineteenth century, the "Fête de la Filerie" was portrayed in a print by O. Perrin, and the author M. Alexandre Bouet describes the pride with which the young spinners accept their prizes. *Galerie Bretonne: Vie des Bretons de l'armorique* (Paris: Isidore Pesron, 1838), pp. 59–64.

one town to another. It seems that women needed a niche in order to earn an income. Those places with thriving markets, such as Nantes and Saint-Malo, provided ample opportunities to female vendors and shopkeepers, in both general retail and in specialty products such as clothing and fashion accessories. Textile production centers, such as Rennes, Landernau, and Morlaix, offered work to countless women, many of whom were unattached and possibly saving up for future marriage. Brest, neither a thriving market nor an industrial center, still offered opportunities to retailers and food providers; its large population of widows had hungry sailors to feed. Quimper, on the other hand, lacked even this niche, and so shows a high number of women in general day-labor, carrying water and delivering letters.

There were also slight changes in women's occupations over the course of the century. For example, several urban centers saw a rise in female tailors. In Nantes, Rennes and Quimper, the total number of both male and female tailors rose as the overall population rose, but the percentage of tailors who were women rose at the same time. In Nantes, the percentage of tailors who were women rose from 24.5 percent to 33.3 percent between 1720 and 1740; the percentage of women tailors in Rennes increased from 9 percent in 1709 to 32 percent in 1753 and 41 percent in 1777; and in Quimper, the percentage moves from 16 percent in 1737 to 26 percent in 1763 and 32 percent in 1772. As the population grew, the demand for tailors, and specifically for women tailors, seems to have grown as well. Since tailors constitute one of the few formally organized groups to include women, this trend reveals a particular opportunity for women to advance as professionals.

Not all trends were positive, however. Nantes shows a growth in the percentage of female day-workers from 9.3 percent in 1720 to 15.2 percent in 1740. The slight rise in the number of unskilled women was matched by an increase in the percentage of female heads of household who were taxed in the lowest bracket: the percentage grew from 42 percent in 1749 to a high point of 58 percent in 1789. Thus, in Nantes, we see an increase in female unskilled laborers alongside what appears to be an overall increase in poverty.[115] In Rennes, manual labor remained stable and low throughout the period, but the percentage of women named without identifying an occupation dropped from 25.3 percent in 1709 to 9 percent in 1739, then rose again to 51 percent in 1777. At the same time, the percentage of taxed women who were in the lowest bracket rose from 43.7 percent in 1709 to 59.5 percent in 1739, but dropped again to 30 percent in 1777. That means that the mid-century point at which most women in Rennes were counted in the lowest tax bracket was the same point at which most women identified themselves as workers. This may simply indicate that women who did not name an occupation were living well off of rents or other

---

115 A growth in the lowest tax bracket might also indicate a positive trend, if it means that people formerly too poor to pay taxes were moving into wage-earning jobs. As there are no figures available for the number of destitute people from one year to the next, the data remains inconclusive. However, several studies point to a worsening economy during this period. See Hufton's *The Poor in Eighteenth-Century France 1750–1789* (Oxford: Clarendon Press, 1975), and, for a primary source, see Alain J. Lemaître (ed.), *La Misère dans l'abondance en Bretagne au XVIIIe siècle: Le mémoire de l'intendant Jean-Baptise des Gallois de la Tour (1733)* (Société d'histoire et d'archéologie de Bretagne, 1999).

resources and that, simultaneously, more people sought out work for wages when the economy was weakest.

In small towns and rural areas, independent women survived but were rarer than they were in the cities. Most women, like most men, married and worked as a contributing member of a family unit. There were certainly elements of a patriarchal social structure—Breton peasant women are said to have stood during meals in order to better serve their husbands. But hard work was expected of everyone in the community, especially in times of hardship. The members of a family were equally invested in each other for the purpose of survival. The division of labor by sex had been established by long practice and proven efficiency, and women and men fulfilled their roles as necessary. At the same time, given the right economic circumstances, some of those who chose to pursue individual activities as merchants or artisans were able to do so.

There is no doubting that women in early modern Brittany had to contend with the limitations of the gender hierarchy. Guilds, for example, were male-dominated hierarchies, and even those guilds that admitted women as equal members never elected women to serve as officers and did not include women in ritual or festive occasions. Thus, even female professionals could never attain true equality with their male counterparts. At any rate, most women worked informally as unlicensed workers or merchants, as did most men, and suffered the harassment of the male-dominated police force. But patriarchy is not simple, nor is it all-powerful. Women may have been disadvantaged in the guilds, but they knew their rights and defended them when necessary. Those outside the formalized sector worked around corporate prohibitions, and managed to practice trades and run shops in spite of the difficulty.

The question of identity, however, is separate from issues of "disadvantage" and "difficulty" in practical terms. Can we not say that a woman had a work identity in spite of, or which accommodated, guild or societal limitations? Could there not have been a women's work identity that had little to do with men's definition of women's roles? Some women kept a profession from early education through marriage and into widowhood. This tended to be true in a very limited number of trades, and only in those identified as "women's work." Mistress tailors, for example, attained the status of true professionals in some cities. Merchants, as well, learned trades and inherited shops from their parents and kept them for life. This strongly suggests evidence of a "work identity" for certain women, that is, a professional identity defined by work, status, and skill. If such work identities existed primarily in trades accepted as "feminine arts," then perhaps we can acknowledge a distinctly feminine work identity recognized both by the women who worked and by the society that accepted women's work as natural.

Consider the example of Françoise Perrine Guyonval, who sued the merchant's guild of Rennes for admission. Guyonval clearly valued her status and identity as a member of the merchants' guild. It was not just her right, but it was the legacy of her parents that she should join the merchant's guild. She had worked in their shop all her life; it was part of who she was. More than that, she had no doubt witnessed her father endure the harassment of the merchant's guild when he was an unlicensed vendor. She must have been there when the *petit marchands* tried to form a new guild, and when her father obediently joined the dominant merchant's guild just before his death. It is no surprise that she might have felt entitled to make demands of the prestigious organization. Furthermore, membership in a guild carried certain privileges and status, whether or not she chose to maintain her own business. Guyonval need not have opened a shop at all in order to pass guild privileges onto her own future children. Her husband's work as *huissier*, or bailiff in one of the courts of Rennes, probably provided sufficient income and social standing. But the combined incomes and prestige offered greater security and doubled what the pair could leave their own heirs.

Guyonval's sense of work identity may be established by her willingness to go to court, but it is further validated by her success at court. When *Parlement* supported Guyonval's claim to guild membership, they also formally recognized her identity as a merchant as well as her right to pass that status onto the next generation. Thus, a feminine work identity need not be incompatible with the other identities usually assigned to women. The identity of "daughter" or "mother" might also include the ability to work, survive, even support a family. Such an identity would not have been exclusive to highly skilled, high-status workers. Even laundresses and porters had rent to pay and children to feed.

Naturally, we historians have viewed women based upon the available sources, and it is true that many pre-modern and early modern sources seem to define women by their relations to others. Thus, it was easy to conclude that women therefore had no distinct identity. In some tax rolls, for example, married women are invisible, and widows are grouped together at the end with no information on their occupations or sources of income. And so, historians wrote about women who had no identity but their marital status. Sadly, for many scholars, the search ended there. However, a different approach to the sources can reveal much about the hidden identities of women. In the *capitation des artisans*, for example, all taxpayers are grouped by trade. Women in this source are identified primarily as artisans, plain and simple. In *fouâge* rolls of the seventeenth century, women are identified simply as heirs and property holders. In judicial court records, women are identified by familial status but also as plaintiffs, defendants, and witnesses. When we approach the sources with a view to finding workers, heirs, and legal claimants, it is not difficult to find sources that identify women on those terms.

Chapter Three

Women under Breton Law

In addition to the economic and religious institutions that guided women's life choices, there were a variety of legal codes, customs, and practices at play in early modern Brittany. At times, these systems were at odds with one another, as when Breton law or local customs contradicted French law. However, the ambiguity, rather than making life more difficult, left some room for interpretation. Any study of women's place under the law has to take this flexibility into account. Thus, though the authors of the *Ancienne Coutume de Bretagne* were certainly influenced by the Roman texts that inspired all French jurists, texts that characterized all women as "irrational and feeble by nature," they were also influenced by the ancient Celtic traditions of rural Brittany.[1] In accordance with these traditions, women could expect a fair share of their parents' estates and the legal right to exploit their own property. To a certain extent, women could even protect their own interests over the objections of their parents and spouses.

It is this relative freedom which made it possible for women to make certain work and life choices. We would not be able to fully grasp women's work without an understanding of their access to resources, their capacity to control resources, and the extent to which they could save and pass on these resources. This chapter will offer an exploration of women's rights under French and Breton law in a variety of situations over the course of the late seventeenth and eighteenth centuries. Women who knew their rights and privileges were fully able to work the system to their own advantage, securing property and protection for themselves and their families.

Through court cases and contracts, we will see evidence of women's comprehension of their own rights and their ability to defend themselves. Identity becomes a key issue here, in both an external and an internal sense. As we have seen in previous chapters, many authorities accepted a narrow view of women as domestic subordinates when it came to honor and social order. A strictly legal view, however, often required addressing women as legitimate heirs, taxpayers, and royal subjects in their own right. Similarly, a woman's ability to recognize and defend her rights was contingent on her identifying herself as an heir, a taxpayer, and a royal subject.

---

1   Jacques Brejon de LaVergée, "Structures sociales et familiales dans la 'Tres ancienne coutume de Bretagne,'" *107e Congrés National des Sociétés Savantes* (Brest: 1982), p. 349.

Law codes and basic rights

The basics of the Breton law code were laid out in the *coutume* of 1330, written more than a century before the duchy of Brittany was absorbed into France. The social and familial hierarchies described there, however, are hardly different from other codes in practice throughout Europe at this time. The privileges of nobility, the advantages of town dwellers, and the primacy of the male head-of-household are plainly established with regard to the ownership of property and the ability to make contracts. The legal incapacity of minor children and of women, particularly married women, had their roots in the feudal definition of duty. As women and children could not be expected to meet the physical demands of service to a liege lord, their claims to property carried less weight, as did their words in legal matters. Over the course of the early modern period, however, old-fashioned notions of chivalry were replaced with the realities of managing financial family affairs. Even the earliest codes had recognized a man's obligations towards his wife, and his technical inability to squander her property.[2] But the later codes, those of the sixteenth, seventeenth and eighteenth centuries, gradually spelled out, in greater and greater detail, a woman's rights over material goods and the limits of her spouse's access to them.

Between 1656 and 1778, several versions of the Breton law code were published, with the later editions greatly embellished with the commentary of jurists Poullain du Parc and Michel Sauvageau. The 1656 edition is an almost verbatim printing of the 1580 *coutume*, in which certain changes from Breton to French practice were firmly established. The most striking example of this is the requirement that a wife get her husband's authorization in order to make a contract. In the *ancienne coutume* of 1330, such authorization was preferred but not essential.[3] Prior to 1580, a wife's right to make a will without her husband's consent was sacrosanct; after 1580, she needed his authorization except when leaving alms to the church. A woman always had the right to defend herself from lawsuits and accusations, but after 1580 she was not able to file suits or accept inheritance without consent.[4] This drastic shift in women's rights supports Sarah Hanley's theory of an increase in patriarchal power in France during the sixteenth and seventeenth centuries. Hanley theorized that the process of political centralization and the rise of powerful jurists as a class led to the consolidation of parental and particularly paternal authority in legal codes. In order to further their families' interests, lawmakers made it easier for the male head of household to control matters of inheritance, marriage, and the buying and selling of property.[5] However, much in Breton law also contradicts the trend, protecting women's rights even from the demands of their families.

---

2   G. Jamont, "Étude sur le droit des gens mariés d'après les coutumes de Bretagne," Thèse de doctorat, Université de Paris, Faculté de droit (Paris: V. Geard & E. Briere, 1901), p. 13.

3   Jamont, "Étude sur le droit des gens maries," p. 21.

4   *Coutumes générales du pays et duche de Bretagne* (Nantes: Ve Pierre Doriov, 1656), Article 449.

5   Hanley, "Family and State in Early Modern France: The Marriage Pact," *Connecting Spheres: Women in the Western World 1500–Present*, Boxer and Quataert, eds (Oxford University Press, 1987), pp. 55–7.

In later versions of the law code, wives were unable to function legally without authorization. However, the *coutume* still offered a way for women to get around a stubborn husband's objections. In her husband's absence, or upon his refusal, a woman could appeal to a judge and be given authority "by justice," or find a curator to act in his stead. An obvious choice for curator was the woman's father, if he still lived. Jeanne Milte, a merchant in Saint-Malo, got her father to authorize the lease on her new shop because her husband was at sea.[6] Authorization by a curator or by justice was confirmed in an act of *Parlement* in 1724, which stated it was necessary to declare that the husband had refused his authority but not necessary that the wife enter an extraneous process in order to claim some other authority.[7] In matters concerning a wife's own inheritance, the court almost automatically granted authorization. Single women were not required to seek authorization as long as they were over the age of 25, but wives were legally in the same category as minors.

The justification for requiring a husband's consent was the fact that he would be held financially responsible, at least in part, for his wife's actions and debts. As the judges in Quimper explained to Charles Bouguion, while charging him with his wife's assault on guild inspectors, "We cannot address the wife without at the same time addressing the husband because he responds civilly for faults committed by his wife."[8] Such financial responsibility is undoubtedly what prompted some men to refuse their authorization, though even the refusal did not always protect them from covering the costs. In 1636, a Saint-Malo woman sued a wet nurse after her baby died of suffocation in the wet nurse's bed. The grieving mother's husband, who was in Paris at the time of the child's death, said he would have refused his consent to the suit even if he had been home. He had objected to his wife's lack of "nature" in using a wet nurse in the first place. Nevertheless, the court ordered him to pay all costs for the investigation and lawsuit.[9] In 1671, a man in Lameur tried to reclaim a piece of property that had once belonged to his wife, but that she had sold on his refusal ten years earlier. The court decided that ten years without the property had not destroyed the man, and declined to overturn the sale.[10] Husbands were held liable with or without their consent.

In a bizarre case in Saint-Malo in 1727, Vincent Philippe sued three *revendeuses* for costs and damages because they had bought furniture and clothing from his wife without his consent. He had three separate inquiries conducted, and each was thrown out of court. The first was questioned because he was seen wearing one of the expensive suits that he claimed had been sold. The second was disqualified when

---

6   ADIV 4 BX 1156, contract of 3 December 1762.

7   *Journal des audiences et arrets du Parlement de Bretagane, Part II* (Paris: G. Martin, 1736), pp. 634–5.

8   ADF 2 E 1520, 7 June 1742. The fact that Bouguion was not even present during his wife's misconduct was immaterial. The judges went on to inform him that his wife could not be cleared of the assault simply because her late-stage pregnancy prevented her from delivering blows upon the inspectors:. "She did worse by exciting the others with her cries and violent encouragement."

9   Michel Sauvageau, *Arrêts et reglemens du Parlement de Bretagne* (Nantes: Jacques Mareschal, 1712), Chapter 195, Book 3, p. 41.

10   Sauvageau (1712), Chapter 162, Book 1, page 92.

it was revealed that one of his witnesses was his own employee, a young woman who had been sent on numerous occasions to sell things for the household to the very same vendors who were now being charged. The court assumed that a trusted servant who had done regular business with the vendors could not fairly testify that the vendors knew they were taking part in an unauthorized transaction. The third investigation, however, had nothing to do with the evidence of the sale but became a battle of spousal authorizations. Philippe claimed that the first two inquiries had been invalid because one of the vendors had never been authorized by her husband to answer the charges. Emmanuel Martin had refused to let his wife, Perrine Turgis, go to court. Though lawyers reminded Martin that a woman could defend herself against accusations without authorization, and furthermore that her actions as a merchant carried his implied consent, he refused to budge. Instead, he charged that the accusations were absurd and unworthy of response, and that Philippe should seek redress for his own wife's unauthorized sale from her dowry or from her family.[11]

The strict need for authorization created some confusing language, as when the mutual donation of goods between a husband and wife carried the legal formula, "this man and his wife, she having requested and been duly and well authorized by him, by common consent and without the undue influence or constraint of anyone but in their free and honest will . . .".[12] She needed his consent even to leave him, "of free will," her worldly goods.[13] It also led to some interesting legal fictions, as in the case of Isabelle Riou, who had sold part of her inheritance in her husband's absence in 1711 but received his authorization retroactively at his return a year later. In 1727, after Isabelle's death, their daughter Renée sued to reclaim the property as her own inheritance on the grounds that her father had not formally consented to the sale. The court agreed that legal recognition of blanket authorizations would be a dangerous precedent and could in theory lead to a husband's free access to his wife's property and inheritance. Thus, ironically, in order to protect the legal control granted to a married woman, the court nullified Isabelle's unauthorized sale of her own property.[14]

In spite of the need for authorization in almost all matters, a woman had the right to work as a merchant "without her husband and without his authorization." This is stated specifically in all versions of the law.[15] The law code assumes that a wife's commerce is separate from that of her husband, and that she alone will be responsible for her debts and contracts. However, if a woman works as a merchant with her husband's explicit permission, then her debts and contracts become their joint responsibility. At least, that is how the law reads. In the case mentioned above, in which Vincent Phillippe sued three merchants, one merchant's husband tried to

---

11 ADIV 4 BX 1117, 1 May 1727–10 January 1728.

12 ADIV 2 ED 20, Mutual donation of Sr. Deschamps and Dlle. Besneray, 24 July 1741.

13 Pierre Hévin stated that a husband's authorization for an act that would benefit him was superfluous, and suggested that overly zealous notaries were at fault. *Consultations et observations sur la coutume de Bretagne* (Rennes: Guillaume Vatar, 1734), p. 116.

14 *Journal des audiences*, p. 573.

15 *Coutumes générales du pays et duché de Bretagne* (1656), Article 448.

thwart the case by refusing to allow his wife to answer the charges. Lawyers for Phillippe argued that the fact of the woman's open shop automatically bestowed her husband's authorization upon all matters involving her commerce, and that in any case she did not need his permission to answer charges.[16] Nevertheless, his refusal appears to have effectively stalled the case.

In daily practice, the issues of authorization and a wife's business obligations were probably handled informally and with few direct challenges. In a strict legal sense, however, there were hundreds of potential pitfalls inherent in this contradiction—that a woman was required to get her husband's consent to make any and all contracts unless she was acting as a merchant, in which case his toleration of her commerce served as implicit consent. This legal paradox and the arbitrary nature of some rulings made it possible for some couples to manipulate circumstances to their advantage, making whichever claim would be of most benefit. In some cases, no doubt, it made more sense to follow the law that stipulated a distinct legal and commercial identity for a wife who practiced a separate trade. This might be especially so in households in which the wife's independent commercial identity was established through guild membership, as some Breton guilds admitted women regardless of their husbands' trade or guild status. But even members of well-off two-income households might at times have found it advantageous to nullify "unauthorized" contracts in order to recoup a loss. A wife's independent work identity might have been therefore most beneficial as something she could assume or reject at will for the good of the household, and not an advantage she used solely for herself.

Marital community

As with other kinds of contractual authorization, the heart of the issue is financial responsibility for debts, and the definition of "community" within marriage. Community includes what both parties have brought to the marriage, things bought or acquired during the marriage, and debts incurred by either party since the marriage. A woman's dowry is technically never entered into the community, because its loss would leave her penniless in widowhood.[17] Nor is any inheritance from her parents entered into community, though inheritance from any other source becomes communal.[18] A woman's debts may be paid from her own goods and from half of the communal goods; a man, as administrator of the community, may dissolve the entirety of his own goods and the community, but cannot touch his wife's inheritance or dowry without her consent.[19]

---

16 ADIV 4 BX 1117, 10 January 1728. To make things even more confusing, the court ruled in 1622 that a man's goods and his half of the community could not be used to pay the expenses of a criminal suit or conviction against his wife without his consent. *Arrêts et Reglemens du Parlement de Bretagne* (1712), Chapter 89, Book 3, p. 16.

17 In practice, of course, a dowry could be used to set up a couple in business or in a home, and often enough it was long gone by the time a woman needed to live off of it in widowhood.

18 *Coutumes générales du pays et duche de Bretagne* (1656), Article 441.

19 Jamont, "Étude sur le droit des gens maries," pp. 25–6; Articles 429, 445, 447.

By 1759, the following note was added to Article 448, which allows a woman to work as a merchant:

> If, being in community, a woman does business without the knowledge of her husband, his obligations are *nulle*. And if he allows her to be a merchant, and make contracts, then what she does in business and in exchange will be valid, and her husband must respond and the debts will be paid from the community and even from the husband's own goods. The debts will come from the goods of the woman, even if they were given to the community, if she enjoys a commerce separate from that of her husband's; if she is merely conducting business on behalf of her husband, then she is not personally responsible for anything beyond the community. And if (she is) a woman who is separated or not in community with her husband, she alone will be responsible for her debts.[20]

Legally, then, a man was responsible for his working spouse's debts only if she had his explicit authorization to engage in commerce. A successful merchant who contributed to the joint property of the marriage would probably have been "tolerated" by her husband. However, if a woman's business failed, and her debts were heavy, it would have been in her husband's best interest to declare she had been working without his knowledge or permission.

Couples could also benefit from manipulating the wife's consent for her husband's actions. The jurist Hévin complained that it was illogical that a wife had to be compensated for the sale of her goods without her permission but would gain automatically from the profits of such a sale that became part of the community.[21] The only legal limit on the wife's consent was that if she had consented to the sale, she could not later claim compensation.[22] This, in theory, made it possible for a woman to withhold her permission until the results of the sale were clear. Thus, a clever couple could keep part of their joint goods untouchable to creditors by ignoring the issue of the wife's permission.[23] If she claimed her goods had been sold without her permission, she either reclaimed the lost property or was compensated, before any creditor, out of her husband's goods.

---

20   Poullain du Parc, *La coutume et la jurisprudence coutumiere de Bretagne dans leur ordre naturel* (Rennes: G. Vatar, 1759), Article 448, supplement. A woman separated or not in community with her husband is solely responsible for her debts, but still needs his consent to make contracts or sell property.

21   Jamont, "Étude sur le droit des gens maries," p. 52; Article 437; and Hévin, *Consultations et observations sur la coutume de Bretagne* (Rennes, 1734), pp. 412–13, 424, and 425–30.

22   *Coutumes générales du pays et duche de Bretagne* (1656), Article 443. Hévin clarified this in a later commentary: a sale made without the wife's consent was to be nullified, and she was not entitled to compensation above and beyond the reinstatement of her property. However, she or her line had to be compensated for the loss of lineage property even if she did consent. *Consultations et observations*, p. 424.

23   Julie Hardwick has objected to this characterization, pointing out that there is no evidence of collusion and that, in practice, women were almost always at a disadvantage. While I agree on both counts, there do seem to be a number of cases in which the couple's legal position is withheld or applied retroactively for maximum benefit. It seems reasonable to assume that this is intentional at least some of the time.

Hévin objected most of all, however, to the fact that a woman never risks total loss while a man does. But of course, that was the point. This chivalrous code was designed to protect the "weaker sex" from the risky activities of men. Nevertheless, community worked both ways. Just as a man was responsible for his wife's debts if her business or her contracts were recognized as communal, a woman was responsible for husband's debts if she was "in community" with him. Accepting community meant accepting all the benefits and paying all the debts therein. In 1710, the widow Perrine Fevre was called before the presidial of Rennes to pay her late husband's amends to a man he had injured in a bar fight a year earlier. In 1715, Elizabeth Caignan sued the tailor's guild of Rennes for back pay owed to her late husband. And in 1726, Olive Biard sued her stepmother for money owed on her father's deathbed care and burial.[24] There were important limitations to a woman's responsibility—she could not be sent to jail for her husband's debts, and she had to be left something to live on if he was convicted of a crime and his goods were confiscated.[25] Guillmette Janue wrote to the presidial in Rennes in 1717 to question their authority in liquidating her husband's entire estate after his conviction of a capital crime. She had had no part in his crime, and she had been left with four children to raise.[26] Her portion should have been left automatically, but she wanted half their community; it is not clear if she got it.

A woman was further protected from her husband's debts if she opted out of the community within 30 days of his death. If she chose to accept community, then she was allowed to keep whatever was left of their joint estate after all debts had been paid. If she renounced community, she got her dowry or her personal possessions, and none of the communal goods, but she was acquitted of all her husband's debts.[27] His heirs then became responsible for his debts, and for making sure that his widow received her portion and her bed and wardrobe. Families were not always so reliable, however, and at times a woman was forced to defend these rights.

It was important that a woman be given access to communal goods and assume a certain measure of her husband's authorization if she was going to act in his stead in business affairs and household matters. Among merchant families, especially, the wife was expected to handle transactions in her husband's absence on a regular basis. Mme. Duhoux-Desages, for example, made clear in her extensive correspondence that she was involved in her husband's commerce as well as her own.[28] Wives were even prepared to handle the affairs of a minor official post; Janne Angelique Moreau, the wife of Julien Louis Menard, *receveur des bois du Roi*, reported that she was out one night "to receive a shipment of building lumber on behalf of her

---

24   ADIV 2 B 1801 (bis) 16 October 1710; 3 B 1442, 10 July1715; and 2 B 1844(2), 28 March 1726.

25   *Coutumes générales du pays et duche de Bretagne* (1656), Article 445; Jamont, "Étude sur le droit des gens maries," p. 40.

26   ADIV 2 B 1844(1), 2 March 1717.

27   *Coutumes générales du pays et duche de Bretagne* (1656), Articles 432, 433, 434, 435, and 436.

28   ADIV 4 C 3, letters of 1702–1748.

husband."[29] In 1720, the *Avocat General* informed the city of Auray that they were forbidden to leave a woman in charge of finances at the Hôtel Dieu. The former *oeconome*'s widow simply had continued in his place after his death and was only brought to the attention of the royal government when she tried to change how alms were distributed to the poor.[30] She had apparently been such a help to her husband that no one really thought about her leaving.[31] In such circumstances, it is not clear if the wife's participation required the formal authorization of her husband. But in all likelihood, spouses probably did without the formalities. In many ways during his life, and for a period after his death, a man's wife was an extension of himself. Without a strong reason to keep their property separate, such as extensive inherited property on both sides or risky ventures made by one or the other, most couples accepted community and all the responsibilities that went with sharing their debts and profits.

Brittany was unique in that, by tradition, community was delayed for a year and a day following the nuptials. Some scholars have dismissed this characteristic as inconsequential since most couples would not have received their dowry or inheritance for some time after the wedding. However, it is a significant feature of the law code since it automatically gives the couple time to settle individual debts and business arrangements. Since brides in early modern Brittany might have entered into marriage with guild membership, shop inventory or land inherited from a parent, the period of non-community seems like a reasonable attempt to avoid complications as the couple established themselves. For a year and a day, a woman had control of her own property. Technically, by law, a woman needed her husband's consent whether or not they were in community.[32] In practice, however, women routinely made contracts for their own affairs after separation or outside of community. The Dame Francoise Decalays, for example, was identified as "non-communaire spouse of Mr. Henri Hedelin" when she contracted for some day-laborers to clear the brush off her land; their marriage contract had stipulated she would manage her own property.[33] Couples also had the option of setting community at will. While drawing up the marriage contract, the families decided whether community would begin after a year and a day, on the day of the wedding, at some future date, or not at all. Poullain du Parc explained in 1778 that any mutually agreed upon arrangement was legal so long

---

29   ADIV 2 B 1844(2), hearing on 12 January 1726. Unfortunately, she and her servants were attacked while she awaited the delivery. She identified her assailant and took him to court, "authorized by the court on her husband's refusal." Clearly, a wife's assistance was not always appreciated.

30   ADIV 1 BF 1224, *Civil Arrêts, Grand Chambre*, 6 August 1720.

31   This offers another example of how the "official" view of women's roles was out of sync with that of popular society.

32   The jurist Michel Sauvageau comments on the potential contradiction between the period of non-community and the fact that the husband is "master of the goods" and entitled to operate without his wife's consent. In fact, this potential conflict is why he recommends doing away with the tradition of "a year and a day" and beginning community on the wedding day. *Observations pour la reformation de la coutume de Bretagne* (Nantes: Jacques Mareschal, 1710), p. 127.

33   ADLA 4 E 2/1294, 4 January 1698.

as it was stipulated before the wedding took place.[34] The marriage contract between the nobles René Marie Le Bel and Marie Francoise Claude Volney states, "it is so declared there will be no community between the future spouses renouncing the custom of the province."[35] Late seventeenth- and early eighteenth-century marriage contracts usually note that the Breton custom of a year-and-a-day would be followed; later contracts most often waive this custom and set community to begin the day of the wedding.[36] This indicates a gradual replacement of the Breton custom with standard French law, and perhaps also signals the contraction of independent rights for married women in the region.

Separation

True "divorce" was forbidden in early modern France, but it was possible to sue for a separation. One either obtained a "separation of goods," in which a couple legally left community but could have stayed together, or a "separation of goods and body," which included physical separation of domiciles. Cases such as these were rare, and usually took place only in dire circumstances. In the Trégor region of Brittany, there were only 160 requests for separation between 1700 and 1725. Of these, 109 separations were requested due to the brutality of the husband; the rest were due to the wife's infidelity, the husband's impotence, or "mutual loathing."[37] Separations were more common in large cities such as Nantes and Rennes, but were still relatively rare. Jamont suggests that judges preferred to grant administrative powers to the wife rather than dissolve a union if the husband's mismanagement was the only problem, though the code itself recommends separation if the husband's affairs are not in order.[38] Similarly, Julie Hardwick found that women suing for separation in Nantes had to prove both excessive violence and financial mismanagement in order to obtain a true separation.[39] The evidence was often produced via the

---

34 Poullain du Parc, *La Coutume et la jurisprudence coutumière de Bretagne* (Rennes: Francois Vatar, 1778), Article 424, p. 235. Specifically, a couple could not claim "non-community" after the wedding if it had not been stipulated beforehand. Without legal notice, community would begin automatically after a year and a day, *retroactively* to the day of the wedding.

35 ADIV 2 EL 153, papers of Lebel family, 1736.

36 Jamont claims the custom of a year-and-a-day to community starts to disappear after 1600, but was universal across Brittany before then (p. 33). In my experience, most contracts follow this custom up to 1700, and then gradually give way to the French custom of starting community on the wedding day.

37 George Minois, "Rupture de fiançialles et divorces dans le Trégor au XVIIIe siècle," *Memoires de la société d'histoire et d'archeologie de Bretagne* 60 (1983): 137-8.

38 Jamont, "Étude sur le droit des gens maries," pp. 217–18; *Coutume de bretagne et usances particulieres* (1725), Article 427, p. 400.

39 Hardwick, "Seeking Separations: Gender, Marriages, and Household Economies in Early Modern France," *French Historical Studies* 21:1 (1998): 175. Laura Gowing found that wives in early modern London could bring charges against their husbands solely on the basis of excessive violence. *Domestic Dangers: Women, Words and Sex in Early Modern London* (Oxford: Clarendon Press, 1996), pp. 222–4.

supporting testimony of friends, family, and neighbors to the effect that the husband was abusive, destructive, and careless with money. The charges of violence alone did not guarantee the granting of a separation, but the mismanagement charges by themselves would only gain her financial rights and not the right to leave. One could sue to dissolve community and stay together, or sue to actually leave the marital home and divide the property—a divorce in all ways except the right to remarry.

The anonymous jurist who commented on the 1725 *coutume* discussed separation at length. If a woman is granted a separation, she has the right to ask for half the community: "but it is more to her advantage to renounce the community rather than leave it to his mismanagement, and leave with her trousseau as if he were dead." By renouncing the community, a separated woman could not be held responsible for debts incurred by her husband that she was not aware of at the time of the separation. At the same time, according to the author, she should not have to renounce unknown profits that were part of the community during the marriage.[40] This left the door open to later claims of reparation from a woman who had renounced the community without ever having benefited from it. Thus, the code was arranged so that women would not be left unnecessarily vulnerable.

The law could just as easily be used against women, however. The same author denounces the automatic separation of goods and domicile when only violence has been proven:. "A violent man who has been a good manager should not be made to dissolve his finances."[41] A separation of domicile without separation of goods would have left women at the financial mercy of the spouses who had abused them. Furthermore, a clever lawyer could in theory make the case that a separated woman should be prohibited from taking her dowry back. Article 451 of the *coutume* states that a woman who leaves voluntarily and is not with her husband "at the time of his death" loses the right to her dowry. The law was designed to punish adulterous wives, of course, but could be interpreted to apply to any case if a family was willing to pursue it.[42] Hélène Chevalier was sued in 1723 for her dowry and part of the marital community by her brother-in-law after her husband's death. She had been shut up in a convent by her husband for five years, but had reconciled with him and been released from the convent before his death at sea. The court ordered that her supposed debauchery before being confined was annulled by their later reconciliation, and that she could not possibly have been with her husband at the time of his death at sea. Therefore, she could not be deprived of her dowry and community.[43]

Women in particularly bad marriages sometimes had to petition more than once for separation. In 1715, Jeanne Coignard wrote to the *maires* and judges of Rennes, begging that her husband be put into prison. His violence began the day of their marriage, she said in her letter, and was continuous during the six years since she had "had the misfortune to marry Jan Perret." Ten months earlier, she had succeeded in obtaining a separation of goods and domicile, agreeing to let Jan take a bed, his clothes, and 13 livres to pay off a debt. After ten months of "peace," Jan had suddenly

---

40   *Coutume de bretagne et usances particulieres* (1725), Article 427, p. 400.

41   *Coutume de bretagne et usances particulieres* (1725), Article 427, p. 400.

42   Minois, "Rupture de fiançialles et divorces," p. 125.

43   *Journal des audiences et arrests* (1736), Chapter 62, Book 1, p. 302.

reappeared, promising to live with her "as an honorable man." Within two weeks, however, he had fallen into his old ways. For four hours on a Sunday night, he had brutalized her, broken the furniture, thrown the food and dishes out the window, and burnt the bill of separation. Her neighbors had rescued her, and served as witnesses to her suit, showing once again how often women depended upon support from outside their households.[44]

In 1710, Sylvie Marain had a similar problem with her husband, Pierre Barabe. He had sold her bed and clothing, had beaten her repeatedly, and had finally kicked her out of their home. She was taken in by a charitable magistrate who later testified on her behalf. Pierre made the further mistake of throwing rocks at the magistrate's windows and attacking the police who came to arrest him. A separation was easily granted, and Pierre was taken to prison for several months. Their case was reopened in March 1711, when Pierre petitioned the court to have his wife committed to a convent. He claimed that he had twice been sent to prison for his violence against her, and that Sylvie was using her legal separation as an excuse for leading a scandalous life. He also produced witnesses to this effect, saying, "this honest man can no longer suffer the vices, evil commerce, and scandals of his wife," and needed the court to grant municipal funds for her imprisonment.[45] The outcome of this lawsuit is not clear, but it, like the case above, illustrate that women in dire circumstances readily turned to their neighbors and to the law to protect themselves.

Few cases are so clear cut, however, and a woman's separation suit could be inspired by greed or spite as easily as by fear. This is especially true among wealthier families in which wives were less likely to face desperate poverty upon separation, and less likely to seek the protection of strangers in the middle of the night. Dame Anne Marie Blanche, wife of Sieur de la Rochemacé, began her suit by requesting the imprisonment of one of their servants for engaging in "scandalous ways" with her husband. Other servants and neighbors claimed to have been confused by the accusations. They insisted that the girl was quite innocent, and the couple had always hurled accusations of infidelity against each other. Their mutual dislike was apparent, and they spent most of their time apart. Never before had a third party been dragged into their quarrels. Dame Blanche's formal charges make little sense, however, if, as her husband claimed, she wanted a separation. By law, a man could seek a separation for his wife's infidelity, but a woman did not have the same right. Furthermore, if a man charged his wife with adultery but was himself guilty of the same crime, his separation would be refused. Thus, Dame Blanche could use such accusations to stop her husband from obtaining a separation, but not for obtaining it herself. It seems evident, nevertheless, that she wanted to get away from him. Typically, she would have needed to prove excessive violence or financial mismanagement, or gotten his consent to separate by mutual agreement. In the end, the proceedings had gotten so unpleasant for all involved that Sieur de la Rochemacé must have consented. Dame Blanche got her separation of goods and domicile, but was ordered to revoke her

---

44 ADIV 3 B 1446, letter of 12 June 1715.
45 ADIV 3 B 1448, 31 January 1710; and, ADIV 3 B 1444, 11 March 1711.

denunciation of the girl in front of six witnesses of the girl's choosing and to pay 500 livres in amends.[46]

The servant in this case was quite lucky to have had the support of her coworkers and the benefit of laws designed to protect the weak from abuse. She may have been a migrant from the countryside, as many servants were, and no doubt had few resources with which to protect herself. Dame Blanche's own circumstances are unclear, as are her motivations in the suit against her husband. But the contrast between her situation and that of the servant is striking. Dame Blanche may have been at the mercy of her husband, and disadvantaged by laws that made it hard for her to leave her husband without his consent. But the servant evidently had as much to fear from a wrathful mistress as she did from a lustful master; either could have destroyed her life.

Cases such as this notwithstanding, in cases of separation of goods alone, a couple could simply agree to separate for whatever reason. George Hardy, medical doctor, and his wife, Anne Aubin, "she, acting with his authorization, living together on the rue Saint George, without prejudice, are respectively given the power to touch, receive, sell, buy, contract, agree, transport, procure, compromise, acquire, and generally deal with and against whomever they deem necessary" in administering their own goods and property.[47] Renunciation of the community was a fairly straightforward process, and may have had more to do with fine-tuning financial issues than with any internal conflict. Community could be reestablished by mutual consent of both parties and did not require any legal or formal procedure.[48] Once again, it is clear that couples were free to decide which arrangement best suited their particular situation.

Mutual donation

As in many legal areas, marriage failures are much more in evidence than successes among police reports and court cases. This creates a rather negative view of marriages in the past. Fortunately, the law also recognized a couple's right to make a "mutual donation" to one another. A mutual donation was an agreement between the spouses that whoever survived the other would have the right to dispose of all the goods of the community and up to a third of the personal goods of the deceased.[49] Its purpose was to give control far beyond the rights gained automatically via community. For example, in a contract from 1771, Jeanne Marchay gave her husband, Michel Trouve, rights to the property she had inherited from her sister; under normal circumstances, a wife's inheritance from a blood relative was untouchable.[50] Pious donations and entailed properties would be automatically respected, and one could designate

46   ADIV 3 B 1453, 15–27 February 1715.
47   ADIV 4 E 530, Notaire Chasse, 9 July 1727.
48   Jamont, "Étude sur le droit des gens maries," p. 218.
49   Poullain du Parc, *La coutume et la jurisprudence coutumiere de Bretagne* (1778), Article 210.
50   ADLA 4 E 2/73, Notaire Auffay, 23 December 1771.

particular wishes in the donation contract.[51] For example, in the mutual donation between Joseph Deschamps and his wife, Bonne Angelique Besnerays, the sum of 1,000 livres was reserved for Besnerays' mother if she was still alive at the time of Besnerays' death.[52] The mutual donation also did not negate debts owed to others by either party, especially if those debts predated the marriage. Such debts had to be paid before the donation could be honored.

Mutual donations usually include references to the "friendship" or *amitié* between the spouses, and it assumes a relative material equality between both spouses.[53] According to the French historian Georges Jamont the mutual donation was one of the few Breton customs to remain intact up to the French Revolution. By the eighteenth century, most of Breton law had been replaced by French and Roman law, which favored children over spouses. But the mutual donation, "inspired by affection" and encouraged by the church, was a common arrangement until the end of the *ancien régime*.[54] The donation contract did not require the husband's authorization to be valid, though permission was typically included. And a couple did not have to be in community to make a mutual donation; a couple could maintain separate goods and use the donation to designate each other as principal heir.[55] A wife was permitted to accept an outright gift from her husband, but not if she intended to keep her dowry. However, a mutual donation was perfectly compatible with the dowry, and a woman could keep her goods as well as whatever she was granted in the mutual donation.[56]

Though it is not entirely clear how these distinctions would have worked in practice, or how they related to community, it is clear that the mutual donation was given priority above all other agreements. A mutual donation was a sacred trust and its validity was challenged only in cases where the state of mind or health of one of the parties was in question. If one party was on his or her deathbed at the time of the signing of the mutual donation, then the donation was automatically invalid, regardless of any other contract between them.[57] Donations between spouses who were clearly unequal in social or financial terms were also routinely challenged, if

---

51   By Act of *Parlement* in 1664, a man must honor his wife's contributions to the church in spite of a mutual donation granting him all of her goods. Sauvageau, *Arrêts et reglemens du Parlement*, Chapter 282, Book I, p. 259.

52   ADIV 2 ED 20, 24 July 1741.

53   According to Hévin, the insistence upon equality between the spouses was absolute. *Consulations et observations*, pp. 271–2, 276–8.

54   Jamont, "Étude sur le droit des gens maries," p. 138. Mutual donations were recognized elsewhere in France, of course, but were not necessarily as ironclad as the Breton version.

55   Poullain du Parc, *La coutume et la jurisprudence coutumiere de Bretagne* (1778), Article 210.

56   Poullain du Parc, *La coutume et la jurisprudence coutumiere de Bretagne* (1778), Article 206. Note that earlier versions of this law prohibited a woman's keeping both the dowry and a donation. See *Coutume Générale Reformée des Pais et Duché de Bretagne* (Rennes: Pierre Garnier, 1693), Article 206. By 1712, Hévin had clarified the distinction between a mutual donation and a non-reciprocal donation from one spouse to the other. *Consultations et observations*, p. 283.

57   Poullain du Parc, *La coutume et la jurisprudence coutumiere de Bretagne* (1778), Article 209.

only because families sought to prevent the contract from costing the loss of vital properties.

In 1717, Renée Huby challenged the mutual donation of her son in a telling case that covered all of these issues. Charlotte-Louise de Frenay married Huby's son, Colomban le Rouxeau, on 24 February 1716. In accordance with Breton tradition, they had set their community to begin a year and a day after the ceremony. They signed a mutual donation in September of the same year, and Rouxeau died in January, 1717, eleven months after their marriage and a month short of community. He died of an illness he had contracted before the mutual donation had been signed, though at the time it had not been clear he would die of it. Furthermore, in purely material terms, Frenay was richer than her husband at the time of his death, making them "unequals" and possibly nullifying their donation. Surely Frenay's relatives would have themselves destroyed the mutual donation if she had been the one to die first. But the thrust of Huby's case against her daughter-in-law was that the couple was not yet in community: "The mutual donation is intended to ensure that neither party is denied the fruits of collaboration," pointed out Huby's lawyers, and in the few months of their marriage, Frenay and Rouxeau could not have enjoyed any "collaboration." Because Rouxeau died before community began, he and his wife had enjoyed only a "habitual community," which amounted to "an actual separation of goods." Therefore, with nothing shared in common, nothing could be given to Frenay as heir to her husband.

Frenay's lawyers countered that usufruct gave certain rights to each spouse, and the mutual donation had concerned primarily those things that the couple had shared in their daily life together:. "The mutual donation is the most honored of all the contracts a husband and wife can make. It is the only way accorded by law for them to give each other reciprocal proof of their warm regard." As for Frenay's wealth, the lawyers found it preposterous for a man's heirs to challenge an exchange that would have worked to his advantage. At any rate, the mutual donation by law had no effect on and could not be affected by community. The court upheld the mutual donation, in all its terms.[58]

Other donations and wills

Mutual donations protect the rights of married couples and the practice is found throughout France. One aspect of Breton custom, however, demonstrates without a doubt that women enjoyed a unique position under the law. Via will or donation, two unmarried women could protect each other financially from the demands of other heirs or kin. This striking arrangement is described following the definition of marriage in the *coutume* of 1725:

> Two unmarried women (*filles*) may be tied by friendship, having together contracted a perpetual society by an act in the form of a testament or mutual donation, reciprocal in all their goods, with the capacity of the survivor to dispose of said goods, on condition

---

58 Sauvageau, *Arrêts et reglemens du Parlement*, Chapter 94, Book I, pp. 435–47.

of the execution of pious legacies contained in said act; such a society and donation was approved by *arrêt* of 1554; however, a similar society and donation made between three *filles* will be null, in case one of the women wants to separate from the other two.[59]

This clause is found at the very beginning of the *coutume*'s section on marriage law, in a section describing how marriage and certain other unions are "natural" and in little need of legal regulation. There is nothing, other than the location of the passage, to suggest that such a union was considered a kind of "marriage." At the same time, it is clearly a partnership, a "perpetual society," between two individuals who are not otherwise related to one another. Their partnership, legally speaking, is expressed like a marriage through a mutual donation rather than through a simple division of property, as one might expect to occur between siblings or cousins. Furthermore, designated as a "perpetual society," such a union goes far beyond a simple testamentary gift from one friend to another. Finally, the fact that the union is permitted between two women, but never three, suggests that it is more than a convenient arrangement between roommates.

While not "marriage," this arrangement, more so than any other defined by law, flies in the face of a "family-state" pact. Surely no one seeking to solidify paternal control over women and resources would support the notion of a perpetual society between women. And yet the clause, written and passed in the sixteenth century, was reaffirmed in the eighteenth, precisely when women were said to have lost the battle against patriarchal encroachment on their rights. The survivor of a "perpetual society," protected by a mutual donation, would keep all of their joint goods along with half of the pair's acquisitions, taking that property firmly away from the donor's family. Few arrangements could be further from patriarchal consolidation than this.

Documentation of such unions is rare, suggesting that the practice itself was rare. However, a few cases survive and they merit our attention. Jeanne Bachelier and Françoise Lucas signed their mutual donation in 1742.[60] The two were identified as *filles majeures et tailleuses*, and they simply note that they live together and share everything.[61] The document reads like a traditional mutual donation: the two swore they were there under no constraint, but made the gift of their free will and because of their "amitié" for one another. They agreed that the survivor of the two would receive "all and each of their goods, movables, effects, and credits," as well as any "acquisitions and conquests" they might have made together after the contract was signed. Catherine Dargent and Jaquette Auduy stated that they sought a mutual donation in recognition of the reciprocal "bonne amitié" they had shared and the many services that they had provided to one another during the "twenty-three or twenty-four years" that they had lived together.[62] Dargent was 60 years old and Auduy was 50 when they signed their mutual donation, and they expected their good health would not last forever. Janne Gandu and Catherine Morice agreed to

59 *Coutume de Bretagne* (1725), 384.

60 ADLA, 4 E 2 663, minutes of the notary, Desbois, 30 July 1742.

61 While it is not clear if the two had been together for very long, Jeanne Bachelier had been named alone as the mistress tailor in an apprenticeship contract two years earlier. ADLA, 4 E 2 663, minutes of the notary, Desbois, 14 October 1740.

62 ADLA, 4 E 2 1631, minutes of the notary, Pilet, 15 April 1744.

share all rent, costs, goods, credits, and debts, and that the survivor should continue to enjoy these things for the rest of her life.[63] This pair noted simply that they had been together *plusiers années*, but their situation is particularly touching. Gandu was identified as the wife of Jan LeMaire, "absent 29 years." The mutual donation notes that in all their time together, the women had shared goods and rent, that they had cared for one another through illnesses, and that they intended to continue doing so.

The donations noted above involved women who did not have much wealth or any other heirs of note. Based on the vulnerability of unattached women in urban areas, it is perhaps no surprise that each of these women contracted a partnership with someone else. However, it is not so difficult to find even fairly well-off women making such arrangements. Dlle. Marie Foüier took great pains to establish through a declaration in 1738 which of the goods in her home belonged to her friend and roommate, Marie Renouard.[64] They had only been together for three years at that point, but Foüier wanted to warn her heirs to leave Renouard's goods alone in case she died and left Renouard vulnerable. Two years later, the two women signed a mutual donation to one another.[65] They included an inventory of their goods totaling 559 livres. The amount is not especially noteworthy, but the list of goods includes such things as "a game table, covered in green cloth," monogrammed handkerchiefs, and silk dresses. It is clear that this was not the home of laborers.

It seems that the mutual donations between women represent a union between them. Unlike donations or bequests from a wealthier woman to a subordinate, which will be discussed below, the mutual donations reveal an equal and reciprocal partnership. Unlike typical roommate arrangements, born out of necessity, the relationships outlined in the mutual donations were long lasting and defined primarily by friendship. In these ways, the mutual donations between women are very much like the mutual donations drafted by traditional spouses. They are reciprocal, they express friendship, and they protect the survivor from the claims of other heirs.

The other testaments and donations left by women in my sample are fairly traditional and corroborate what has been noted in other studies of women's wills. The wills are typically written on behalf of widowed or single women, rather than married women. The benefactors often include children and siblings, but are just as likely to include people of unclear relation to the testator. The legacies might include a pious gift or a request for religious services, but also note seemingly modest goods to be left to particular individuals. Finally, the wills serve not just as a means to settle outstanding debts, but as a forum for otherwise quiet women to acknowledge their emotional debts and personal relations.[66]

---

63   ADLA, 4 E 2 515, minutes of the notary, Cocquard, 12 May 1742.

64   ADLA, 4 E 2 662, minutes of the notary, Desbois, 3 June 1738.

65   ADLA, 4 E 2 663, minutes of notary, Desbois, 3 April 1740.

66   Martha C. Howell, "Fixing Movables: Gifts by Testament in Late Medieval Douai," *Past and Present*, 150 (February 1996): 3–45; Giovanna Benadusi, "Investing the Riches of the Poor: Servant Women and Their Last Wills," *American Historical Review* 109:3 (June 2004): 805–26.

Numerous wills include a special gift for those who cared for the testator during an illness. Renée Valotiere, after bestowing the bulk of her modest fortune on the Ursulines, left the sum of 57 livres to Marie Jollivet, "la veuve Houssayé." Their relation is unclear. Both women were widowed, but nothing else is explained except that Marie Jollivet should get Valotiere's clothing and pay the surgeon out of the aforementioned sum, "payment for which la Houssayé is not responsible."[67] Perrine Dugué, after a lengthy illness, paid for a mass for her soul, left money for her sister to give to the poor and additional sums towards prayers for long-dead relatives and other debts, and finally asked that, if there was money left over, that something be given to her niece "for being at her bed."[68]

Marie Monnier, identified as a *fille majeure lingére*, had her will drawn up as she prepared to take a room at the hospital. Monnier left everything to her widowed sister, Louise, who had come to care for her three years earlier when Monnier first fell ill. The assets included all of Monnier's household and personal goods as well as 180 livres, which Louise was free to use "as she sees fit."[69] Monnier clearly had no other heirs and was happy to recognize her sister's help and affection by declaring Louise the recipient of this modest collection. In this case, as in those above, it makes sense that someone facing death would want to acknowledge her caretakers, especially if there were no other heirs.

In other cases, however, the presence of other heirs did not deter women from leaving special legacies. Perrine Giraud, a widowed cloth merchant, asked first that her daughter, Michelle Liejard, sell the silver goblet and cup to pay for masses for her soul. Then Giraud noted that all her clothes, linens, and a gold chain should go directly to Michelle "for faithful help and service, particularly in her commerce and household, since (Giraud's) widowhood and recent illness." Giraud's will went on to state that her other children had no claim on these items, having already received their inheritance, presumably when their father had died. The rest of Giraud's will lists outstanding business-related debts.[70] In this case, Giraud used her will to ask one final service of her daughter Michelle and then to acknowledge Michelle's devotion. Since Breton law at this time still stipulated partible inheritance, Giraud needed to note that this legacy was particular, for services rendered. It was to be considered separately from the equal portions due each of her other children.[71]

Marguerite de Villiers earmarked the sum of 100 livres for her niece, so that the young woman could "invest and learn a trade appropriate to her state." Only after having established this sum did Villiers move onto her surviving children and grandchildren.[72] It is not clear if Villiers was acknowledging any special service on the part of her niece, but it seems clear that Villiers wanted to ensure that the girl had a secure future. Thus, in addition to acknowledging devotion, women used their wills to care for the next generation.

---

67 ADIV 4 E 500, papers of the notary, Chasse (22 April 1687).

68 ADLA 4 E2/1294, papers of the notary, LeBreton (15 September 1698).

69 ADLA 2 E 3496, *Titres de familles*, Monnier (4 June 1777).

70 ADLA 2 E 3222, *Titres de familles*, Giraud (1 June 1708).

71 See below, in this chapter, for a description of partible inheritance.

72 ADLA 4 E 2/658, papers of the notary, Dubois (28 March 1725).

Finally, it was common for women to use their wills to acknowledge the "good and agreeable" services of their servants and, perhaps, to pay long overdue wages. As in some of the cases noted above, there was no difficulty when there were few other heirs. Marie Aguesse, an unmarried *lingere*, left all of her goods and a sum of money to her faithful domestic, Marie Janneau. Aguesse did have a number of siblings, and her papers reveal some complex land, rent, and merchandise arrangements between them. However, her bequest to Janneau was uncontested by the siblings and it must have served Janneau very well. Only four years after Aguesse's will was written, Janneau was registered in the *maîtrise* of Nantes as a *tailleuse*; ten years after that, Janneau was still listed in the *capitation* tax roll as a single woman working at the same trade.[73]

Sometimes circumstances warranted action beyond a standard will, and those cases called for a simple donation.[74] Marie Dorsemene wanted to acknowledge the services and companionship of her *fille de chambre*, and seems to have anticipated the future interference of other heirs. Thus, she chose to register a donation in favor of her servant. Dorsemene, the widow of a master *boulanger*, declared that Therese Briand had lived with her since before the death of her husband. She states that Briand had continued in faithful service since the death of her husband, and had, indeed, sacrificed much to do so. Dorsemene adds further legitimacy to her donation by stating that the women had promised the late master, on his deathbed, to care for each other. Dorsemene then proceeded to list every item in her household that was meant for Briand. She notes, with precise attention, that Briand had inherited an armoire from her own parents that closely resembled a second armoire that Dorsemene was giving to her. Therefore, she warned her relatives not to confuse the two armoires and accuse Briand of stealing. Finally, Dorsemene declared that neither her heirs nor the heirs of her late husband had a right to demand anything of Briand after Dorsemene's death.[75]

Jeanne Celeste LeTourneau left all of her goods and money to the sisters, Renée and Marguerite Rios. LeTourneau had been a *pensionnaire* with the Rios sisters for 12 years already and hoped to stay with them until the end of her life. LeTourneau wanted to thank the sisters for all their care and attention. In return, they promised to feed her, get medical help for her if it should become necessary, and make funeral arrangements if she died in their home. Up until this point, there is little distinction between this donation and a traditional will. The final stipulations of the donation are distinct from a will, however, in that they stated a contingency plan in case of separation. If LeTourneau decided to move out, if one of the sisters died before her, or if the sisters decided to separate from LeTourneau, then they would receive 200 livres for expenses and the three would go their separate ways.[76]

---

73 ADLA 2 E 4, *Titres de famille*, Aguesse (10 May 1773); AMN HH 81, *Maîtrise* registers for Nantes (1779); ADLA B 3530, *Capitation* tax roll for Nantes (1789).

74 I designate this a "simple" donation to distinguish it from the mutual donations discussed above.

75 ADLA 4 E 2/72, papers of the notary, Auffray (8 March 1766).

76 ADLA 4 E 2/72, papers of the notary, Auffray (31 December 1770).

The relationships revealed by these testaments, donations, and mutual donations share certain similarities with the marriages protected by traditional mutual donations. Cohabitation is what denotes community between two women in a perpetual society, as it does between a husband and wife. Cohabitation often includes care during sickness and attendance at the deathbed. Both of these acts have been acknowledged in bequests from one woman to another, and they are worth special notice because they are acts required by law of a wife if she is to be considered the heir of her husband. In fact, a wife's absence from her husband's deathbed was grounds for disinheritance.[77] Thus, the community and care between women, especially between women with no spouses or heirs, takes on an additional intimacy that, in a traditional marriage, would have been required by law.

Partible Inheritance

Many of the rights accorded to a married woman had the potential to pit a widow against her own children. The practice of allowing one spouse to make the other principal heir via mutual donation seems to be at odds with another important Breton custom, that of partible inheritance. In Brittany and other regions in northern France, the estate and debts of a parent were divided equally among all surviving children.[78] The presence of a mutual donation, more often than not, meant that children had to wait for the death of both parents in order to inherit their portions, unless other provisions had been made in the donation contract. In theory, Article 211 of the *coutume* invalidated a mutual donation if the surviving children had no other means of support. In practice, however, it often took a lawsuit to settle conflicts between claims.

In spite of potential conflicts, however, the concept of partible inheritance was favorable to women because it assured access to resources that, elsewhere in Europe, were the sole property of male heirs. Articles 583 through 588 of the *ancienne coutume* describe the details of inheritance law as it pertained to "the bourgeois and others of the third estate," including the recommended order of inheritance. Each child should get an equal portion, but all male children, in order of age, were to get first choice and would be followed by the female children, in order of age. Generally speaking, the oldest male child was expected to get the principal dwelling.[79] In practice, however, as long as the portions were equal in value, partitions were made based on much more than gender or birth order. If an heir had chosen a religious calling, for example, or intended to pursue some kind of commerce in the city, then

---

77   *Coutumes générales du pays et duché de Bretagne* (1656), Article 451.

78   See E. LeRoy Ladurie, "A System of Customary Law: Family Structure and Inheritance Customs in Sixteenth-Century France," *Family and Society* (Baltimore: Johns Hopkins University Press, 1976), p. 89; and Suzanne Desan, "'War between Brothers and Sisters': Inheritance Law and Gender Politics in Revolutionary France," *French Historical Studies*, 20:4 (Fall 1997): 602.

79   *Coutumes générales du pays et duché de Bretagne* (1656), Articles 583, 587, and 588. Note that nobles were covered in separate articles, as it was necessary to designate an heir to the title. Titled estates were reserved for the oldest male child.

fields and farmhouses were better left to whichever child was actually living at home. According to Janne Hamelin's will, which was described in the introduction to this book, her oldest son was a priest and her oldest daughter was married, having already accepted the monetary value of her portion at her wedding. Thus, Hamelin's home and textile business inventory were left to the remaining two girls who were already maintaining the shop.[80] Such investments, along with training and guild membership, would not have been wasted on girls in Brittany. All were part of a custom of establishing children.

Some families allowed the heirs to draw lots. The eldest son was sometimes entitled to choose first, or allowed to trade his lot for a more preferable one. In 1709, Louis Ovieux and Marie Hamoy drew up an inventory of six equal properties to be divided among their six children. Each of the properties included some kind of lodging, either an apartment or some small house, and a garden, field, or section of woods. They were certified to be exactly equal in value, a maneuver that required one house and one field to have been split into two portions a piece. The two unmarried sons were to get first choice of the lots; they were followed by the two married daughters, one of whom was older than her brothers; and whichever lots remained would be held in trust for the remaining unmarried children who were still minors.[81] In such an arrangement, it was entirely possible that one of the daughters would gain control of the primary dwelling.[82]

As was explained under the system of marital community, an inheritance from a parent was the sole and untouchable property of the heir. This was true even in cases in which a woman was deprived by law of her dowry and other forms of property. Renée de Nebout was confined to a convent by her father-in-law after her husband was murdered; she was accused of adultery and suspected of having had a part in her husband's death. Under Article 450 of the Breton code, De Nebout lost the right to retain her dowry or benefit from any part in the marital community. Nevertheless, when her own cousins tried to claim her inheritance, she sued and won the right to keep it. At the heart of her lawyer's case was the argument that, unlike condemnation, banishment, or entry into a convent, confinement to a house of retreat, even perpetual confinement, was not a 'civil death.' De Nebout lost the privileges of an "honest" married woman, but not the basic rights of a free person. Her relatives were ordered to repay her the price of the property they had confiscated.[83] De Nebout was clearly entitled to the property; she understood her rights and was able to defend herself in spite of numerous disadvantages.

---

80   ADIV 4 E 500, notary Chasse, 24 April 1687.

81   ADLA 4 E 2/791, notary Fresnel, 8 September 1709. The choosing of "lots" could mean simply choosing the preferred portion, but was occasionally overtly described as "drawing lots" from a hat. The *Ecomusée* of modern-day Rennes, a preserved farm, was inherited in this manner by the oldest daughter.

82   Barbara Diefendorf found that non-noble families were much less likely to favor sons. "Women and Property in Ancien Règime France: Theory and Practice in Dauphiné and Paris," *Early Modern Conceptions of Property* (London: Routledge Press, 1995), p. 174.

83   *Journal des audiences et arrests du Parlement de Bretagne* (1736), Chapter 2, Book I, p. 57.

Most of the precedent-setting cases of property law involved noble families. This is not surprising because they had property and the means to protect and transmit it. However, the same basic rights of inheritance were enjoyed by the "third estate," and this ability to pass resources on to the next generation offered a certain amount of social mobility. Janne Ubedal of Saint-Malo moved to Rennes in 1707 at the age of 20. She spent almost four years working as a servant in various homes around the city before opening a shop. In 1713, Janne's roommate was being investigated on charges of debauchery, and Janne was considered suspicious by association. The police questioned Janne closely about her background and her activities since her arrival in Rennes. When asked repeatedly why she had left servitude, Janne explained that she had been waiting for her inheritance. She had always had the intention of becoming a merchant, but had to wait for her late father's tenants to send her some money. As soon as her portion came through, she "left the life of a servant" and invested in the shop of the old Widow Deschamps. Together, for the previous two years, the two women had sold butter, salt, and buckwheat crepes. Unfortunately, due to her roommate's scandalous ways, Janne was ordered to serve three months in the tower and then return to her parish of origin.[84]

Presumably, not all such enterprising young women fell into ruin. The right to attain and control inherited resources, assuming there were resources to inherit, was well protected by law. In fact, the rights of a woman as an inheriting daughter were so well protected that unmarried adult women rarely served as the subjects of legal commentary. It was only when a woman's rights and obligations intersected with someone else's, as with a spouse's or a sibling's, that she became a cause for concern. A single woman in her majority, which was set at the age of 25, was free to consent to marriage, make contracts, and buy or sell property on her own. This was true in the case of the *lingere*, Aguesse, whose generous bequest to her servant allowed the young woman to leave service and become a tailor.[85] Sadly, legal and financial independence in no way guaranteed security, as Janne Ubedal discovered. She was free to inherit and to choose the life of a merchant over servitude, but was undermined by her roommate's dishonorable conduct. Her autonomy from the household had left her in a precarious position.

The right to inherit undoubtedly allowed many merchants and tradeswomen to establish themselves; several probably inherited a business, or its inventory, or the funds to pay guild dues. And, while property law clearly favored men in terms of access to community and the ability to freely make contracts, women were far from incapacitated. Widows, unmarried women, and in many cases, married women as well were able to manipulate their property as they saw fit within certain parameters. As was the case with the patriarchal institutions of the marketplace, the limitations on women's rights under early modern Breton and French law were real enough. But those limitations were not strict enough to prevent women from making and acting on their choices. Women, even women from fairly humble families, understood their rights and maximized their opportunities for success.

---

84   ADIV 3 B 1451, 11–22 May 1713.

85   ADLA 2 E 4, *Titres de famille*, Aguesse (10 May 1773); AMN HH 81, *Maitrise* registers for Nantes (1779); ADLA B 3530, *Capitation* tax roll for Nantes (1789).

Sexual crimes and conflict

Aside from property law, the other body of law pertaining explicitly to women concerns matters of sexual honor and protection from sexual predators. Sexual dishonor was defined in two ways—*mauvaise vie*[86] and outright prostitution. In cases concerning sexual dishonor, women were often presumed guilty and regarded as a danger to social order. By contrast, sexual crimes usually involved the rape or seduction of a minor, and in these cases women were often perceived as the innocent victims. Exceptions to this perception were cases in which an older woman was charged with the rape of a younger man, especially if his parents decided to pursue charges. Both aspects of sex law were founded on the chivalric principle that the vulnerable had to be protected. This chivalry was aided, of course, by a strict sense of social hierarchy that required the prevention of inappropriate marriages via *rapt* or seduction.

The *ancienne coutume* declares that anyone who rapes or seduces a minor son or daughter may be condemned to death.[87] This law was perfectly in accordance with the royal Ordonnance de Blois of 1639 and the Marly Declaration of 1730, both of which affirmed capital punishment for "ravisseurs" and total disinheritance of clandestine marriages.[88] The purpose was to prevent accusations of rape from being used as a pretext for marrying without consent or forcing marriage between social unequals. However, in spite of the fact the Breton law repeated the royal edicts, Marly was specifically directed at Brittany because it was one of the few places in the eighteenth century where those condemned for the crime of *rapt* could opt for marriage with the victim in order to avoid death.[89]

The Declaration of Marly in 1730 was something of a turning point in Breton law. Prior to Marly, according to a study done by Muriel Rolland, it was possible to get a conviction for rape based almost entirely on a woman's declaration, and pregnancy was evidence enough to prove seduction. Generally speaking, a woman's good reputation served to give her word some weight.[90] And in cases in which marriage between the seducer and the seduced was out of the question, such as when a noble or wealthy man was accused of impregnating a teenaged servant, then pregnancy and a simple declaration from the girl were likely to result in a financial commitment of some sort. In any case, there was a code of honor in which the injured girl was given the benefit of the doubt. For example, the judges in Quimper went so far as to chastise Sieur Ciminic for seduction, corruption of a minor (his servant), using his

---

86   Literally, "evil life," but referring to dishonorable conduct.

87   *Coutumes générales du pays et duche de Bretagne* (1656), Article 498.

88   Ordonnance de Blois printed in *Coutumes générales du pays et duche de Bretagne* (1656); Marly Declaration printed in Sauvageau's *Coutumes de Bretagne, nouvelle edition* (1742).

89   Muriel Rolland, "Des femmes séduites face à la justice: le *rapt* de séduction en Bretagne aux XVIIe et XVIIIe siècles," *Memoires de la société d'histoire et d'archeologie de Bretagne*, 76 (1998):. 294.

90   Rolland, "Des femmes séduites," pp. 274–7.

wife's own bed to do so, and for "ignoring the laws of hospitality" that should have ensured the safety of those living under his roof.[91]

Understandably, there were limits to this code of honor, and a real tension between the need to protect the weaker sex and the distrust of women's testimony. In 1652, the *Parlement* in Rennes reversed a lower court's decision to award damages to a minor servant, damages that had been based entirely on her accusations against her master's son. They decided that her declaration was grounds for an investigation, but could not be used for a definitive condemnation.[92] Ten years later, the court also decided that accusations had to be accompanied by proof of the victim's age, since the law only applied to minors, and a midwife's certification that the victim was pregnant.[93] But the language of the law and the course of several cases show that seduced women were regarded as vulnerable and in need of safekeeping. Even the son of an officer in the presidial, Pierre Le Masson, was condemned to death for the seduction and impregnation of a young woman he had been "frequenting" for years under the promise of marriage. On his appeal in 1724, the *Parlement* gave him the option of marrying the young woman, but all parties eventually accepted a financial settlement.[94]

In the years leading up to and following the Marly declaration, however, the focus had clearly changed. The women were less likely to be regarded as innocent victims and more likely to be investigated for debauchery. In the words of the anonymous jurist of 1725:

> A ravisher is one who takes a woman or girl by force and violence without her consent: He must be punished with death, for this is a capital crime; but one could not claim that a woman or girl who followed voluntarily was ravished; in this case, only the minority of the girl or marriage of the woman makes it a crime, and then it is one of seduction . . . so that a man may accuse his wife of adultery but also accuse the one who seduced her.[95]

The Marly declaration, as well, made it clear that "illicit commerce" had to be separated from seduction in order to avoid unfairly condemning someone. Marriage was no longer an option, even if the victim and her family agreed to it, and true *rapt* was a capital crime. Thus, the focus of investigations was less and less about a woman's vulnerability and more about her possible compliance and personal guilt. This shift in responsibility away from the seducer, and away from marriage as a solution, may be evidence of an increase in patriarchal power. As powerful lawmakers sought to consolidate parental control over marriage, they recast seduction as illicit

---

91   ADF 49 J 824, 17 February 1748. This case was after the declaration of Marly, and suggests that the older values were upheld longer than Rolland has suggested, at least in the smaller towns.

92   Sauvageau, *Arrêts et reglemens du Parlement* (1712), Chapter 8, Book I, p. 11.

93   Sauvageau, *Arrêts et reglemens du Parlement* (1712), Chapter 84, Book I, p. 45.

94   ADIV 1 BN 1418 and 2 B 1844 (2), 13 January 1723; see Rolland's discussion of this case, p. 289.

95   *Coutume de Bretagne et usance particulieres de quelques villes* (1725), Article 623, p. 553.

sex and made true *rapt* a capital crime in order to eliminate the possibility of forced, unsuitable marriages.[96]

In the early decades of the eighteenth century, the shift from criminal rape cases to investigations of honor put women's activities and relationships under a microscope.[97]   In this new atmosphere, legal acts designed for one purpose now served to document women's sex lives. The *declaration de grossesse* had been instituted at the end of the sixteenth century as a way of preventing infant abandonment. Unmarried pregnant women were identified and pressured to name their sexual partners so that new parents could be forced to support their illegitimate children. In the eighteenth century, *declarations* were still used to identify fathers for financial purposes but were also used to investigate women for *mauvaise vie*. Disturbingly, many *declarations* and other honor inquiries revealed probable cases of rape in which women were charged with dishonorable conduct while their attackers were not pursued. In Rennes in 1710, the unrelated declarations of Ann Leheure, a 21-year-old laundress, and Janne Guichart, a 22-year-old servant, revealed that a local law clerk was the father of both illegitimate children. The women did not know each other, but told similar stories of delivering merchandise to the lawyer's home, finding the clerk alone there, and being violently attacked by the man. In both cases, the police merely took the man's statement that he had nothing to do with the pregnancy.[98] The same was true for the cases of Marie Francoise Penhar, a 20-year-old *tailleuse* and daughter of a wealthy merchant, and a 21-year-old servant named Louise Lefloe Lemoine, both of Saint-Malo and both victims of violent rape at the hands of Sieur de Chastellier Bandon. In 1719, Penhar was raped at sword-point at the country home of Madame de La Lande Magon during a weekend outing, and subsequently disowned by her father. The servant, Lemoine, was attacked soon after she began working for Bandon in 1736; when she became pregnant, he shut her into a room and force-fed her abortifacients. Neither declaration was followed by a suit against Bandon.[99] In both cases, the repeated violence of the men in question passed without comment while the honor of the women was investigated.

Successful rape convictions depended upon overwhelming evidence and perfect circumstances. One such example is the case of Julliene Hernier, the wife of a military officer in Rennes in 1714. Hernier was accosted by a man on a horse as she made her way to the wet nurse's house outside of the city to see about her baby's health. When he told her to get on his horse, she told him that she was married, desperately needed to care for her baby, and was four months pregnant with her second child; she tried to go on her way. He pursued her, and beat and raped her savagely. Workers in a nearby field heard her crying out to the Lord and her husband, though no one came to her aid. They found her, and took her to a doctor, who certified her injuries for the court. Later that day, two servants reported to their master that they had been attacked by

---

96   Hanley, "Family and State in Early Modern France: The Marriage Pact," p. 57.

97   Honor trials will be covered extensively in the next chapter as an aspect of sociability.

98   ADIV 3 B 1443, both statements in April 1710.

99   ADIV 4 BX 1157, Penhar's statement of 22 October 1719; Lemoine's of 24 January 1737.

a man on a horse and surely would have been raped if they had not worked together to fight him off.

Hernier and the two servants were all respected women, and word got around their neighborhoods quickly. When a horse trader from Saint Brieuc arrived at a tavern in Rennes, Hernier was taken to identify him. He claimed that he had only offered her a ride on his horse and that she was injured when she fell off of it. He tried to escape, and was held up by a young girl, a servant at the tavern, who hung onto the reins of his horse. The man was arrested and convicted of rape. The sentence is missing from the file, but there is a very good chance he was executed. He was an outsider who had attacked the well-liked, faithful, and pregnant wife of a soldier. Several witnesses swore that they had heard her cries for help, and the two servants testified that he was the same man who had attacked them. The man was probably lucky not to have been beaten to death by the crowd on the night of his arrest.[100]

Another case, however, demonstrates what can happen when a woman faces charges of *rapt*, or seduction of a minor. Just as a female rape victim could hope to see justice done only when the circumstances were perfect, a woman charged with rape was at a disadvantage. Most of the time, if a woman was facing such charges, it was because she was involved with a younger man of higher social standing. In such cases, a woman was expected to protect herself against a family with better connections and more resources under a law code that often favored paternal control over marriage. Andrée Rabin faced such a battle when she became involved with the son of a wealthy widowed merchant who was trying desperately to save her family's fortune.

Guillemette Desages was the widow of Jean Baptiste Desages, the Sieur de Duhoux and a successful shipping merchant in Saint-Malo.[101] Together, they had built a fortune in Spanish and New World trade and at the opening of the eighteenth century were counted among a handful of upwardly mobile families. However, at Jean's death in 1701, Guillemette was left with a number of minor children and scattered business interests. Her business correspondence shows her growing anxiety over political conflict with Spain and the stubborn refusal of her agent in Cadiz to pay her for several shipments of merchandise. In the course of the next 20 years, Desages lost Atlantic trade contacts in a multitude of wars, lost a number of ships to the Spanish king, and was irreparably defrauded by her Spanish correspondent. Historian Andre Lespagnol traced the bleak rise and fall of the family's fortune, noting that by 1720 Guillemette Desages had "fallen back into the ranks of the lower bourgeoisie which had produced her."[102]

However, Desages did not go down without a fight. For years she pursued the agent who had cheated her, via every possible contact and lead, finally giving up when she found that he had died. None of his heirs or creditors in Spain could be

---

100   ADIV 2 B 1843 (3), 15 February 1714.

101   Desages is the family name and Duhoux is the title. Court records refer to the family simply as Desages. Business records refer to them as the Duhoux merchants. The wife refers to herself as Mme. Duhoux-Desages in her own correspondence.

102   Lespagnol, *Messieurs de Saint-Malo: Une élite négociante au temps de Louis XIV* (Rennes: Presses Universitaires de Rennes, 1997), p. 720.

persuaded to pay back a French widow, in spite of her numerous pleas for mercy for her "pitiable situation."[103] Back home in Brittany, Desages also had trouble controlling her agents in Nantes and Paris, and spent the last decade of her life battling for the rent on her property in Rennes.[104] She took the fights personally, and often referred to the establishment of her children and the honor of her family as her top priorities. Thus, it should be no surprise that she also fought to control her children and their marriage prospects.

Appropriate alliances were always a key feature of the upper echelons of society, but are especially important to newly wealthy families. In 1708, only seven years after her husband's death and before there were any signs of financial trouble, Desages became aware that her oldest son was romancing the carpenter's daughter at their estate in Pleurtuit. Jean was 24 years old at the time, destined to be the next Sieur de Duhoux, and had taken up residence at Pleurtuit because it would become his primary residence upon accepting the title. He had gotten to know the carpenter, Jean Rabin, during extensive renovations on the manor, and had met Jean's daughter, Andrée, when he accompanied Rabin home for dinner. For two years, Jean ate regularly at the Rabin's home and afterwards went for long walks with Andrée. It was a match formed out of daily contact and mutual attraction. By 1708, Jean had declared his intention to marry Andrée, and Desages was quick to call in the authorities.

Before the seneschal at Saint-Malo, Desages and her lawyer made a case against Jean Rabin, Andrée's father, for permitting the youngsters to meet. It should have been obvious to all, she argued, that her son's "birth, considerable alliances in Saint-Malo and attractive fortune" made such a match impossible. She accused Rabin of introducing the couple on purpose, and demanded the protection of her family's honor. The court thus forbade Jean Desages to visit the Rabins or contract a marriage with the young woman, warned the Rabins not to tolerate his visits under any pretext, and prohibited all priests, rectors, and curates from performing a wedding ceremony.[105]

When Jean continued to visit Andrée in the months that followed, his mother escalated her attack. Jean was two months shy of his 25 birthday, and his legal majority, but Andrée was a year and half older than her suitor. Thus, in October, Dame Desages filed charges of seduction of a minor against Andrée and named her father as an accomplice. Moved by the "affection which she has for her son" and for "the honor of her family," Desages was "obliged to oppose such an alliance, for this Rabin woman is a simple peasant."[106] She complained again in December and demanded an investigation.

The seneschal's officer visited Pleurtuit and spoke with ten witnesses, all of whom confirmed each other's story. Jean and Andrée were hardly engaged in scandalous behavior—among the damning evidence was testimony that the two went to church together and that Jean had once kissed Andrée's cheek during the buckwheat harvest

---

103   ADIV 4 FC 3, see especially the letter to Reverand Father Joseph, 12 February 1725.

104   ADIV 4 FC 3, these letters span 1734 to 1746, including the last letter she wrote.

105   ADIV 1 BN 1048, *arrêt de Parlement*, 27 August 1708.

106   ADIV 1 BN 1048, memo of 22 October 1708.

and told everyone he was going to marry her.[107] At one point during the officer's investigation, Jean emerged from the Rabin house and approached the witnesses. He read over the copies of their statements, laughed, and turned to the officer, saying, "Tell my mother I am here, and then tell her I am coming back tomorrow."[108] Some witnesses reported that Jean's valet had threatened them for testifying against his master, but that Jean himself had prompted them all to be completely honest, "but do not say more than you know to be true."

The law was very clear in a matter such as this. The Blois Ordonnance of 1640, reaffirmed by the Marly Declaration of 1730, required parental consent for any marriage and allowed for the disinheritance of disobedient children. The children of marriages performed without parental consent could be legally regarded as bastards, and the priests who performed clandestine marriages were liable to strict punishment. In 1708, the Desages were still in a good social and financial position, and Jean's mother undoubtedly had high hopes for his chances on the marriage market. *Parlement* met twice to discuss the charges and on 7 March 1709 ordered the judges in Saint-Malo to enforce the verdict against the Rabin family. By 12 April, Rabin had been taken into custody and his goods were confiscated to pay court costs and damages. Andrée was sent to the Saint Charles convent in Dinan.[109]

Guillemette Desages was trying to protect her business and her family's fortune when she sued Andrée for seduction. As she wrote to Jean de la Peine, the agent in Spain who was soon to defraud her, "I have the greatest fear of times without money."[110] She wrote those words the same week she filed her third and final charges against the Rabins, years before she found herself returned to a relatively humble social status. Desages had fought long and hard to give her children some kind of security and a chance to rise even higher in the ranks of society. But it was a difficult battle for a woman to fight alone, as her agents abandoned her, her investments dried up, and her children rebuffed her. She lacked the authority, the contacts, and the resources to control all of her assets. And so, this case pitted one vulnerable woman, Desages, against another, Andrée, and neither was able to protect herself. In the end, Desage's victory came to nothing. Jean was impoverished by his own personal investments with the elusive Spanish correspondent and it is unclear if he ever married. In 1737, he was living in simple apartments in a house owned by someone else. By then, Desages had moved in with her oldest married daughter.[111] Andrée Rabin, fortunately, was not destroyed by the ordeal. She was eventually released from the convent and married to Pierre Sevestre, a farmer from her village.[112]

---

107   ADIV 1 BN 1048, testimony of Jaquemine Bauchet, Janne LeBret, and Janne Merien, 29 December 1708.

108   ADIV 1 BN 1048, report of 29 December 1708.

109   ADIV 1 BN 1048, Parlementary registers 9 February and 7 March, 1709; seneschal of Saint-Malo, 13 March and 11 April 1709; letter of supplication from Rabin and Daughter, 12 April 1709.

110   ADIV 4 FC 3, letter of 24 December 1708.

111   ADIV 4 FC 3, letter of 25 February 1725; ADIV C 4069, Capitation of Saint-Malo, 1737.

112   ADIV 62 bi 340, *Tables d'etat civil de Pleurtuit,* 7 November 1713.

In the law codes that governed sexual crime and honor, just as in the laws of property and inheritance, there was a delicate balance between the need to protect women as vulnerable members of society and the desire to curtail their responsibility over material goods and the fates of others. All such limitations were based on the view of women as child-like and unpredictable. Jamont's study of property law and Rolland's study of sexual crime both suggest that the medieval version of Breton law was more favorable to women, with the more restrictive French codes being implemented later. But even at the end of the *ancien régime*, the limitations were not insurmountable, and women were able to pursue justice as a matter of course. Their access was not freely gotten, as they always needed intermediates or the court's sanction to pursue their own cases. Even so, women did not hesitate to address authorities when necessary to protect their rights and correct abuses.

In situations in which there was a physical attack or destruction of property, women were quick enough to call in the police. Quarrels with neighbors, rival vendors, or relatives sometimes came to blows, and required official action. Even repeated insults and threats caused some to take their cases to the authorities. Most such cases in the police archives are relatively minor, however, and were usually settled with a warning or a small fine. Other cases, such as conflicts with guild or city officials, were addressed to a higher authority. The *poissionieres* of Nantes, for example, wrote to the *intendant* to complain that the new municipal fish market did not meet the agreed upon specifications.[113] These fish merchants were frequently at odds with the local police and city fathers, once going so far as to circulate a wax caricature of a commissioner.[114] Nevertheless, they knew their rights and made free use of every level of authority in their conflicts with each other, with outsiders, and with the police themselves.

Women could, and did, act in concert with one another in the corporative structures of the market and in their social lives. But women were more likely to face the law as individuals. Of course, women had to be willing to address authority for the very reason that they were vulnerable. The fish merchants did not have the prestige of a guild, but they were quick to join forces in order to protect themselves. Other women had even less support. Janne Lettant ran a tavern by herself in Saint-Malo while her husband was at sea. In 1700, she was attacked by a drunk when she refused to serve him after hours. Five years later, another *aubergiste* in the same situation was attacked and robbed by two armed men while her two small daughters and her young apprentice cowered in a stairwell.[115] In these cases, women were obviously isolated and vulnerable.

In order to survive, a woman had to have a support network or the means to protect her own interests. When Marie-Jacquette Antequil wrote her husband at sea, she recounted numerous tales of harassment from the previous owner of her shop. It seems the man wanted to buy it back, and was threatening her daily for her refusal to sell:

---

113   ADLA C 318, signed *memoire*, no date.
114   AMN FF 120, police complaint of 18 June 1726.
115   ADIV 4 BX 1095, 11 April 1700; 4BX 1102, 5 December 1705.

Monsieur Lemarquand marries his cousin, the widow, tomorrow, and that is why he wants the shop back . . . he came over here to insult and abuse me, without much purpose because I have no dispute with him or with any other. It is pure jealousy. I asked him if he would back up his words before a judge and he said yes. On that I got a surety against him from the court . . . you see the grief a woman gets for not having a man. But God blessed me, for the more I cried, the more was yielded.[116]

Just as the law codes themselves were a fine balance of chivalry and distrust of women, so a woman seeking justice often had to maintain a fine balance between demanding her rights and appealing for mercy.

Conclusion

In reviewing women's position in Brittany relative to their position elsewhere, a few points stand out. The first and most striking aspect of Breton law with regard to women is the system of partible inheritance. Access to resources, and the right to control those resources, gave Breton women greater latitude as they negotiated society and the economy. Unlike German, Italian, or English women, and unlike women in most parts of France, *Bretonnes* had the capacity to open their own shops, pay guild dues, or buy and sell property: the inability to do such things is a leading cause of women's second-class status in pre-modern societies. Most restrictions under Breton custom concerned a woman's rights in relation to her spouse and his family. A single woman over the age of 25 had the right to make contracts, choose her calling and live alone or with other single women; the realities of a weak economy and a violent society might have made life difficult for a single women or a widow, but there was nothing codified in law that curtailed her autonomy.

There were certainly changes in Breton law over the course of the early modern period, and some of those had to do with the political centralization of France in the sixteenth and seventeenth centuries. There is some evidence of what has been called the "family-state pact" in some of the legal developments outlined in this chapter.[117] Trends signaling the pact, such as the shift away from forced marriage as a solution to cases of seduction, or an increase in a husband's control over his wife's economic activity, are as visible in Brittany as they are in Paris. This is hardly surprising. Brittany may have enjoyed a certain level of independence, as many provinces did, but it was still a part of the French justice system. Lawyers who worked in the *Parlement* of Rennes had worked or studied in Paris.[118] In all likelihood, they remained part of the socio-legal circuit that influenced the growth of patriarchy which Hanley has noted in French law. Thus, in the seventeenth century, Breton women needed their husband's consent to make contracts or wills, though they had not needed such authorization in earlier centuries. A woman's right to work as a merchant with or

---

116   Phillippe Henwood, "Marie-Jacquette Pignot: une femme de marin à Saint-Malo au XVIIIe siècle," *Memoires de la société d'histoire et d'archeologie de Bretagne*, 76 (1998): letter of August 1746.

117   Hanley, "Family and State in Early Modern France," pp. 55–7.

118   Collins, *Classes, Estates and Order in Early Modern Brittany*, pp. 75–6.

without her husband's consent remained intact throughout this period, but it was much modified and clarified by the mid-eighteenth century in order to protect men's property from their wives' debts. And the practice of postponing marital community for a year and a day after the wedding gradually disappeared over the course of the seventeenth and eighteenth centuries, to be replaced by the French custom of beginning community on the wedding day. Perhaps this simplified matters for most couples, as it was a choice freely made when drawing up the marriage contract. But it also signaled a decrease in a woman's autonomy regarding her property and debts at the time of marriage.

At the same time, there remained several advantages for women under Breton law with regard to inheritance and property. Unmarried or widowed women could maintain businesses, manage property, and make contracts without difficulty, and married women whose husbands proved uncooperative had access to other legal representation. Finally, women were able to make wills and donations, secure in the knowledge that the gifts were protected even from competing heirs.

As for women in the court of law, there can be no doubt that women lacked full and equal access to justice in early modern Brittany. Obviously, women could not create law nor could they serve as lawyers. Nevertheless, women were far from incapacitated. In numerous cases outlined above, women understood their positions in society, and the rights implied in those positions, and successfully pursued justice in order to protect their interests. Laws and customs may have been patriarchal in nature, but women from a variety of backgrounds and social classes were able to recognize their rights and fight to defend them.

Chapter Four

Social Life and Honor

"One goes to the tavern for news and the laundry for gossip." So goes a popular saying in Brittany dating from the eighteenth century.[1] Implicit in this distinction between the world of men and that of women is the idea that women have no serious reason to socialize with one another. Women do not meet to discuss the day's issues but to gab about their neighbors. At best the gathering is child-like and harmless. At worst it is a dangerous breeding ground for immoral thoughts and activities. In this chapter, we will explore women's social lives with an eye to uncovering the relationship between sociability and issues of honor, companionship, and survival. We will study female sociability from an external perspective—that is, how women's friendships were viewed by men, the community at large, and authority figures; and from an internal perspective—how women's friendships, with other women or with men, provided emotional and financial support and contributed to a sense of identity.

It is easy for the historian to forget that women in pre-modern societies maintained close personal relationships beyond their immediate family circles. Margaret Hunt blames a too-eager dependence upon eighteenth-century prescriptive literature, which by its very nature locates a woman's "highest happiness" in total devotion to the needs of her family and her "current and future heterosocial and heterosexual relations."[2] Indeed, moralists in the early modern period, from church leaders in the seventeenth century to the enlightened thinkers of the eighteenth century, recommended a chaste, silent, and retired life for married women and unwed maidens alike. Sieur de Vigoreux echoed the sentiments of a multitude of Renaissance writers when he noted in 1617 that the "ideal marital situation finds women 'shut up in their homes.'"[3] Seventeenth-century nobleman François de Saligne de la Mothe-Fénelon feared the moral decay of France and offered up the isolation of women both as a way to "preserve the world from feminization and a way of saving women from the corruption of the world."[4] Enlightened writers such as Montesquieu and Rousseau repeated these sentiments, with such claims as "there are no good morals for a woman outside of a withdrawn and domestic life."[5]

---

1   Paul-Yves Sébillot, *La Bretagne et ses traditions* (Paris: Maisonneuve et Larose, 1998), p. 105.

2   Hunt, *The Middling Sort: Commerce, Gender, and the Family in England, 1680–1780* (Berkeley: University of California Press, 1996), p. 75.

3   In James Farr, *Authority and Sexuality in Early Modern Burgundy (1550–1730)* (Oxford University Press, 1995), p. 50.

4   Joan Landes, *Women in the Public Sphere in the Age of the French Revolution* (Cornell University Press, 1988), p. 27.

5   Landes, *Women in the Public Sphere*, p. 72.

If historians err in depending too heavily on prescriptive literature, we are not alone. Contemporary elites and authority figures also bought into the narrow and idealized vision of women, leaving them out of touch with popular notions of women's identities. This, at least in part, explains the reasoning behind the legal restrictions placed upon women in any era. But it also explains how so many of us retain a simplistic view of women's lives in the past, believing that they really were isolated from the world outside their doors. In most official sources, women are identified by marital status because that was the only status that mattered to courts and clerks. However, in sources by and about women, they are identified by occupation first and then marital status or place of residence. Women identify themselves by their own names and occupations, and they identify their neighbors and peers in the same fashion. In order to gain a clear view of the complex nature of women's identities, therefore, we need to look at them from a variety of perspectives.

A woman's relationships outside the family were treated as suspect or dismissed as frivolous, and "gossips" were regarded with the utmost contempt. Mary Wack shows the potential subversive quality of gossip as depicted in sixteenth-century religious plays in the English town of Chester: women who gather to drink commiserate about hard work and bad husbands and challenge each other to resist authority.[6] The capacity for gossip to cross race and class boundaries among women gave it an additional subversive power. Kathleen Brown found that the African slaves and Native American and poor white servants of a Virginian woman accused of infanticide were considered guilty by association: "shared domestic routines, gossip, and a common knowledge of the female body were sufficient conditions for collaboration."[7] Even when women's gossip was not considered in itself a danger, it was still something that had to be kept separate from men's important and pure speech. As Rousseau put it, "We need not be much disturbed by the cackle of women's societies. Let them speak ill of others so long as they like, provided they do so among themselves."[8]

And yet, women did, of course, have fulfilling and supportive friendships with each other in a variety of settings. Yves Castan, in his treatment of social life in Languedoc, recognizes the reputation of women as gossips and the implied criticism in that assessment. But he goes on to note that women's association always took place within the context of their work, at communal ovens and shops, or in the church, where they could meet "without reproach."[9] A woman's primary social network naturally would have consisted of her kin, especially in the patriarchal culture of southern France described by Castan. However, it is clear that women maintained relationships, even close friendships, with neighbors and coworkers in spite of cultural inhibiting factors.

---

6   Wack, "Women, Work and Plays in an English Medieval Town," in Susan Frye and Karen Robertson (eds), *Maids and Mistresses, Cousins and Queens: Women's Alliances in Early Modern England* (New York: Oxford University Press, 1999), p. 38.

7   Brown, "'A P[ar]cell of Murdering Bitches': Female Relationships in an Eighteenth-Century Slaveholding Household," in Frye and Robertson (eds), *Maids and Mistresses, Cousins and Queens*, p. 88.

8   In Landes, *Women and the Public Sphere*, p. 85.

9   Castan, *Honnêteté et relations sociales en Languedoc (1715–1780)* (Paris: Librairie Plon, 1974), pp. 174 and 199.

An active social life could be a liability or a source of support. If a woman's relationships were perceived as dishonorable, no matter what their true nature, the impact on her and her family could be disastrous. Thus, even neighborhood and working relationships between women had to be entered into with care. At the same time, women's friendships with each other could serve as a refuge from boredom, economic difficulty, and marital discord. Women worked side-by-side in homes and at fountains, roomed together when incomes were scarce, and stood up for each other in local squabbles. Thus, women's community could be simultaneously a source of comfort and a guide for behavior, and as such it seriously influenced a woman's sense of identity. As Kathleen Brown has put it,

> Even as they lived, worked and socialized among men, women constituted their own critical communities through gossip and visiting. Women's sense of who they were usually depended upon whom they defined as their female peers and what those friends, neighbors and kin said about them.[10]

At the same time, women belonged to a wider community that included men both as superiors and as equals, and mixed-sex sociability had positive and negative aspects to it. Questionable contact with men could lead to a woman's downfall, but mixed socializing also provided opportunities for men and women to meet potential mates or make matches for friends and family members. In this chapter, we will discover the extent to which a woman's social life enabled her to make sustainable choices about her work life, her independence, and her home life.

Honor and the Limitations of Social Life

Masculine "honor" was, in early modern culture, a complicated issue, involving such attributes as courage, hard work, and trustworthiness.[11] These aspects of masculine honor stand independently of one another, and loss of one kind of honor for a man did not necessarily entail loss of all honor. Female honor, by contrast, has been powerfully linked to chastity, the primary virtue. And chastity is evident in obedience and demure behavior. Julie Hardwick, in her study of notarial families in early modern Nantes, notes that widows often relinquished control of their households to adult male children "in order to retain the guarded speech and behavior that were regarded as pillars of female honor."[12] Legal rights and financial power were less attractive to these women than the maintenance of an "honorable" status.

---

10   Brown, "'A P[ar]cell of Murdering Bitches," p. 89.

11   See Farr, *Hands of Honor: Artisans and Their World in Dijon, 1550–1650* (Ithaca: Cornell University Press, 1988); Cynthia Truant, *Rites of Labor: Brotherhoods of Compagnonnage in Old and New Regime France* (Ithaca: Cornell University Press, 1994); and Robert A. Nye, *Masculinity and Male Codes of Honor in Modern France* (Berkeley: University of California Press, 1998) for in-depth examples of masculine honor.

12   Hardwick, *The Practice of Patriarchy: Gender and the Politics of Household Authority in Early Modern France* (Philadelphia: University of Pennsylvania Press, 1998), p. 138.

Control of feminine honor was a keystone of maintaining social order. When a woman's honor was in question, she was more than a social misfit—she was a potential criminal. Feminine deviance of any kind was linked with sexual behavior, as if the loss of one virtue guaranteed the loss of all virtue. Charges against women, even in clear-cut cases of petty thievery or other crimes, carried sexual overtones. In Rennes in 1676, a fishmonger named La Jolie, arrested for seditious behavior in the *Papier Timbré* riots, was exiled to the Antilles along with 22 other "problem" women, all of them prostitutes.[13] Georg'ann Cattelona notes that, while both men and women could be confined to prison for "begging, vagabondage, and crime, women alone were incarcerated for sexual misconduct."[14] Through numerous police investigations and court cases, authorities occupied themselves with rooting out all dishonorable women, from wayward daughters and adulterous wives to professional prostitutes. A typical legal *memoire* from 1672 instructs all rectors, vicars, priests, and notaries to denounce anyone connected with scandalous women and all those who "welcomed and tolerated" such women.[15] Punishment for those convicted of crimes of dishonor could include imprisonment, loss of property, or, in extreme cases, exile. Often, a woman arrested for leading "une mauvaise vie" had little to no legal protection. Conviction for moral crimes rarely required more evidence than the original denunciation and supporting testimony.

However, this is not to say a woman's honor was based entirely on sexuality. Castan found that in the south of France, feminine honor included piety as a Christian, skill as a household manager, and devotion to one's children.[16] It is true that each of these traits may operate in conjunction with obedience to one's spouse, and, by extension, with sexual fidelity. But in order to gain a deeper understanding of female honor, we need to move beyond the tendency to ascribe all aspects of honor to sexuality. Women were as quick to defend themselves from accusations of dishonesty or thievery as they were to defend themselves from accusations of debauchery. They rightly saw that a loss of "good reputation" of any sort could lead to a loss of livelihood.

Numerous complaints registered with the police of Nantes attest to the high value placed on a woman's reputation as an honest worker. In 1664, Catherine Phelipeau, a cloth merchant, complained that an assailant had accused her of stealing pieces of cloth. Such charges, according to Phelipeau, were contrary to her honor: "The *suppliante* has always been a merchant and has worked with honor and without reproach," she has lived "30 years in this parish, where her father and mother were wed," and such accusations could lead to her becoming "bankrupt."[17] In 1680, when a widowed laundress named Renée Gaultier went to drop off the linens she had

13   *Moi, Claude Bordeaux . . . journal d'un bourgeois de Rennes au 17e siècle* (Rennes: Éditions Apogée, 1992), Entry 14 July 1676.

14   Cattelona, "Control and Collaboration: The Role of Women in Regulating Female Sexual Behavior in Early Modern Marseille," *French Historical Studies* 18/1 (1993): p. 14.

15   ADLA B 6672 *Memoire de Nicolas Heron . . . Official de Nantes*, 29 October 1672.

16   Castan, *Honnêteté et relations sociales*, p. 164.

17   ADLA B 6670, Police of Nantes, 8 November 1664.

finished for some *compagnon* cabinetmakers and pick up her pay, a man called her names: "whore," "procuress," and "thief." As Gaultier saw it, "these were injuries against the honor and good reputation which allow her to honestly earn a living for herself and her daughter."[18] A century later, such complaints were still typical. In 1761, a servant named Françoise Sotin was accused of theft and filed a complaint against her accusers. They had "called her all kinds of names, all to the injury of the honor and reputation of an honest girl who had served in a number of considerable houses where no one has ever complained about her."[19] Working women of different backgrounds, across several decades, used exactly the same language to defend themselves and their ability to support themselves. "Honor and good reputation" for a woman certainly included a sexual component, but also entailed honesty and hard work.

Unfortunately, for some women the loss of honor in any sense could lead to total devastation. A simple denunciation, unchallenged by the accused or by credible witnesses, almost always resulted in a conviction for the vaguest of crimes: *mauvaise vie*. Commonly defined as "sexual misconduct," *mauvaise vie* also carried with it the implied charges of dishonesty, destruction, disturbing the peace, and upsetting the social order. *Mauvaise vie* was a serious charge, and almost impossible to fight. Every aspect of one's social life could be used as incriminating evidence. The following story offers us a glimpse of the ways in which one's honor was intertwined with one's sociability.

Louise Piel dite Dujardin was the young wife of a domestic servant in Rennes in the 1750s.[20] She worked as a cloth bleacher in the local textile industry and employed at least one live-in employee, a *brodeuse* [embroiderer]. Her husband worked as a cook in the entourage of a noble and was frequently away, leaving Louise alone with their two children and her servant. In his absence, Louise was known to have friends over—other local women and men who came to supper and stayed most of the night, singing loud songs and disturbing the neighborhood. In 1751, a local couple accused Louise of debauching their daughter, Michelle, and Louise was subsequently jailed on little more evidence than local reports of these noisy evening suppers.

Michelle, the "ruined" young woman, was never investigated. The testimony of her parents was enough to make it a police matter, and the authorities wasted no time in arresting Louise and building their case against her. The outlines of what happened on the night in question are supported equally well by Louise, her worker, and her friends and neighbors. Michelle arrived on Mardi Gras to ask Louise for piecework as a *brodeuse*. Louise explained that she preferred not to put out piecework, but would hire Michelle by the month and give her room and board. Michelle stayed to discuss the terms and, as it was getting late, agreed to stay for supper and spend the night rather than walk alone across town. They were joined at dinner by the two children, the *brodeuse*, and a local *lingere*. The next day, Michelle went home and returned a week later to say that her mother disapproved of her working away

---

18   ADLA B 6675, Police of Nantes, 30 July 1680.
19   ADLA 2 E 3318, *Titres de famille*, 22 August 1761.
20   All documents pertaining to this case are in the AMR, Liasse 360.

from home. She left and, as far as Louise was concerned, the matter was settled. Michelle's parents filed charges a week later.

It was the testimony of her neighbors that destroyed any chance Louise had for escaping punishment, though no one reported any kind of disturbance the night of Michelle's visit. Furthermore, the neighbors doubted Michelle's character quite apart from anything Louise had done. Michelle had been staying at the retreat for penitent women in recent weeks and was rumored to have broken the bars of her window to escape. Michelle's own parents admitted that their daughter had been housed in the retreat, but claimed it was under Louise' influence that Michelle left the home for girls and entered into "evil ways."[21]

However, the state of Michelle's soul was not really at issue as long as her parents vouched for her. Nor was the night of Michelle's supposed corruption at the heart of the matter. What was really the key to Louise's guilt or innocence was the honor of her household in the absence of her husband. Her neighbors all had the same complaint—Louise had lots of people over, sometimes late at night, and they were always noisy. One older woman, a widow who lived by herself, stated that men with swords often came to visit Louise in the middle of the night. The local clockmaker's apprentice claimed in his statement that he once followed two girls and a military officer to Louise's door because "everyone knew" that Louise was dishonorable and he wanted to see inside her apartment. The clockmaker's wife, a glovemaker by trade, went even further and said that Louise was "the biggest whore in Rennes." The woman's apprentice and servant agreed with her, claiming they had seen men come and go freely from the apartment.

All of the neighbors agreed that Louise was herself a prostitute and that she procured young women for men callers. As proof, many referred to an incident that had occurred only two days before Louise was arrested. Late on a Sunday evening, a young woman was heard to cry out. She ran out onto the steps from the doorway, and appeared to be crying and disoriented. Louise and two young men took her by the arms and pulled her back into the apartment. Soon after, the young men hurried away. To the one neighbor who had witnessed the affair, it seemed obvious that a young woman was being beaten into submission. Other neighbors, interrogated a day later, had not seen or heard anything but agreed that this must have been the case. Meanwhile, the police had already taken the testimony of the injured girl and had recorded both her version and that of Louise, who was questioned while in custody. According to her side of the story, the girl had struck her head on the doorway while dancing. Sick from the injury, she first tried to go home then almost passed out. Louise took her in and nursed her head injury. In fact, the girl was still in bed at Louise's apartment because she was too weak to go home.

After Louise's arrest, anyone associated with the household was tormented by the neighborhood. A friend of the sick girl had the misfortune to visit on the day of the police investigation. A neighbor, seeing her arrive, shouted at her that the police were on their way to arrest everyone in Louise's apartment. Terrified and weeping,

---

21   AMR Liasse 360: Complaint filed by Gille Duvant and Marie Denya (3 March 1751); testimony of neighbors and employees (4, 5 March 1751); interrogation of Louise (6 March 1751).

the girl ran to the cellar and tried to hide under the staircase. The police found her there. When the police questioned her, she testified that she occasionally bought thread from Louise for her own work as a seamstress but rarely spent time there. When questioned, she went on to say that she knew Michelle had come to find work after breaking out of the home for wayward girls. On her own, the girl added that Louise was an honorable woman.

Naturally, there is no way to know what really happened at Louise's place. It is possible her social gatherings were as innocent as she and her friends claimed they were. The three women freely admitted that they met for late suppers a couple of nights a week. Their parties were rowdy, perhaps, and disturbing to the neighbors, but not inherently sinful. On the other hand, her neighbors may have been telling the truth. Louise may have been entertaining a steady stream of soldiers and sailors with young women who had been corrupted against their will. We will never know for certain. It was her word against theirs.

Louise, however, was not truly on her own because she was married. Louise's husband, Jean, was far away at the time of her arrest, but he hurried to her side and set to work getting her released. He wrote a letter to the court exclaiming his surprise and dismay over his wife's imprisonment.[22] He stated that he was shocked by the accusations--her parents were "honest folk of Rennes," and he himself had never noticed anything amiss in her conduct. If, in his absence, Louise had gotten into some kind of trouble, it was due to her nature—"full of joy, generous, and loving the company of her friends for dancing and other legitimate pastimes." He noted that through her profession as a bleacher and as the employer of several girls who do embroidering piecework, Louise had made many friends and acquaintances. It was due to this active social life that people made "false and unjust" assumptions about Louise and her "evil ways." Jean blamed "certain enemies" who sought to ruin his wife, and went on to question the character of Michelle. "If she went to my wife," he wrote, "it was to ask for work. If she then went elsewhere, where her parents dare not say in public," his wife could not be held responsible.

However, Jean had to do more than vouch for her good character in order to get Louise released; he had to reassure the court that he would take control of Louise. He wrote about the accusations: "if it's true, if one supposes for a moment that the accusations of debauchery are true," he hoped that the court would "accord" him his rights to the "chastisement, care, and conduct of his wife." If Louise was at fault, Jean assured the court, he would take care of her himself. That was exactly what the authorities needed to hear. Louise was released into her husband's custody. The final verdict stated that Jean was in charge of his wife's conduct, that the two were ordered to live together in a single domicile, and that if they did not comply they both would be punished.[23] Thus, the natural order was restored—the wife was put under the control of an appropriate guardian, and the husband was commanded to assume his responsibilities as that guardian. To the authorities, this was the preferred state of affairs even if it threatened the livelihoods of both husband and wife.

---

22   AMR Liasse 360: Letter from Jean Baptiste Allain dit Dujardin (18 March 1751)
23   AMR Liasse 360: Sentence and release of accused (20, 21 March 1751).

This sort of situation was not unheard of elsewhere in early modern Europe. In the book *The Holy Household*, about Reformation Augsburg, Lyndal Roper describes many situations in which the "natural order" of the household was supported, by force, if necessary, by the town council.[24] Women, because of their irresponsible and child-like natures, were expected to submit docilely to the authority of their husbands. Men, because of their innate and God-given strength, were expected to behave like good sovereign leaders—gentle and caring, but firmly in control. When men and women strayed from these instinctive roles, the civil authorities were there to push them back into line.

That is what the court in Rennes did in the case of Louise Piel and in others like it. At issue was not necessarily the seduction of Michelle, whether or not that crime actually occurred, but the fact that Louise was a "masterless woman" who surrounded herself with other masterless women. To the early modern legal mind, the situation was fraught with potential dangers, especially once there was evidence of misconduct. Women were weak by nature. When a source of corruption was identified, it had to be dealt with immediately.

It is important to note that there was a difference between this state of affairs and earlier situations in which unattached women were automatically assumed to be guilty. Medieval writers categorized women as virgins, wives, or widows. Anyone who did not fit into these definitions was, by default, a prostitute and could be treated as such.[25] That was not the case in early modern Breton cities, where numerous unattached women lived without harassment. There were no laws against single women living together, for example, as there were in some German cities.[26] But unattached women were, nevertheless, in a precarious position. Once accused, they had few means by which to protect themselves and their guilt was more or less assumed. And, while there was no prohibition against women living together, the conviction of one woman for dishonorable behavior cast a shadow of guilt over all of her associates. Such was the case for Louise and her friends in the face of accusations from the neighbors.

For contrast, let us compare Louise with one of her neighbors, the glovemaker who had referred to Louise as the "biggest whore in Rennes." Both women were married, with children, and they were both tradeswomen, with a number of employees. The mistress glovemaker was married to the clockmaker. She and her husband each had apprentices in their respective crafts, and an additional servant who helped the mistress run the household apart from her workshop. The main difference between the two women was that Louise was left to her own devices and enjoyed a social

---

24   Roper, *The Holy Household: Women and Morals in Reformation Augsburg* (Clarendon Press, 1989).

25   Sharon Farmer, "'It is not Good that [Wo]man Should Be Alone:' Elite Responses to Singlewomen in High Medieval Paris" and Ruth Mazo Karras, "Sex and the Singlewoman" in *Singlewomen in the European Past, 1250–1800* (Philadelphia: University of Pennsylvania Press, 1999).

26   Merry Wiesner, "Having Her Own Smoke: Employment and Independence for Singlewomen in Germany, 1400–1750," *Singlewomen in the European Past*, p. 197.

life outside of her marriage, while the mistress glovemaker was a proper wife and conformed to social expectations of her role as such.

In fact, the woman's violent dislike of Louise was possibly a product of the contrast between them. Merry Wiesner has noted the common role of women as accusers of other women in sixteenth-century witch hunts. She says, "Women gained economic and social security by conforming to the standard of the good wife and mother and by confronting women who deviated from it."[27] A good woman was chaste, pious, obedient, and married. A bad woman was willful, independent, aggressive, and sexually out of control. Certainly, both Louise and the glovemaker were somewhat independent as successful tradeswomen. Perhaps, then, the best way for the glovemaker to emphasize that she was a good wife was to point out that Louise was not. Indeed, though everyone in the neighborhood was eager to denounce Louise when offered the opportunity, only the mistress glovemaker used harsh language and violent terms to describe what she considered to be a "blight" on their community.

Police archives are full of stories such as Louise Piel's, in which the home of a widow, spinster, or independent wife was targeted for suspicion of dangerous social and sexual activity.[28] Many of the stories ended the same—the accused woman, unable to defend herself by any legal means, was jailed and her property was confiscated. Undoubtedly, charges were warranted in numerous cases. As Olwen Hufton has indicated, poverty and lack of support forced many hungry women to fall back on prostitution for survival.[29] But clearly, the standards of evidence in these cases were not high. These were merely trials by suspicion, in which a couple of damning reports from any source were enough to lead to conviction. The eighteenth-century jurist Joly de Fleury wrote that "a woman can be considered a prostitute if she receives into her home people of all ages and of any condition at all hours," while Jousse, another legal theorist, claimed that rumor was not enough to support conviction.[30] But these matters were not precise, and judges could be persuaded of anything when faced with persistent accusations.

A few words about the French criminal procedure are in order. In the early Middle Ages in France, both the accused and the accuser in a criminal case were imprisoned pending the trial, and each was allowed to make a case before the judge.

---

27   Wiesner, *Women and Gender in Early Modern Europe* (Cambridge University Press, 1993), p. 229.

28   For an idea of the frequency of these charges, consider the police archives of Nantes, showing 125 charges against individual women or couples, 1735–1750 (AMN FF 271), 74 charges, 1752–1780 (AMN FF 272), and an additional 30 charges filed by relatives, 1711–1760 (AMN FF 269). In Rennes, surviving police archives show two to three investigations a year in the 1750s (AMR Liasses 360 and 415); archives of the presidial of Rennes show nine cases ending in imprisonment and confiscation of goods, 1701–1703 (AMR Liasse 413) and six cases, 1712–1716 (ADIV 3 B 1443–1446).

29   Hufton, *The Poor of Eighteenth-Century France* (Oxford: Clarendon Press, 1974), p. 317.

30   Marie-Christine Morel, *Les femmes et la justice au milieu du XVIIIe siècle à Rennes (1751–1759)* Memoire de maitrise d'histoire, Université de Haute Bretagne, 1990–91, pp. 25–8.

This system made people wary of pressing charges, however, and over time people were permitted to make "denunciations" rather than accusations. A denunciator was never jailed, and in fact became a part of the justice system, directing authorities to other potential witnesses. Even so, both sides were eventually presented before a judge and the accused was able to face the accuser.[31]

A national reform of the justice system was introduced in 1539 by the king, François I, based, ironically enough, on a system first introduced in Brittany. In the interests of efficiency, civil and criminal procedures were now conducted almost entirely in writing. Depositions were taken by sergeants or interrogators, signed by the witnesses, and presented *en masse* to a judge. Only when all of the testimony was collected did the accused appear before a judge. At this hearing, the judge conducted a final interrogation of the accused, and sent the findings, again entirely in writing, to a royal *procureur*, or second-judge.[32] In order to guarantee that the accused would speak the unadulterated truth, he or she was imprisoned during the entire investigation and forbidden to receive advice from any source.[33] Secrecy guarded both the denunciators and their evidence. And though the trial procedure allowed for a "confrontation" phase, in which the accused may face the denunciators, the judge would have, by that point, already reviewed all of the testimony and chosen which witnesses were required to appear for the confrontation. Thus, the accused never heard all of the pertinent testimony, and was given no chance to answer it.[34]

Over the course of the seventeenth and eighteenth centuries, royal courts gradually extended their jurisdiction over a wider and wider territory. In Rennes, which was typical of many administrative centers, the Parlement and the Presidial, both royal courts, had an influence over municipal affairs. Local affairs were under the administration of the police, or a local court run by the seneschal or a provost. The police force worked in conjunction with the lower court to maintain local order, and only turned municipal affairs over to the higher, royal courts if a great deal of money or important people were involved.[35] The higher courts in the eighteenth century followed a more elaborate procedure than the one outlined above because so much was at stake. But the simple criminal procedure based upon denunciation was followed in lower courts right up to the French Revolution.[36] Enlightened *philosophes* such as Voltaire and Montesquieu were vocal critics of the justice system, which they characterized as "barbaric."[37]

And yet, if all French citizens were potential victims of an unjust system, women were doubly so. Not only were they arrested at the first accusation, restricted from seeking counsel, and unable to face their accusers, but they were crippled by the legal

---

31   A. Esmein, *Histoire de la Procédure Criminelle en France et spécialement de la Procédure Inquisitoire depuis le XIIIe siècle jusqu'a nos jours* (Frankfurt am Main: Verlag Sauer & Auvermann KG, 1969), pp. 108–10.

32   Esmein, *Histoire de la Procédure Criminelle*, pp. 140–42.

33   Esmein, *Histoire de la Procédure Criminelle*, pp. 228–31.

34   Esmein, *Histoire de la Procédure Criminelle*, p. 367.

35   James Collins, *Classes, Estates and Order in Early Modern Brittany* (Cambridge University Press, 1994), pp. 108–17.

36   Esmein, *Histoire de la Procédure Criminelle*, p. 217.

37   Esmein, *Histoire de la Procédure Criminelle*, p. 354.

assumption that their testimony was less creditworthy than that of a man. Women charged with crimes against honor were presumed guilty from the outset. Women were also particularly disadvantaged by the low standards of proof necessary to make a case. Eyewitness testimony was considered the purist form of evidence, but in most trials that meant a firsthand account of criminal activity. In honor cases, it was often sufficient to prove that a woman had been in the wrong place or in the wrong company. It is no wonder that women were quick to file complaints against slander.

There were two types of charges in the search for dishonorable people. One was the charge of leading a "mauvaise" or "scandaleuse" life; this charge was leveled against particular women, living singly or with other unattached women, who were suspected of having "soldiers and students" visit for nights of drinking and debauchery. Louise Piel dit Dujardin faced these charges, as did many unattached or unsupervised women. Anne Rouxel, a 21-year-old *tailleuse* living in Rennes in 1751, was sent back to her parents' home in the countryside. She had come to the city looking for work and had roomed briefly with La Gerard and her sisters, girls of dubious reputation. Rouxel testified that she had left the Gerards when she saw their scandalous ways and intended to move in with an honorable *fileuse* named Lafleure. The police, however, considered her too much of a risk and gave her three days to leave town.[38]

Sometimes, as with Anne Rouxel, the charges were less about blatant prostitution than they were about simple dishonor.[39] Genevieve Poislan, a *lingere* in Nantes, was tracked all over town and arrested because she continued to accept visits from "several bad women" and a man named Denancy, who caused "numerous scandals." When Poislan could not be found in the room she rented, the police questioned a young woman coming down the stairs. She told them she was visiting a *fileuse* who lived in the same house, but that she knew Poislan, and directed the police to the shop of a *tapissiere* [rugmaker] in the next parish. They arrested Poislan there.[40]

The unifying factor between these cases was the "masterless" condition of the women in question. In 1704, Janne Meneu, a widow, and her daughter Marie Renard, were denounced by neighbors for having soldiers over to drink and pass the night.[41] That same year, the sisters Mathurine and Renée Yvon, *fileuses* who roomed with their employer, a *teinturier* [dyer], were accused of "harboring badly dressed people [*malnottés*] and vagabonds."[42] In 1753, Marguerite Coligner, a 40-year-old *fileuse* who spoke only Bas-Breton, was banished from Nantes for suspicion of "une vie scandaleuse." Her husband was a driver and was often gone. Marguerite was left

---

38   AMR Liasse 360, 7 May 1751.

39   Jurists made a finer distinction between an actual prostitute, who received several male visitors, and a girl who had lost her virtue to a single individual. In these police cases, however, both prostitutes and dishonored women were charged with "mauvaise vie."

40   AMN FF 271, 5 October 1740. There is no indication that Poislan's working associates were investigated for misconduct.

41   AMR 415/1, 4 October 1704.

42   AMR 415/1, 25 May 1704.

with a child and no source of her income but her spinning. Neighbors complained that she had frequent guests, mostly soldiers.[43]

Even family members turned in women who were suspected of dishonorable behavior. In 1711, Louis and Magdelaine Duplessis Mesle, the oldest surviving children of Jacques Daniau Sr. Duplessis Mesle, wrote to the *intendant* of Brittany to complain that a soldier was living with their widowed mother.[44] In 1747, Pierre Rolland, *cordier*, accused his wife, Louise Guilmot, of being wanton. He claimed he no longer allowed her to come home so she would not disturb their children, and he was supported by several witnesses who reported having seen Louise with "ten or twelve sailors."[45] It is possible that these people turned in their relatives out of a fear of being tainted by their misconduct. But family members could also manipulate charges out of spite. Servan Boullas and his wife Servanne Herry wrote to the judge in Saint-Malo, begging that their daughter be released from the women's prison. Servanne had had a terrible fight with the girl, and, "in her rage," had made false accusations against her before the police. Now, she was sorry for her angry words and revoked all accusations.[46]

The second potential honor charge was of having a "maison debauchée" [debauched household]; this charge was directed against couples or entire households who harbored "ill-dressed girls" for the pleasure of others. Innkeepers were especially susceptible to these charges. In 1735, Madame Desbrosses of Nantes was charged with running an improper cabaret because certain girls were seen there in the company of men. One witness testified he wanted to go in just for a drink, but was pushed out by several armed men.[47] In 1751, Julie Echer, a *toileuse*, and Catherine Jeunesse, a *tapissiere*, went to the cabaret owned by Dubois and his wife. The women went to the cabaret accompanied by two soldiers, but claimed they left after seeing how much debauchery and scandalous behavior Dubois allowed there.[48]

Anyone could be charged with having a dishonorable home. The standard elements, again, were women, noise, and armed men. In 1753, Hubert dit Desilles and his wife, listed as *chirurgians* [surgeons], were the subjects of a complaint filed jointly by seven of their neighbors in Rennes. The two were accused of hosting scandalous girls and men at "all hours," making noise, and hurling insults at others in the neighborhood.[49] Robinet and his wife, a couple in Nantes, were accused of harboring girls and men who came to the neighborhood, "insulting the neighbors and attacking simple folk, brutalizing them with swords and intimidating them with

---

43   AMN FF 272 #2, 26 May 1753.

44   AMN FF 269 #1, 22 December 1711.

45   AMN FF 269 #2, 12 August 1747.

46   ADIV 4 BX 1157, 1 October 1725.

47   AMN FF 271 #9, 31 December 1735.

48   AMN FF 271 #114, 11 August 1751. Note that the female witnesses in this case did not hesitate to testify that they had attended a cabaret in the company of two soldiers. This suggests a certain tolerance of young women "dating" as long as no charges were filed against them.

49   AMR Liasse 365, 26 January 1753.

pistols and fists."[50] Apart from the obvious dangers of having armed men drink and fight in the neighborhood, people feared that honorable women would be corrupted. Neighbors of the Coullaud household in Nantes feared for their own niece, an honest girl who lived and worked in the same building. Customers "of all qualities and professions" seeking the Coullaud woman occasionally walked into the wrong apartment and made "terrifying demands."[51]

Most of the debauched households investigated were quieted through the imposition of fines. Multiple complaints led to more serious punishment. Cabarets could be shut down, for example, and the owners jailed. The very nature of a cabaret, however, meant that these business owners worked on the verge of debauchery. As a matter of course, they had to defend themselves from such charges.

Individual women, by contrast, could be completely ruined by a bad reputation. And so, it is heartening to know that authorities also responded to accusations of slander when women filed them. A woman had to act quickly to a public assault on her character, lest the rumor gain enough momentum to destroy her. On 25 January 1702, Guilmette and Marguerite Juglot, *tapissieres et honneste filles*, awoke to find that someone had attached a libel to their workshop door, accusing them of being whores. The two women took the sign to the police, who began interviewing their neighbors to search for the culprit. Witnesses reported that two school boys were hired by a neighbor, Jan Andre Babson, to put the sign on the shop, for some unknown reason. The Juglot sisters claimed that the libel would hurt business and the chances for one of them to marry. Babson was fined and told that more grievous injury would have warranted corporal punishment.[52] Clearly, the potential threat to their livelihood was serious enough that the Juglots had to take the initiative to save their "honor and good reputation."

Mere accusations were enough reason to call in the police. When Enrette de la Verdure accused Anne Henry of being unfaithful to her husband with other married men, police came in to interrogate the neighbors. Who was telling the truth? Who was the troublemaker? Overwhelmingly, in this case, witnesses supported the accused, Anne and her husband, Anthone Orescue. The old La Verdure was always insulting people, neighbors said, and Orescue and his wife were good neighbors. Most witnesses were upset to have heard Anne crying after La Verdure had insulted her. Like Babson in the previous case, La Verdure was fined for having made false accusations.[53]

In some cases, slanderers were clearly aware of their power to destroy someone. René Buron and his wife, Janne Le Rai, tailors, worked methodically to ruin a young *brodeuse* named Merguerite Crosnier in 1691. According to witnesses, the two sought out all of the tailors and cloth merchants in the parish of Saint Leonard's in Nantes and warned them against doing any business or socializing with Crosnier. "They said Crosnier was a liar and a whore and I will not say what else," swore a tailor's wife, Marie Pareau. Janne le Rai went to Crosnier's employer and told him he should

---

50   AMN FF 271 #21, 17 August 1745.
51   AMN FF 272 #10, 21 July 1761.
52   AMR 415/2, 25 January 1702; sentence 9 February 1702.
53   AMR 414, 10 July 1731.

fire the girl, saying, "She will only cause you scandal." Pierre Boullai, a philosophy student boarding in the home of a tailor, overheard Le Rai telling another woman, "I will put La Crosnier in the *sanitât*." The specific complaints against Crosnier were never specified, but their relentless attempts to spread their "warnings" forced Crosnier to file a complaint against them.[54]

Such accusations went well beyond the kind of slander Laura Gowing describes in her book, *Domestic Dangers: Women, Words and Sex in Early Modern London.*[55] In London, it was not unusual to sue someone for uttering the phrase "whore" as an insult, and Gowing makes a strong case for seeing sexual slander as a gauge of women's place in society. The charge "whore" was certainly bandied about as a casual insult in Brittany. Fights between neighbors or marketplace rivals were full of this insulting language, and the implications were serious enough to warrant lodging a complaint against the slanderer. But the name-calling, in itself, was rarely cause for punishment in Brittany. Only repeated and violent abuse, or foul language that included taking the Lord's name, were prosecuted by the police. Honor cases, on the other hand, went well beyond the issue of slander because they often included actual charges. Calling someone a "whore" in the street can certainly damage that person's reputation, and reputation was a serious matter for early modern women. But denouncing someone as a whore to the police almost certainly ruined that person's life.

Some women fell victim to apparently false charges and lost everything, even with the help of supportive neighbors. Georgine Riant was a widow who rented out horses and carriages from her stable in Rennes. Her nearest neighbor, an innkeeper named Fleurigard, had been trying for years to buy out her business and attach it to his hotel. Finally, he denounced her and her daughter as prostitutes. Riant and her daughter were very popular—in fact, her daughter was a licensed mistress tailor with an impressive following of courtly customers who wrote letters on their behalf. However, the two women were convicted of "mauvaise vie," branded with a fleur-de-lis, and banished from the city. Their home and business were auctioned off.[56]

Anne Nerriere was a certified midwife living in Rennes in 1712. She had been trained in Paris under the sponsorship of her mother, a retired midwife, who also presented her for licensing before the surgeons' guild of Rennes. Nerriere was married, but her husband's whereabouts were never mentioned. The two women lived together just outside the city walls in a neighborhood known as "Saint Michel," where they had an ongoing dispute with their neighbors, Jan Dauphine and Perrine Le Batard, who owned a tavern. At the request of these neighbors, Nerriere was accused of debauchery, arrested, and stripped of her license and most of her worldly goods. Nerriere's story is more complex than some because of the extent to which

---

54   ADLA B 5843, *Prevoté*, 22 September 1691.

55   Gowing, *Domestic Dangers: Women, Words and Sex in Early Modern London* (Oxford: Clarendon Press, 1996).

56   ADIV 3 B 1452, 12 August and 15 October 1714. The fleur-de-lis signified that the women were convicts, and that their lives were the possession of the king should they ever be arrested again.

she fought back and the overwhelming evidence that should have supported her appeal.

Nerriere was arrested on 2 January 1712.[57] Nearly a month passed before her mother, Janne Hamon, was able to gather witnesses and appeal to the police. Nerriere and Hamon claimed that Perrine Le Batard, the accuser, wanted to be a midwife and frequently harassed and insulted Nerriere in order to drive her from the neighborhood. Le Batard's false accusations against Nerriere were motivated by jealousy, Hamon said, and by a desire to cover up her own scandalous activities. Le Batard was said to harbor prostitutes at the tavern, and was suspected of delivering babies in secret, without a license and without reporting them to the proper authorities. Hamon insisted on a full investigation of the false accusations and the private lives of the accusers, and filed formal charges with an officer of the presidial.[58]

In the days following Hamon's supplication, statements were taken from witnesses identified by Hamon and Nerriere. Pierre Boullas, a chamberlain wigmaker, reported that he often drank at Dauphine and Le Batard's pub. One night, a drunk friend of Dauphine's announced that he was going upstairs "to kiss a pregnant girl." Nerriere was there, tending to the woman in labor, when the drunk pushed his way into the room. Several cries were heard, and Nerriere was seen pushing the man out of the room; she slapped him twice and returned to her patient. Later that night, Dauphine and Le Batard offered the witness money to sign a paper denouncing Nerriere. He said he refused because he did not know if it was true. Boullas' statement was corroborated by his 18-year-old stepson, who was with him that night.[59]

Guy Morion, Sieur de la Pommeroye—a master surgeon of Rennes—reported that he went to Nerriere's place on one occasion to help her with a difficult delivery. He was intercepted by Le Batard, who offered him a drink and told him Nerriere was running a bordello. He commented that he did not think that was true, but thought no more about it. René Goupil, a sergeant in the royal guard, testified that Le Batard offered him a drink while he was on his way to church. At the same time, she asked him to sign a complaint against Nerriere, but he did not know Nerriere and he had his doubts about the tavern. Goupil's wife added that she had once seen a pregnant woman enter the tavern and emerge a day later with a newborn baby. When Le Batard and her "patient" encountered Nerriere in the street, the women argued with each other, and Le Batard seemed badly shaken by the encounter.[60] Practicing midwifery without a license was a serious crime, and it is possible that Nerriere threatened to report Le Batard for her illicit activities.

Janne Morice, an apprentice *tailleuse*, reported that she once visited Le Batard's tavern to buy a jacket; Le Batard also worked as a *revendeuse* on the side. Morice had decided the jacket was too expensive, but Le Batard said she could have the jacket if she went upstairs to see something. In the room upstairs, Morice saw a young girl with a new baby who was accompanied by two men. One of them grabbed Morice as soon as she entered the room and she had to fight him off. He said he had mistaken

---

57   ADIV 3 B 1450, *procès verbal* of 2 January 1712.
58   ADIV 3 B 1450, letter of 25 February 1712.
59   ADIV 3 B 1450, statement of 27 February 1712.
60   ADIV 3 B 1450, statements of 27 and 28 February 1712.

her for someone else, but she fled. Days later, when she had returned to haggle for the jacket, Le Batard apologized for the earlier confusion. She repeated her offer of the jacket, and asked Morice to tell the police she had been attacked at Nerriere's apartment.[61]

Nerriere's own supplication was received by the police a few days later. In it, she asked that all the new information, as well as her mother's *memoire* to the presidial, be considered in the case against her. The accusers had fewer and less reliable witnesses, and were themselves guilty of certain crimes.[62] On the same day, Dauphine and Le Batard sent a new denunciation against Nerriere, bemoaning her "scandalous conduct, false counter-accusations, and pretended witnesses." They went on to say that Nerriere's countersuit was null because it was filed in the wrong jurisdiction. Their denunciation was a local police matter, whereas the presidial was a higher court that handled criminal procedures such as sedition, illicit assemblies, and grand theft.[63]

Unfortunately for Nerriere, the sentencing court agreed that the countercharges were being handled by a different court and could have no effect on the proceedings against Nerriere. On May 7, after having been held in jail for four months, Nerriere was convicted of "abusing her profession as a midwife and leading a life of prostitution." She, along with several other prostitutes, was to be led by the wrists through the market for three days, wearing a sign identifying her as a whore. She was forced to pay for the costs of the trial through the confiscation and liquidation of her goods, and her elderly mother was to be likewise arrested and interrogated.[64]

Sadly, Nerriere and her mother disappear from the sources at this point. They are not among the tax roles or parish records for Rennes in any of the following years; it is likely that they became dependent on charity or left the city, hoping to start anew somewhere. As the details of this case show so clearly, lone women were in a precarious position and faced losing everything when accused of crimes of dishonor. Nerriere and her mother received much-needed support from their neighbors, and still it was not enough to save them. Nerriere was trained and licensed by a respected guild, having been established by her mother in a profession, and her good work could not save her either.

In an interesting footnote to the case, Le Batard was accused two years later of exposing a newborn in an alley behind her tavern. The original complaint was filed by Hamon at the time of her daughter's sentence, but the later investigation does not include statements from either Hamon or Nerriere. On November 21, 1714, police took several statements from witnesses who saw the baby or had information concerning Le Batard's activities as an unlicensed midwife. Le Batard was accused of taking the money intended for the baby's entrance into the hospital and throwing the baby in a ditch during the night. On 4 December, when police went to Le Batard's

---

61   ADIV 3 B 1450, statement of 28 February 1712.

62   ADIV 3 B 1450, letter of 3 March 1712; the file no longer contains any of the testimony against Nerriere.

63   ADIV 3 B 1450, letter of 3 Mars 1712. For the differences between courts, see James Collins, *Classes, Estates and Order*, pp. 108–17.

64   ADIV 3 B 1450, sentence of 7 May 1712.

tavern to arrest her for interrogation, they found that she and her husband had disappeared. By 23 January 1715, the case had been transferred to the royal court and neighbors were complaining about the police lock on the abandoned tavern. On March 2, Jan Dauphine had been captured, charged with fleeing arrest, and made to pay court and investigation costs. Le Batard was apparently never arrested.[65]

Nerriere's case, like many others, had been built upon accusations from someone who stood to gain financially from the removal of the accused women. It is clear that false accusations were an obvious, almost easy, means to get rid of unwanted rivals. The vulnerability of so many women meant that it was almost impossible to defend oneself against charges of misconduct.

In the sixteenth and seventeenth centuries, accusations of witchcraft had been enough to warrant investigation. In the enlightened age, when witchcraft had become a mere theological issue best left to ecclesiastical courts, secular lawmakers, with the support of average citizens, found that accusations of sexual depravity were sufficient to control the behavior of errant women. The "crime" may have changed, but the methods of detection and punishment remained remarkably similar.[66] The accused were usually misfits who could be jailed on the most cursory evidence in the form of formulaic testimony by witnesses. This kind of trial by suspicion is certainly not confined to the early modern era—the searches for Jews during the Holocaust or communists during the Cold War operated in much the same way. But the similarities between a sixteenth-century witch-hunt and an eighteenth-century whore hunt are strongest in that they both targeted non-conformist women and relied on evidence that could be neither proven nor disproven. A comparison of these two otherwise very different phenomena is useful because it reveals so much about how persecution functions.

Robin Briggs's significant study on *Witches and Neighbors* explores the routine followed in the average European witch trial.[67] Briggs admits that there is a certain amount of misogyny apparent in the witch-hunt phenomenon. But he also finds that witch-hunts were a general way of resolving conflict in small communities in which neighbors were direct competitors who had to interact intimately on a regular basis. Thus, the accusers were, more often than not, women who knew the accused and held some ill will against her: "Aggressiveness and competitiveness by women were primarily expressed in relation to other women."[68] Accuser and accused often blamed each other for the "excessive pride" and un-neighborliness that was at the heart of their grudge. Neighbors rallied around an accuser who was taking on a deviant or unpopular member of the community, but also worked to protect a "good" neighbor

65   ADIV 3 B 1450, original complaint, no date; 3 B 1452, 21 November, 4 and 19 December 1714; 23 January and 2 March 1715.

66   Significantly, the change in rhetoric also meant that far more people could be charged—accusations of dishonorable conduct held up much better in court than did accusations of witchcraft. I am grateful to Katherine Crawford for suggesting this line of thinking to me. It warrants further investigation.

67   Briggs, *Witches and Neighbors: The Social and Cultural Context of European Witchcraft* (New York: Penguin Books, 1996), pp. 21–3.

68   Briggs, *Witches and Neighbors*, p. 268.

who was unjustly charged. The social lives of women and the relationships between women are thus played out in the realm of potential criminality.

Briggs concludes that witch trials were not "a deliberate criminalization of women," but part of a broader move to exert moral and social control over troublemakers by labeling and punishing all unwanted behavior. Perhaps the same could be said about the honor trials of the eighteenth century. In a number of honor investigations, neighbors complained as much about "un-neighborly behavior" as they did about actual threats or disturbances. In fact, several of the *maison debauchées* were inns guilty of refusing service to people who later testified against them, and girls leading scandalous lives were also said to be rude and insulting to others.

The comparison between witch-hunts and honor trials is not as much of a stretch as it may seem. In addition to the similarities of the two processes—anonymous and vague denunciations, a standard lexicon of accusations, and the general non-conformity of the accused—there is the inherently sexual and criminal nature of witchcraft itself. For some witch investigators, illicit sexual activity was enough to warrant suspicion of sorcery. In a pamphlet entitled, *La Montaigne*, Jesuit and "missionary to Brittany" R. P. Maunour gave detailed instructions for confessors in search of sorcerers.[69] Demons access their victims through dreams, Maunour explained, and tempted them to assemblies with pleasures of the flesh. Thus, when one interrogates a virgin, one must ask her about her dreams: did she dream of beasts or men? Did they offer her gifts and make promises to her, as lovers do? Did she feel their weight on her body when she slept? Did she like to reflect on these dreams during the day?[70] If the penitent is married, the questions turn to children: how many children does she have and did she sacrifice any of them to the devil? The interrogator was to specifically address abortion:

> If this is a woman who had aborted, ask her, How many children have you lost? Did the evil one tell you that you had too many children, that people would mock you because you were not able to feed them? Did you desire the death of (the child) you carried in your womb?[71]

These questions are almost identical to those asked by police in a typical honor investigation, the one difference being that positive answers in a witch-hunt carried demonic as well as criminal implications.

In a modern, skeptical age, we are prepared to dismiss the validity of witchcraft accusations, but we frequently accept charges of dishonorable conduct at face value. The vast majority of those accused and punished either as witches or as sexual criminals were women. I am simply trying to highlight the tenuous nature of these cases. Whether or not honor investigations were a "deliberate criminalization of women," they singled out women based upon standards that would have never

---

69   ADIV 1 F 1040, *La montaigne, ouvrage du R. P. Maunour de la comagnie de Jesus, missionaire de Bretagne, mort en odeur de sainteté dans le bourg de Plevin Paroisse de l'évêché de Quimper* (7 November 1751).

70   Ibid., pp. 9–10.

71   Ibid., p. 18.

been used against men. The accused were often guilty only of being different and vulnerable, or of having led uncontrolled social lives.

Women had to be careful about their social conduct in a way that men did not. But it would be foolish to conclude from this that women could never enjoy social lives outside the home. Louise and her circle of friends were not so different from other women in early modern cities. Married women who lived with their husbands met others through daily contact in the neighborhood, at shops and fountains, and at church. They, like widows who lived with grown children, supplemented their household relations with friendships that passed the time and eased life's burdens. For young women and widows living alone, or wives whose husbands were absent, contact with the world at large would have been necessary for survival.

Women's friendships

Beyond illuminating the attitude toward women's honor in the eighteenth century, the cases above also reveal to what extent women enjoyed social lives outside of marriage and motherhood. It's clear from their testimony, either against or in defense of one another, that women were involved with neighbors, coworkers, and religious or social peers on a day-to-day basis. Certainly, small communities by their very nature created intimacy. Privacy was a rare commodity, and antagonism was to be expected. However, familiarity also bred friendship. In the words of Anna Letitia Barbauld, an eighteenth-century writer, "a friend is never chosen. A secret sympathy, the attraction of a thousand nameless qualities . . . a similarity of circumstances—these are the things that begin attachment."[72]

The social spheres of women in early modern Brittany differed dramatically from small towns and villages to large cities. In villages, where inhabitants tended to marry and stay within a certain distance of natal homes, social networks were built primarily on kin, households, and neighbors. These networks could easily extend beyond the immediate family but maintained a local context. Households could be made up of single parents and children, siblings, distant relatives, and hired hands.[73] Neighbors had constant and intimate contact with one another. At sewing bees and spinning bees, where women gathered in the evenings to share lamplight and friendly competition, or at natural gathering spots around fountains, markets, and churches, women met and socialized with others like themselves.

Some authorities, who envisioned the household as the purest example of "natural order," were suspicious of anything that fell outside of that miniature hierarchy, even within the confines of village life. Spinning bees, for example, were frequently portrayed across Europe as a medium for immorality. A houseful of women, working late into the night, was not only likely to have encouraged a certain frivolity among the workers themselves but also served as a temptation to local men.[74] Moral reformers

---

72   Barbauld, *Memoirs, Letters and a Selection of Poems* (Boston: Osgood, 1874).

73   François Lebrun, *La vie conjugale sous l'ancien régime* (Paris: Armand Colin, 1975), p. 82.

74   Jane Schneider, "Rumpelstiltskin's Bargain: Folklore and the Merchant Capitalist Intensification of Linen Manufacture in Early Modern Europe," *Cloth and Human Experience* (Smithsonian Institute Press, 1989). p. 193.

criticized the popularity of these women's work parties well into the industrial age. The earliest condemnations likened these and any nighttime gatherings to witches sabbaths, with clear diabolical and immoral purposes.[75] In 1619, the catholic Synod of Saint-Malo condemned *veillées*, in which villagers gathered for spinning, storytelling, and flirting, as "assemblies of the night invented by the prince of darkness whose sole aim is to cause the fall of man."[76] Prohibitions against *veillées* were repeated in other synodal statutes and by an *arrêt* of the *parlement* of Brittany in 1670. Again, we see the demonic implications of women's social gatherings. By the mid-eighteenth century, however, the implications of evil had been more or less dropped from church ordinances.[77] Instead, churchmen now interpreted these rural festivities, as well as the habit of women to sit in the shade of the church to "sew, spin and gossip," as signs of ignorant disrespect of the holy church, best met with improved education.[78]

In villages, social life revolved around kin and near neighbors. In large cities like Rennes and Nantes, the potential pool of companions for women expanded remarkably. Relatives were the first source of support, and women often stayed with sisters, cousins, or aunts and uncles. Françoise Simon, who kept a journal in seventeenth-century Rennes, described taking in her cousin's daughters after her cousin died of the plague.[79] Renée Vissaicher, an elderly widow living in Rennes in 1704, petitioned to have her niece released from the convent for repentant girls, where her employer had sent her. Vissaicher refused to accept the injustice or the expense and had decided to take her niece home.[80] Elizabeth Giraudais of Nantes signed a contract with her niece, Louise Giraudais, to establish repayment of room, board, and the cost of apprenticeship as a *lingere*.[81] And even the unfortunate Louise Piel dit Dujardin, arrested for the corruption of a young girl, could count on the support of family connections. A woman named Toussainte Nicolas petitioned for temporary custody of Piel's daughter, listing herself as "une tante à la mode de Bretagne," and declared her intention to protect the young girl from scandalous influences while her mother was incarcerated.[82]

---

75   Amaury Chanou, "La religion souterraine à Saint-Malo en 1434," *Annales de Bretagne et du Pays d'Ouest* 102:2 (1995): p. 110.

76   François Lebrun, "La religion de l'evêque de Saint-Malo et de ses diocesains au début du XVIIe siècle, à travers les statuts synodaux de 1619," Extrait de *La religion populaire*, Colloques Internationaux du Centre National de la Recherche Scientifique (Paris, 1977), p. 45.

77   "Ordonnances synodales du diocese de Vannes publiées dans le synode générale," (Vannes: Jaques de Heuqueville, 1695); "Ordonannces synodales du diocese de Saint-Malo renouvellées et confirmés dans le synod," (Saint-Malo: Jules Valais, 1769); and "Statuts et ordonnances de monseigneur . . . evêque et comte de Dol," (Rennes: Vatar, 1741.)

78   Alain Croix, *Cultures et religion en Bretagne aux 16e et 17e siècles* (Rennes: Éditions Apogee, 1995), p. 251.

79   *Moi, Claude Bordeaux* (entry April 1647).

80   AMR 415/1, 14 January 1704.

81   ADLA 4 E 2/70, 1753.

82   AMR Liasse 360: Letter from Toussainte Nicolas (13 March 1751) "à la mode de Bretagne" means she was probably a cousin of either Louise or her husband, Jean.

Neighbors, too, could be a natural source of support. Julie Hardwick, Marie Yvonne Crépin, and Roderick Phillips found, in separate studies, that women escaping violent situations or suing their husbands for separation could count on neighbors, especially women neighbors, for help and solace.[83] Phillips believes that "separate spheres" of sociability called men to guildhalls and taverns and left women especially open to the friendship of other women.[84] But it may have been the natural tendency of women to look out for each other if their lives were similar and they felt empathy for one another, particularly in cases of domestic violence. In particularly violent episodes, neighbors usually intervened, like the woman in Rennes who yelled through her neighbor's door during an argument, "If you kill her, I'll testify against you."[85]

Neighbors could also be helpful in other circumstances. In some of the honor cases above, well-liked women could count on neighbors to testify to their good reputation. In other cases, a woman's neighbors and friends might help her thwart guild inspectors and police. In Rennes in 1702, the surgeon Sieur Basmeulle, his wife, and a local *cordier* conspired to hide Janne L'ainé Malouine from police. It is not clear why the woman was being sought, but Basmeulle and several of his neighbors led investigators through a maze of apartments and shops, hoping to give Malouine a chance to escape. After she had been captured, Basmeulle was forced to admit that he and his family had been hiding her.[86]

At times, neighbors were so involved in helping a friend that they physically attacked inspectors in an attempt to drive them off. In 1761, the tailors of Nantes attempted to seize the goods of Mlle. Le Chevrie, who was found working illegally. On their way out of the building, the inspectors were attacked by "several women who were opposed to the confiscation." Especially violent was a woman named La Guy, who threw herself bodily at the officers.[87] In 1768, police inspectors interrupted the baptism of Monsieur Fargellau's baby to inquire about the unlicensed midwife who had been given the honor of carrying the newborn to church. Women relatives and friends attacked inspectors, forcing them to seek refuge in a nearby bakery.[88] The flip side of all this, naturally, were the neighbors who actually denounced or physically attacked each other rather than assist each other. But anyone who needed help was as likely to get it from neighbors as they were to get it from family in these close-knit communities.

Women frequently found work together, roomed together, and provided jobs for other women. P.J.P. Goldberg found that women in medieval England often

---

83   Hardwick, "Seeking Separations: Gender, Marriages, and Household Economies in Early Modern France," *French Historical Studies*, 21/1 (1998); Phillips, "Women, Neighborhood, and Family in the Late Eighteenth Century" *French Historical Studies* 18:1 (1993).

84   Phillips, p. 2.

85   Crépin, "Violences conjugales en Bretagne: la repression de l'uxorcide au XVIIIe siècle," *Memoires de la Société d'Histoire et d'Archeologie de Bretagne* 73 (1995): 170.

86   AMR 415/2, 18 September 1702.

87   AMN HH 170 #74, 15 July 1761.

88   AMN FF 253 #1 and #2, 15 April 1768.

migrated into towns in pairs, searching for work after agricultural jobs disappeared.[89] They traveled with sisters or friends from their home villages. In seventeenth- and eighteenth-century Brittany, such women seemed able to create networks once they arrived in town. The attempts were not always successful, as we saw above in the example of Anne Rouxel, the young *tailleuse* banished from Rennes in 1751 for having stayed briefly with other women of bad reputation, or in the case of Michelle, who had sought work with Louise Piel dit Dujardin and became the center of a scandal. In 1713, Janne Ubedal welcomed Cecile Teiller as a roommate shortly after Teiller's arrival in Rennes. Teiller was the wife of an absent sailor, and she paid her part of the rent by sewing, spinning and making mattresses. Unfortunately, Teiller was also pregnant. Since neighbors and authorities could not adequately discern whether her husband had set sail recently enough to be the expectant father, both women were charged with "mauvaise vie" and banished from the city.[90]

In spite of such potential difficulties, women seemed to seek out apartments and rooms in buildings occupied by other women. The *capitation* tax roll of Saint-Malo was organized in such a way as to keep track of the owner and all tenants in each building. Therefore, we have a record of the women and men who rented rooms or apartments in the same house. As one might have expected, there is usually no correspondence between the occupations of neighbors in the densely populated sections of a large city. However, it was not unusual to find several widows or a cluster of unmarried women in a single building near the market quarter. In 1740, for example, a house on the Rue de Notre Dame had four tenants, all of them widows with occupations: two *couturieres,* one bleacher, and one petty merchant. Near the cathedral, Gilette and Etienette Themoin, two widowed sisters, were roommates, and their tenant was a third widow. All of the women were *couturieres*. Guilmette Girard, a bleacher; Julienne Mallet, a *couturiere*; Julienne Poisson, a *poulailliere* [chicken vendor]; and Perrine Guerin, a widowed day-worker all shared a house on the Rue de Saint Benoit.[91] They had in common their status as unmarried or widowed women and their relatively low incomes.

Police reports issued by guild officers in search of contraband reveal the extent to which women worked together. Marie Avia and Marie Anne Gard, "tailleuses et non maitresses," had their work confiscated in 1757 in Nantes.[92] Marie Le Noire, another *tailleuse*, insisted that the dresses found in her apartment belonged to her roommate, a legitimate apprentice who worked "à la journée pour Mlle. Jeanne Goiaux."[93] Mlle. Brisonette justified her own work by identifying her employer, LaHay Gabory, who was a member of the tailor's guild.[94] And Mlle Le Breton, former roommate and apprentice to a *maitresse tailleuse*, Mme Boupeau, claimed to have inherited Boupeau's apartment and guild privileges when the latter had left for America eight

89   Goldberg, *Women, Work and Life Cycle in a Medieval Economy: Women in York and Yorkshire, 1300–1520* (Oxford: Clarendon Press, 1992), p. 300.
90   ADIV 3 B 1451, interrogation of 11 May 1713.
91   ADLA B 3605, Saint-Malo *Capitation* roll, 1740.
92   AMN HH 170 #66, 6 April 1757.
93   AMN HH 170 #75, 4 September 1762.
94   AMN HH 170 #44, 2 April 1753.

years earlier.[95] Anne Chauvigne and Marie Momusseau were roommates and *lingeres* who served as co-mistresses to a new apprentice in 1712; according to *capitation* tax rolls, the two were still living together in 1740.[96]

In the absence of formal corporative institutions, some women banded together in informal ways. Though most merchants registered with the *greffier* at Nantes individually, Magdelaine Larzen, Janne Pavoir, and Janne Richard, three married grain vendors who lived on the same street, registered together in 1750. Only Larzen's husband, a "wheat measurer," had a related trade; professionally, these three neighbors had more in common with each other than with their husbands. In Saint-Malo in 1748, seven women filed a complaint against the police commissioner on behalf of the *marchandes de suifs et chandalles de Saint-Malo* [tallow and candle vendors].[97] They were concerned about the fines levied against women who sold more than ten *livres* of candles without permission from the police, on the grounds that the police were rarely around to accept registration. In Nantes, the *poissonieres*, fish vendors, regularly filed complaints or wrote *memoires* in order to criticize police activity, request better market conditions, or settle differences with other merchants.[98]

This is not to suggest that women were always supportive of each other. The marketplace was in many ways the realm of women, and there was a clearly established hierarchy among these women. The *poissonieres* of Nantes were split into camps, and their "collective action" was often aimed at other fish vendors in disputes over territory and privileges. According to a *memoire* written in 1771, "In this business, there are mistresses and there are servants. The *dames compteuses* [accountants] have the right to command and the poor *revendeuses* [vendors] are forced to obey."[99] In a dispute between two *boulangeres* in the Halles of Rennes in 1715, witnesses among the other bakers clearly took sides. One side swore that Janne Rocher had started the fight by throwing old bread in Guillemette Robas's face; the others swore that Robas responded to a mere comment from Rocher by swinging a stick at her head.[100] And in 1716, six women who worked for the *lavandiere* [laundress] Michelle Tienrot got into a territorial dispute on the riverbanks where people spread their clothes to dry. Two local servants apparently took a prime spot to do their household linen and the professional laundresses beat them for it.[101]

In 1732 in Saint-Malo, a number of women shopkeepers petitioned the police to restrain the activities of all the *marchandes revendeuses de linge* [secondhand linens vendors] of the city. Led by Marie Sohier and representing "all the *marchandes* of jewelry, fine linens and drapery," especially those who held shops on the Rue des

---

95   AMN HIII 171 #4, 21 May 1772.

96   ADLA 2 E 3205, Table of *titres de famille*, 1 July 1712; ADIV C 4145, Capitation for Nantes, 1740.

97   ADIV C 1453.

98   AMN FF 135, police decision regarding market territory in 1750; AMN FF 136 two cases concerning foreign competition and abuses of distributors in 1771; ADLA C 318 undated *memoire* to *intendant* requesting improvements to fish market.

99   AMN FF 136 *Mémoire* to commissioners, no date.

100   ADIV 3 B 1446, 9 March 1715.

101   ADIV 3 B 1454, 22 February 1716.

Halles, the petitioners requested that something be done about the numerous street vendors who spread their wares in front of their open shops on market days: "Every Tuesday and Friday, they come to sell their linens, yarns and thread in front of our shops. . . impeding those who approach and making so much noise that one cannot converse with those who have come to do business. . .". When challenged, the street merchants allegedly became abusive. The shopkeepers asked that the police, and archers, if necessary, direct the vendors to a more agreeable location so that they all might do business in peace.[102]

The cases above illustrate that it was not uncommon to find women engaged in collective action against other women. The multilayered identities of real women do not necessarily leave room for what modern scholars would call "female solidarity." As much as early modern women may have had in common with one another, their actions were also dependent upon competing familial, economic, and local loyalties. The Saint-Malo shopkeepers in the example above had little sympathy for the street vendors, in spite of the fact that they all could be described as "female merchants" and no doubt had many of the same problems.

At the same time, there is no denying that women could be a resource for one another. Women were friends and roommates, coworkers, and neighbors. Women provided training for young girls and financial support for relatives, friends, and servants. The women in these examples were not just passing time together, but seeing each other through violence, sickness, and death. Whether through choice or circumstance, women were able to forge alliances with each other quite apart from their relationships with natal or marital families. Women who were widowed or married to men who left for long periods quite naturally created emotional ties that did not require the presence or participation of men.[103] Unmarried women who sought work or living quarters may have felt most comfortable approaching other women for help and business. Work-related contacts, religious activity, similar backgrounds, or similar problems—all these factors would have led easily to social interaction between women and the creation of support networks.

Women's relationships with men

Urban life gave women access to more than greater work opportunities and more elaborate relationships with one another. It also opened up the potential marriage market. In rural areas, women and men were more likely to get married, get married young, and marry someone known by, or even chosen by, their parents.[104] Marriages among the elite, either landed gentry or wealthy bourgeois, were equally likely to involve a parental arrangement between a young woman and a much older man. For artisans and working class women, cities offered some independence, as well

---

102   ADIV 4 BX 1156, letter to judges, January 1732.

103   "Georg'ann Cattelona Responds to Elinor Accampo" forum on Women, Social Relations and Urban Life, *French Historical Studies* 18:1 (Spring 1993): 61.

104   Martine Segalen, *Fifteen Generations of Bretons: Kinship and Society in Lower Brittany, 1720–1980* (Cambridge: Cambridge University Press, 1991), p. 48.

as greater choice in marriage partners, including the choice not to marry at all.[105] Of course, relations between women and men have never been restricted to holy matrimony. In this regard, the social patterns in Brittany are comparable to those in other parts of France in the early modern era. The large and diverse population of a city increased the opportunities for casual interaction between the sexes, leading to simple familiarity and, on occasion, to sexual liaisons. While illicit sexual relationships in the countryside usually involved servants and their employers, urban dalliances seem to have occurred most often between "coworkers"—domestics with each other, weavers with spinners, tailors with *tailleuses*, and so forth.[106] Whatever their nature, relationships grew out of everyday contact.

It would be wrong to paint too rosy a picture of independent life for women in the early modern period. Often, the only historical evidence of sexual activity is found in records concerning illegitimate pregnancies and abandoned or killed infants. Many of these cases involved relationships in which the female partner was at a clear disadvantage. As in most rural areas, the majority of cases recorded in the *declarations de grossesse* for the barony of Chateaubriant were servants.[107] Most women claimed to have given in to their masters or their masters' sons under the promise of marriage, more so than any threat of violence. But their abandonment during pregnancy, and the effort they expended getting the expectant fathers to pay for their care, eloquently reveals their delicate position. Women in the cities were just as vulnerable to seduction and outright rape. Mathurine Ineut, described as "une pauvre fille imbecile," lived with her uncle in Rennes in 1702. She collected twigs for a living. Her neighbor, a court lawyer named Esqu. Le Gousles, pushed himself on her several times. The record only indicates he was informed of his responsibility to pay the midwife.[108] Marguerite Inglot, a servant at the home of the Procurer in Rennes, was raped repeatedly by her master's son, who took the key to her bedroom from the kitchen.[109]

Most "declarations," however, do not involve cases of force but of promises; a balanced view of seduction must take into account the negotiations that led up to the woman's consent. Janne Huguarel, the widow of Claude Robert, was impregnated at the *L'icon d'or* tavern by Julien Le Coq Breston after he had promised to marry her

---

105   Goldberg, *Women, Work, and Life Cycle*, p. 259; Pamela Sharpe, "Literally Spinsters: A New Interpretation of Local Economy and Demography in Colyton in the Seventeenth and Eighteenth Centuries," *European History Review* 44 (1991): 46-65. Given a favorable economy, Goldberg and Sharpe suggest, many women could have remained unmarried out of choice and not out of lack of opportunity, as has been suggested in the past.

106   Based on illegitimate pregnancies: Lebrun, *La vie conjugale*, pp. 98–9; Jacques Depauw, "Illicit Sexual Activity and Society in Eighteenth-Century Nantes," *Family and Society: Selections from the Annales, Economies, Sociétiés, Civilisations* (Baltimore: Johns Hopkins University Press, 1976), p. 146.

107   ADLA 2 mi 583 B 13096, 1743–1778. "Declarations de grossesse" were recorded in all parishes in an effort to prevent abandonment or murder of unwanted babies. Expectant mothers were expected to provide the name of the baby's father and the circumstances of conception.

108   AMR 415/2, 5 December 1702.

109   AMR 415/1, 22 February 1731.

and advance her 60 *livres* for her "commerce."[110] Janne Bourgeau dite La Bellegarde, a bleacher new to Rennes, was pregnant by the master wigmaker who owned her building and had promised to pay her rent.[111] In cases of clear social inequality, in which marriage was unlikely, promises were usually financial in nature. Janne Barber, a 20-year-old *lingere*, was promised a "pension" by Sieur Abbe Chotard; 24-year-old dye-worker Françoise Malarde was promised "100 *ecus* to to start up a cabaret" by Sieur Guerentonnet.[112]   But by far, the most frequent promise was marriage. Julienne Beauge, a *bouchere* [butcher] who lived with her aunt, frequently went out with Pierre Andre. They met because he delivered herbs to her kitchen, and he had promised to marry her someday.[113]   Gabrielle Ferriniere had lost her lover, Jean Franco, a carpenter's apprentice, when he left for the Americas and died during the voyage. He had promised to send for her when he had established himself.[114] Georgine Bourné, a worker in the yarn mills [*moulins à fil*], used to meet her partner, a tailor's apprentice named Dufrene, in the fields near a church. He had promised to marry her.[115]

It is possible that many of these promises were never offered, and the women were just trying to protect themselves. Honor might have yet been preserved if matrimony was expected. But there were also several cases in which women made no mention of promises. Janne Miennette, a *cordonniere* [rope maker] who lived with her sisters, spent time with a *cordonnier* named François Nigor. She swore he had given her no gifts and had made no promises, but that she went to him twice at his apartment and let him into hers once when her sisters were away.[116] Jaquette Chale, a servant, had no explanation for why she had given in to the pastry chef, Jan Le Chaud, except that he rented a room in the same building that she did.[117] Thus, just as it would be wrong to suggest that independent women led easy lives, it would be wrong to suggest that all these women were victims. Premarital sex was hardly tolerated, but neither was it unheard of, and none of the testimony in these cases suggests concern on the part of the women over their loss of virtue. Ironically, a voluntary *declaration de grossesse* put women in control of the situation and headed off accusations of *mauvaise vie*. None of the women who came forward on their own seems to have been confined or punished for doing so.

An unmarried woman was required by law to name the father of her child, lest the baby become a burden on society. The pressure undoubtedly led some women and the midwives who cared for them to lie. In Nantes in 1729, the rector of Saint Similian parish wrote a letter to the police secretary. The widow Durand, in hard labor and confined to a bed, had confessed that she had made a false declaration. The father of her child was Francois Bretonniere, a brother of the church, and not

---

110   ADLA 2 mi 582 B 13096, 25 January 1749.
111   AMR 415/1, 3 June 1732.
112   ADIV 3 B 1447, 9 January and 24 April 1716.
113   AMR 415/1, 3 January1730.
114   AMN GG 747, 27 April 1726.
115   AMR 415/1, 19 September 1729.
116   AMR 415/1, 19 December 1729.
117   AMR 415/1, 20 August 1731.

Jean Egereau, as she had originally reported. Facing a difficult labor that she might not survive, Durand had wanted to confess and clear Egereau of responsibility. The rector named himself and "Mlle Bonnami, the wife of a ship's captain" as witnesses to this new declaration, and invited the officer to come interrogate the woman himself as she could not go out.[118]

In spite of the pressure to conform to a certain kind of sociability, one limited to the making of honorable families, it is clear that women were frequently in contact with men in a variety of settings. There was more to male-female relations than the above tales of seduction might suggest. *Veilliées* were nighttime gatherings in the countryside, where men passed the time with songs and storytelling while women spun and sewed. These were an easy companion to the spinning bees at which women competed against one another and sometimes attracted a male audience.[119] Taverns, most often considered a masculine reserve, attracted female customers who mingled with friends and neighbors. Not surprisingly, authorities kept a careful watch on all of these venues, and other mixed-sex gatherings, because of the obvious temptations inherent in free association. Gatherings of men were not subject to the same scrutiny, or at least not the same kind of scrutiny. Disorderly men had the potential for violence, so groups such as *compagnonnages* were watched for signs of uprising.[120] Disorderly women were sexual deviants, breaking up marriages, challenging the natural hierarchy of the home, and having illegitimate children who became a burden on society. Thus, in theory, the preservation of order and honor required that all women's social activity be monitored. Men might be welcomed at spinning bees, but women who attended men's fêtes or spent too much time at taverns were frowned upon.[121] Regardless of these inhibiting factors, however, men and women could socialize freely enough. According to Yves Castan, men in southern France during this period reported casual, even racy, conversations with women as part of village interaction.[122]

There may have been room for platonic friendships between men and women as neighbors or coworkers, but sources reveal very little about such relationships. It is clear, however, that mixed-sex gatherings and everyday business offered the kind of socializing that could lead to marriage. Just as so many of the reported cases of illegitimate pregnancies concerned couples who were "coworkers," many marriages took place between people who knew each other from work or who shared a certain status and work environment. Thus, a laundress might meet a dockhand, not because

---

118   AMN GG 747, 29 June 1729.

119   Jane Schneider, "Rumpelstiltskin's Bargain," p. 193. Spinning bees and other female competitions are commonly understood to have served only to attract potential husbands. While this is a likely element of the games, I believe they functioned primarily as a way for women to socialize with each other.

120   Cynthia Truant, *Rites of Labor: Brotherhoods of Compagnonnage in Old and New Regime France* (Ithaca: Cornell University Press, 1994) and William Sewell, *Work and Revolution in France: The Language of Labor from the Old Regime to 1848* (Cambridge: Cambridge University Press, 1980).

121   Anne Fillon, "Frequentation, amour, mariage au XVIIIe siècle dans les villages du Sud du Maine," *Annales de Bretagne* 93/1 (1986): 50.

122   Castan, p. 168.

they did the same work, but because they both worked on the piers. Servants met and married other servants but also formed relationships with porters who made regular deliveries. In 1755, Anne Sues, a *tailleuse journaliere*, met and married Jean L'hermit, a *garçon* ferryman, after moving to his neighborhood near the Chapelle de Bonticour in Nantes.[123] Sometimes the marriage of one sibling into a new circle created the contacts that led to subsequent marriages, as when a girl was hired by her newlywed sister to work as a servant in an *auberge* and ended up married to the second son of the host.[124] Such family contacts might also have been responsible for the marriage of Françoise Perrine Rubot, a *couturiere* in Saint-Malo to Nicolas Thomas Sebire, a ship's officer: their witnesses were the bride's older sister and her husband, also a *tailleuse* and a ship's officer.[125]

Social status and wealth were important determining factors in these matches. As noted at the beginning of this section, the daughters of wealthy merchants, landed gentry, and military officers were most likely to marry into families equal to their own. There was often a greater age disparity between elite brides and grooms, with the bride being younger, and the bride's status was indicated by her father's title rather than by her own occupation, if she had one. By contrast, the laboring classes always noted both the bride and groom's occupations in parish registers. These brides almost always had to earn enough on their own to start a household and so were likely to have an occupation, marry later, and choose a mate without even citing a parent as witness to the ceremony. Once again, it would surprise no one that poorer people had to combine incomes in order to survive, and that the two-income households of the poor are no great find. But I find that this marriage pattern exists even among artisans and shopkeepers in Brittany. Among these middling sorts, it was not unusual to find a merchant or tradeswoman, literate and in possession of guild membership, married to a lawyer or craftsman.[126] Thus, while elite marriages seem to have served as financial alliances between families, matches among poor and middling classes seem more likely to have emerged from some kind of social contact. This observation is not a new one, but it bears repeating so as to emphasize the relationship between women's sociability and marriage.

As noted in Chapter One, there is a certain amount of correspondence between the occupations of spouses in reported two-income households. In Rennes in 1739, for example, 26 per cent of men and 20 per cent of women who sold cloth and clothing were married to spouses who also sold cloth or clothing. However, in that same year, 33 per cent of male cloth and clothing merchants were married to women who worked as general laborers, carrying water or delivering bread.[127] In these cases, it is probably not the work itself that dictated the social contact but some other context, such as the neighborhood. For the cities of Brest in 1740 and Morlaix in

---

123   ADLA 4 E/2 70, 1 February 1755. Marriage contract, Notaire Auffray.

124   Fillon, "Frequentation, amour, et mariage," p. 53.

125   ADIV 5 mi 1301 R 738, marriage acts in Saint-Malo, 1739.

126   This thesis is part of a work in progress and based upon patterns in the marriage acts of Saint-Malo (ADIV 5 mi 1301 R 737–50) and several parishes in Rennes (AMR GG 2 mi 1–120).

127   ADLA B 3560 *Capitation* tax roll.

1739, most two-income households were headed by men who worked on ships or distant farms, belonged to a military unit, or had no recorded occupation of their own.[128] In these situations, it is clear that the wife's occupation, usually in retail or food sales, was necessitated by the husband's absence or poor income. There is no way to tell how or where the couple met, but again, their contact seems to have had little relation to their occupations. These cities were large enough to have offered the freedom from small town restrictions and parental control, as well as a variety of social settings. Ironically, it is likely that the gathering places, both public and private, that so disturbed seventeenth- and eighteenth-century moralists were the very environments in which city dwellers were able to meet potential mates.

Conclusion

From the Middle Ages through the early modern period, some religious and municipal authorities believed that a woman's only proper social outlets were the members of her immediate family and household. According to the encyclopedist Desmahi, the definition of an "honest woman" was very clear:

> Her glory is to live in obscurity. Confined to the duties of wife and mother, she devotes her days to the practice of unheroic virtues: occupied with running her family, she rules her husband with indulgence, her children with gentleness, and her servants with kindness.[129]

There were efforts to limit women's sociability to fit that narrow definition. Some efforts were more successful than others. Though there were women who were punished for straying from the proscribed boundaries of home life, everyday life was much more varied than we have imagined. Non-"traditional" households did exist; women, as well as men, enjoyed a multitude of relationships in work, church, and neighborhood; and, a certain amount of illicit social and sexual contact appears to have been the norm. Scholars have too often accepted the prescribed view of women as the authentic one, or gone to another extreme and dismissed all evidence of patriarchal structure. A truer portrait encompasses both the structure and the fluidity of human society. In the village, household chores became a uniting activity, as when spinning, gathering water, or going to market became the contexts for female sociability. In larger cities, women sought each other out for support, for work, and for comfort. There is an undeniable and complex connection between women's working lives and their social lives. Just as the "wrong" social contact could lead to the destruction of a woman's home and livelihood, as when her honor was in doubt and she was perceived as a danger, the "right" social contact could establish her in an occupation, introduce her to potential marriage partners, and see her through sickness and poverty.

---

128   ADIV C4117, Brest *Capitation* roll of 1740; ADLA B 3631, Morlaix *Capitation* of 1739.

129   Quoted in Lieselotte Steinbrügge, *The Moral Sex: Women's Nature in the French Enlightenment*, trans. Pamela E. Selwyn (New York: Oxford University Press, 1995), p. 31.

Conclusion

A better understanding of women's lives in the past can only be achieved if we try to put aside our assumptions about women. The generalizations we have accumulated after decades of research undermine our efforts. The generalizations to which I refer include such concepts as "separate spheres," the family economy, and woman as "deputy husband." These ideas are part of the picture, to be sure, but they are not the entire picture. We need to look at what the sources have to offer and be open to surprises. Only then will we be able to see the variations of human experience within our models as well as the richness of what falls outside of our models.

The nature of women's work in early modern Brittany was as much a product of cultural ideals as it was a result of either reproductive necessity or patriarchal practices. A point of this project has been an attempt to consider the meaning of women's traditional occupations by exploring the work and life choices available to women in one economic region over the course of a century. It has long been noted that women tend to be found performing particular tasks, either with or without wages, and there have been many attempts to explain why that should be. Theories encompass women's natural capacities, the demands of family life, the dangers of unaccompanied travel, and the mandates of the typical male hierarchy. It is my belief that the explanation includes all of these elements but cannot in reality be accounted for by any single cause. Furthermore, any explanation would have to take into account women's tastes and choices, and their desire to be identified as both honorable and feminine.

Like most pre-modern societies, Brittany had its share of patriarchal institutions. In the words of the *Avocat General* of the king, in ordering the town of Auray to remove a widow from her husband's former post: "it is against all regulation and unheard of that a woman should serve as financial officer to the Hôtel Dieu because that is a function for which her sex renders her absolutely incapable."[1] Administrative, educational, and legal professions were absolutely closed to women, meaning that most sources of authority were male-dominated. And yet many formal market organizations were surprisingly open to women. Guilds in most Breton cities admitted women via family connections or for a set payment, albeit while limiting their activities within the corporation. Certain guilds, notably those in Rennes, Brest, and Quimper, admitted women as full members and respected their membership regardless of marital status. Furthermore, women had an authority and a presence in the streets and markets that was, at times, recognized by authorities in need of aid or information. Additionally, law codes and customs in Brittany assured women a certain access to resources and a right to justice. Through inheritance and manipulation of marital community, a woman was able to exploit property to her own ends. In the face of patriarchy, the *bretonne* was disadvantaged, certainly, but not helpless.

---

1   ADIV 1 BF 1224, remonstrance of 6 August 1720.

Religious sensibilities and traditional mores are difficult to define, but they clearly exert a powerful influence on behavior and on women's choices regarding work, domestic life, and friendship in the early modern era. A sense of honor, specifically women's sexual honor, was an ever-present guide for women in their contacts with men and with each other. Over the course of the period under examination, roughly the mid-seventeenth to the late eighteenth centuries, women's sexual honor took on a greater importance in the ongoing struggle to maintain religious and social order. The diabolical nighttime gatherings of the sixteenth century became the frivolous and flirtatious spinning bees of the eighteenth. The chivalric laws designed to protect women from sexual predators and abusive masters were modified in later years, as the weaker sex became less of a victim and more of a willing accomplice in sin. Since the mere suggestion of scandal could threaten a woman's livelihood, women were well advised to avoid even the appearance of illicit conduct. Thus, just as a woman might think twice before entering a tavern full of sailors, as much for safety's sake as for the impression it might make to her neighbors, perhaps she would refrain from pursuing obviously masculine groups and trades.

Numerous Breton women were able not only to survive, but also to prosper, in spite of multiple disadvantages and limitations. It therefore makes sense to take another look at our assumptions about women's agency and identity in the face of cultural structures that seemed set against them. Breton women did conform to the patterns revealed in other studies of women in terms of the trades they represented and their overall economic and legal vulnerability. However, Breton women also offer a contrast to women elsewhere in Europe in the eighteenth century. They enjoyed a relatively favorable access to family resources as well as the right to operate in the market. Perhaps, then, Brittany is a special case that can have little impact on general conclusions about women in Europe during this time period. And yet, a closer look at other regions and cultures might reveal a similar range of opportunities.

By the eighteenth century, ideas about the natures of women and men were firmly entrenched: "Woman is fragile like a reed and weak like a bit of flax." This proverb was recorded in mid-century in a French-Breton dictionary.[2] Such distinctions extended even to the fiber that peasants worked with. In 1731, an agent in Vitré wrote to the *intendant* that there were two kinds of hemp fiber, according to spinners, "female hemp, which is softer, more fine and easier to work with than the male fiber, which is thick, coarse, and harder to handle."[3] These definitions of masculine and feminine no doubt had an influence on what was deemed appropriate for men and for women. Sewing, for example, was considered a feminine occupation, and the only rural men who sewed were those who could not or would not work in the fields. Thus, Breton peasants liked to joke that it was fitting that the tailors' fête was celebrated on the day of the trinity, since it took three tailors to make a real man.[4]

---

2   *Dictionnaire Français-Breton ou Français-Celtique du dialecte de Vannes* (Leide, 1744), p. 163. It continues, "Let man confess, in good faith, that he is more wicked than she."

3   ADIV C 6195, letter of 23 August 1731.

4   Paul-Yves Sébillot, *La Bretagne et ses traditions* (Maisonneuve et Larose, 1968), p. 88.

Such symbolic associations, when compounded with a narrow and strictly enforced code of honor, would have been very powerful indeed. And yet, under the right circumstances, even a bit of soft, fine fiber revealed an inherent strength without which those Breton sails could not have powered France's ships.

Bibliography

Archival sources

Archives départementales d'Ille-et-Vilaine, Rennes (ADIV)
  Series 2 B 1801–15 Audiences and Sentences
  Series 3 B 1426–54 Police of Rennes
  Series 4 BX 1068–158 Police of Saint-Malo
  Series C 1286–4145 Intendancy
  Sous-series 2 E Family papers, various
  Sous-series 4 F C 3 Correspondence of Mme Duhoux-Desages, 1702–46
  Sous-series 4 E Notaries, various
  Sous-series 5 E 18–28 Corporations of Rennes
  5 mi 1301 reels 737–41 Marriage Acts of Saint-Malo
Archives municipales de Rennes (AMR)
  Liasses 190–99 Merchants and artisans of Rennes
  Liasses 305–16 Religious Houses of Rennes
  Liasses 360–418 Police of Rennes
  Fonds Privés 7 Z 1–8 Poorhouse of Rennes
  Fonds Privés 11 Z 1–194 Mercers of Rennes
Archives départementales de la Loire-Atlantique, Nantes (ADLA)
  Series B 3502–639 Capitation Rolls
  Series C 12–661/1 Commerce and Industry
  Series D 22 Charitable Schools
  Sous-series 5 E Corporations of Nantes
  Sous-series 4 E Notaries, various
  H depot 749–60 Prison at Nantes
  2 mi reels 582-583 B 13096 *Declarations de Grossesse*, Chateaubriand
Archives municipales de Nantes (AMN)
  Series FF 60, 135–6, 253–72 Police of Nantes
  Series GG *Declarations de Grossesse*, Nantes.
  Series HH 35–175 Corporations of Nantes
Archives départementales du Finisterre, Quimper (ADF)
  Series 1 C 35 and 36 Toile Bureau of Locronon
  Sous-series 2 E 1501–20 Corporations and Communities
  Sous-series 49 J 613–824 Police and Criminal Procedures in Quimper
Archives départementales du Côte d'Armor, Saint Brieuc (ADCA)
  Series B 3736–8 Cloth bureau at Quintin

Printed Primary Sources

Barbauld, Anna Letitia, *Memoirs, Letters and a Selection of Poems* (Boston: Osgood, 1874).

Boislisle, A.M. (ed.), *Correspondance des Contrôleurs Généreaux des Finances avec les Intendants des Provinces* (Paris, 1883).

Bouet, M. Alexandre, *Galerie Bretonne: Vie des Bretons de l'armorique* (Paris: Isidore Pesron, 1838).

Corps d'observations de la société d'agriculture, de commerce et des arts, établie par les États de Bretagne (Rennes, 1760).

Coutume de Bretagne et usances particulieres de quelques villes et territoires de la même province (Nantes, 1725).

Coutume Génerale Reforme des Pais et Duché de Bretagne (Rennes, 1693).

Coutumes Generales du pays ey duche de Bretagne, en 1580, reformées et rediges (Nantes, 1656).

Dictionnaire François-Breton ou François-Celtique du dialecte de Vannes, enrichi de themes (Leide, 1744).

Hévin, Pierre, *Consultations et observations sur la coutume de Bretagne* (Rennes, 1734).

Le Peletier, Dom Louis, *Dictionnaire de la langue Bretonne ou l'on voit son antiquité* (Paris, 1752).

Lemaître, Alain J. (ed.), *La Misère dans l'abondance en Bretagne au XVIIIe siècle: Le mémoire de l'intendant Jean-Baptise des Gallois de la Tour (1733)* (Société d'histoire et d'archéologie de Bretagne, 1999).

Moi, Claude Bordeaux. . . journal d'un bourgeois de Rennes au 17e siècle (Rennes, 1992).

Ordonnances synodales du diocese de Vannes publiées dans le synode général, tenu à Vannes le 22 septembre 1693 (Vannes, 1695).

Ordonnances synodales du diocese de Saint-Malo, renouvellées et confirmés dans le synode de l'annee 1769 (Saint-Malo, 1769).

Poullain du Parc, A.M., *La coutume et la jurisprudence coutumiere de Bretagne dans leur ordre naturel* (Rennes, 1759).

Sauvageau, Michel, *Coutume de Bretagne. Nouvelle édition, augmentée considerablement* (Rennes, 1742).

————,*Tres ancienne coutume de Bretagne* (Nantes, 1710).

Statuts et reglemens des corps d'arts (Nantes, 1723).

Statuts et ordonnances de monseigneur l'illustrissime et reverendissime messire Jean Louis Bebouschet de Souches, evêque et comte de Dol (Rennes, 1741).

Secondary Works

Abreu-Ferreira, Darlene, "Fishmongers and Shipowners: Women in Maritime Communities of Early Modern Portugal," *Sixteenth Century Journal*, 31:1 (Spring 2000): 7–23.

Aston, Trevor, *The Brenner Debate: Agrarian Class Structure and Economic Development in Pre-Industrial Europe* (New York: Cambridge University Press, 1985).

Badinter, Elisabeth, *L'amour en plus: Histoire de l'amour maternal (XVIIe-XXe siècles)* (Paris: Flammarion, 1980).

Baernstein, P. Renee, "In Widow's Habit: Women between Convent and Family in Sixteenth-Century Milan," *Sixteenth Century Journal*, 25:4 (Winter 1994): 787–807.

Barber, Elizabeth Wayland, *Women's Work: The First 20,000 Years* (New York: W.W. Norton & Co., 1994).

Barron, Caroline, "The 'Golden Age' of Women in Medieval London," *Reading Medieval Studies*, 15 (1990).

Benadusi, Giovanna, "Investing the Riches of the Poor: Servant Women and Their Last Wills," *American Historical Review*, 109:3 (June 2004): 805–26.

Bennett, Judith, *Ale, Beer, and Brewsters in England: Women's Work in a Changing World, 1300–1600* (Oxford: Oxford University Press, 1996).

———, "Misogyny, popular culture, and women's work," *History Workshop Journal*, 31 (1991): 166–88.

———, "Women's History, a Study in Continuity and Change," in Pamela Sharpe, (ed.), *Women's Work: The English Experience, 1650–1914* (London: Edward Arnold, 1998).

Bennett, Judith and Froide, Amy M., "A Singular Past," *Singlewomen in the European Past 1250–1800* (Philadelphia: University of Pennsylvania Press, 1999).

Berg, Maxine, *The Age of Manufacture, 1700–1820* (New York: Oxford University Press, 1986).

———, "What Difference Did Women's Work Make to the Industrial Revolution?" *Historical Workshop Journal*, 35 (Spring 1993): 22–44.

———, "Women's Work, Mechanisation and Early Phases of Industry in England," in Patrick Joyce (ed.), *The Historical Meanings of Work* (Cambridge: Cambridge University Press, 1987).

Bideau, Alain, "La mort quantifiée," *Histoire de la population française: tome 2, de la Renaissance à 1789* (Paris: Presses Universitaires de France, 1988).

Bluche, François and Solnon, Jean-François, *La véritable hiérarchies sociale de l'ancienne France* (Geneva: Librairie Droz, 1983).

Bossenga, Gail, "Protecting Merchants: Guilds and Commercial Capitalism in Eighteenth-Century France," *French Historical Studies*, 15 (Fall 1988): 693–703.

Brejon de Lavergnee, Jacques, "Structures sociales et familiales dans la très ancienne coutume de Bretagne," *107e Congrés National des Savantes* (Brest: 1982).

Brekilien, Yann, *Les paysans bretons au XIXe siècle* (Paris: Hachette, 1966).

Briggs, Robin, *Witches and Neighbors: The Social and Cultural Context of European Witchcraft* (New York: Penguin Books, 1996).

Brown, Judith, "Note on the Division of Labor by Sex," *American Anthropologist*, 72 (1970): 1075–6.

———, "A Woman's Place Was in the Home: Women's work in Renaissance Tuscany', in M. Ferguson, M. Quilligan, and N. Vickers (eds), *Rewriting the Renaissance: The Discourses of Sexual Difference in Early Modern Europe* (Chicago: University of Chicago Press, 1986).

Brown, Kathleen M, "'A P[ar]cell of Murdering Bitches': Female Relationships in an Eighteenth-Century Slave-holding Household," in Susan Frye and Karen Robertson (eds), *Maids and Mistresses, Cousins and Queens: Women's Alliances in Early Modern England* (New York: Oxford University Press, 1999).

Bruzulier, Jean-Luc, "L'illégitimité et l'abandon à Vannes entre 1760 et 1789," *Annales de Bretagne,* 96:4 (1991): 397–405.

Cahn, Susan, *Industry of Devotion: The Transformation of Women's Work in England, 1500–1660* (New York: Columbia University Press, 1987).

Castan, Yves, *Honnêteté et relations sociales en Languedoc (1715–1780)* (Paris: Librairies Plon, 1974).

Cattelona, Georg'ann, "Control and Collaboration: The Role of Women in Regulating Female Sexual Behaviour in Early Modern Marseille," *French Historical Studies*, 18:1 (1993).

———"Georg'ann Cattelona Responds to Elinor Accampo" forum on Women, Social Relations and Urban Life, *French Historical Studies* 18:1 (Spring 1993): 61.

Cerutti, Simona, *La ville et les métiers: Naissance d'un langage corporatif, Turin, XVIIe-XVIIIe siècle* (Paris: Editions de l'école des hautes Études en Sciences Sociales, 1990).

Chappell, Carolyn Lougee, "'The Pains I Took to Save My/His Family': Escape Accounts by a Huguenot Mother and Daughter after the Revocation of the Edict of Nantes," *French Historical Studies,* 22:1 (Winter 1999): 1–64.

Chaunou, Amaury, "La religion souterraine à Saint-Malo en 1434," *Annales de Bretagne et les pays d'Ouest*, 102:2 (1995): 107–12.

Chojnacka, Monica, *Working Women of Early Modern Venice* (Baltimore: Johns Hopkins Press, 2000).

Clark, Alice, *The Working Life of Women in the 17th Century* (London: 1919).

Coffin, Judith G, "Gender and Guild Order: The Garment Trades in Eighteenth-Century Paris," *Journal of Economic History*, 54:4 (December 1994): 768–93.

———, *The Politics of Women's Work: The Paris Garment Trades, 1750–1915* (Princeton: Princeton University Press, 1996).

Collins, James, *Classes, Estates, and Order in Early Modern Brittany* (New York: Cambridge University Press, 1994).

———, "The Economic Role of Women in Seventeenth Century France," *French Historical Studies*, 16:2 (Fall 1989): 436–70.

———, *The State in Early Modern France* (Cambridge: Cambridge University Press, 1995).

Craig, Béatrice, "Les affaires, sont-elles affaires des femmes?" *Histoire Sociale/ Social History*, 34:67 (November 2001): 277–81.

———, "Patrons mauvais genre: femmes et enterprises à Tourcoing au XIXe siècle," *Histoire Sociale/Social History*, 34:67 (November 2001): 331–54.

———, "Women and the Family Business: The Case of Tourcoing in the Nineteenth century," Carleton Conference on the History of the Family, Ottawa, May 1997.

Crépin, Marie-Yvonne, "Violences conjugales en Bretagne: la répression de l'uxorocide au XVIIIe siècle," *Memoires de la société d'histoire et d'archeologie de Bretagne*, 73 (1995): 163–75.

Croix, Alain, *L' age d'or de la Bretagne, 1532–1675* (Rennes: Éditions Ouest-France, 1993).

——, *La Bretagne aux 16e et 17e siècles: La vie–La mort–La foi* (Paris: Maloine, 1981).

——, *Nantes et le pays nantais au xvie siècle: études demographiques* (Paris: J. Touzot, 1974).

Crowston, Clare Haru, *Fabricating Women: The Seamstresses of Old Regime France, 1675–1791* (Durham: Duke University Press, 2001).

Davis, Natalie Zemon, "Women in the Crafts in 16th Century Lyon," in Barbara Hanawalt (ed.), *Women and Work in Pre-industrial Europe* (Bloomington: Indiana University Press, 1986).

——, "Women on Top," *Society and Culture in Early Modern France* (Stanford: Stanford University Press, 1965).

Depauw, Jacques, "Illicit Sexual Activity and Society in Eighteenth Century Nantes," in Robert Forster and Orest Ranum (eds), *Family and Society: Selections from the Annales, Economies, Sociétés et Civilisations* (Baltimore: Johns Hopkins University Press, 1976).

——, "Immigration feminine, professions féminines et structures urbaines à Nantes au XVIIIe siècle," *Enquêtes et documents du Centre de recherches sur l'histoire de la France Atlantique*, 2 (1972): 37–60.

Desan, Suzanne, "'War between Brothers and Sisters': Inheritance Law and Gender Politics in Revolutionary France," *French Historical Studies*, 20:4 (Fall 1997): 602.

De Vries, Jan, "Between Purchasing Power and the World of Goods: Understanding the Household Economy in Early Modern Europe," in Pamela Sharpe (ed.), *Women's Work: The English Experience, 1650–1914* (London: Edward Arnold, 1998).

Diefendorf, Barbara B., "Women and Property in *ancien régime* France: Theory and Practice in Dauphin and Paris," in John Brewer and Susan Staves (eds), *Early Modern Conceptions of Property* (London: Routledge, 1995).

Doyle, William, *The Oxford History of the French Revolution* (New York: Oxford University Press, 1989

Dumont, Dora, "Women and Guilds in Bologna: The Ambiguities of 'Marginality'," *Radical History Review*, 70 (1998): 4–25.

Dupuy, A. "Les Epidemies en Bretagne au XVIIIe siècle: chapitre III, les médecins-l'administration," *Annales de Bretagne*, 2 (1886):195–7.

Erickson, Amy Louise, "Common Law versus Common Practice: The Use of Marriage Settlements in Early Modern England," *The Economic History Review*, New Series 43:1 (February 1990): 21–39.

Esmein, A., *Histoire de la Procédure Criminelle en France et spécialement de la Procédure Inquisitoire depuis le XIIIe siècle jusqu'à nos jours* (Frankfurt am Main: Verlag Sauer & Auvermann KG, 1969).

Fairchilds, Cissie, *Domestic Enemies: Servants and their Masters in Old Regime France* (Baltimore: Johns Hopkins University Press, 1984).

Farge, Arlette, *Fragile Lives: Violence, Power and Solidarity in Eighteenth-Century Paris*. Carol Shelton (trans.) (Cambridge, MA: Harvard University Press, 1993).

Farmer, Sharon "'It is not Good that [Wo]man Should Be Alone:' Elite Responses to Singlewomen in High Medieval Paris" in Judith M. Bennett and Amy M. Froide (eds), *Singlewomen in the European Past, 1250–1800* (Philadelphia: University of Pennsylvania Press, 1999), 82–95.

Farr, James, *Authority and Sexuality in Early Modern Burgundy (1550–1730)* (New York: Oxford University Press, 1995).

———, *Hands of Honor: Artisans and the World in Dijon, 1550–1650* (Ithaca: Cornell University Press, 1988).

Ferrieu, Xavier, "Les Vatar ou trois siècles d'imprimerie à Rennes," *Memoires de la société d'histoire et d'archeologie de Bretagne*, 62 (1985): 223–84.

Fillon, Anne, "Frequentation, amour, mariage au XVIIIe siècle dans les villages du Sud du Maine," *Annales de Bretagne*, 93:1 (1986): 45–76.

Forster, Robert, and Ranum, Orest (eds), *Family and Society: Selections from the Annales, Economies, Sociétés et Civilisations* (Baltimore: Johns Hopkins University Press, 1976).

Frain, E, *Moeurs et coutumes des Familles Bretons avant 1789* (Rennes: Librairie Plihon, 1883).

Frye, Susan and Robertson, Karen (eds), *Maids and Mistresses, Cousins and Queens: Women's Alliances in Early Modern England* (New York: Oxford University Press, 1999).

Gallet, Jean, *Seigneurs et paysans bretons du moyen age à la revolution* (Rennes: Éditions Ouest-France, 1992).

Garlan, Y. and Nières, C., *Les revoltes Bretonnes de 1675: papier timbre et bonnets rouge* (Paris: Éditions Sociales, 1975).

Gélis, Jacques, "L'accouchement au XVIIIe siècle: Pratiques traditionelles et contrôle médical," *Ethnologie Française*, 6: 3/4 (1976): 325–40.

Goldberg, P.J.P., "Women in Fifteenth-Century Town Life," in John A.F. Thomson (ed.), *Towns and Townspeople in the Fifteenth Century* (Wolfboro, N.H.: Alan Sutton, 1988).

———, *Women, Work and Life Cycle in a Medieval Economy: Women in York and Yorkshire, 1300–1520* (Oxford: Oxford University Press, 1992).

Gowing, Laura, *Domestic Dangers: Women, Words, and Sex in Early Modern London* (Oxford: Clarendon Press, 1996).

Gullickson, Gay, "The Sexual Division of Labor in Cottage Industry and Agriculture in the Pays de Caux," *French Historical Studies*, 12:2 (1981): 177–99.

Hafter, Daryl, "Female Masters in the Ribbon-Making Guild of Eighteenth-Century Rouen," *French Historical Studies*, 20:1 (Winter 1997).

———, "Gender Formation from a Working Class Viewpoint: Guildswomen in Eighteenth-Century Rouen," *Proceedings of the Annual Meeting of the Western Society for French History*, vol. 16 (1989).

———, "Women Who Wove in the Eighteenth-Century Silk Industry of Lyon', *European Women in Pre-industrial Crafts* (Bloomington: Indiana University Press, 1995).

Hanawalt, Barbara (ed.), *Women and Work in Pre-Industrial Europe* (Bloomington: Indiana University Press, 1986).

Hanley, Sarah, "Engendering the State: Family Formation and State Building in Early Modern France," *French Historical Studies*, 16:1 (Spring 1989): 4–27.

————, "Family and State in Early Modern France: The Marriage Pact," in Marilyn J. Boxer and Jean H. Quataert (eds), *Connecting Spheres: Women in the Western World, 1500 to the Present* (New York: 1987).

Hardwick, Julie, *The Practice of Patriarchy: Gender and Politics of Household Authority in Early Modern France* (Philadelphia: Pennsylvania State University Press, 1998)

————, "Seeking Separations: Gender, Marriages and Household Economies in Early Modern France," *French Historical Studies*, 21:1 (1998).

Henwood, Philippe, "Marie-Jacquette Pignot: une femme de marin à Saint-Malo au XVIIIe siècle," *Memoires de la société d'histoire et d'archeologie de Bretagne*, 71 (1998): 321–39.

Hill, Bridget, "Women's history: a study in change, continuity, or standing still?," in Pamela Sharpe (ed.), *Women's Work: The English Experience, 1650-1914* (London: Edward Arnold, 1998).

Hoffman, Philip, *Growth in a Traditional Society: The French Countryside 1450–1815* (Princeton: Princeton University Press, 1996).

Howell, Martha C., "Fixing Movables: Gifts by Testament in Late Medieval Douai," *Past and Present*, 150 (February 1996).

————, "Women, the Family Economy, and the Structures of Market Production in Citiesof Northern Europe During the Late Middle Ages," in Barbara Hanawalt (ed.)*Women and Work in Pre-Industrial Europe* (Bloomington: Indiana University Press, 1986).

————, *Women, Production, and Patriarchy in Late Medieval Cities* (Chicago: The University of Chicago Press, 1986).

Hufton, Olwen, *The Poor of Eighteenth-Century France, 1750–1789* (Oxford: Clarendon Press, 1974.)

————, *The Prospect Before Her: A History of Women in Western Europe, Volume 1, 1500–1800* (London: Harper Collins, 1995).

————, "Women Without Men: Widows and Spinsters in Britain and France in the Eighteenth Century," *Journal of Family History*, 9 (Winter 1984).

Hull, Isabel, *Sexuality, State and Civil Society in Germany, 1700–1815* (Ithaca: Cornell University Press, 1996).

Hunt, Margret, *The Middling Sort: Commerce, Gender and the Family in England, 1680––1780* (Berkeley: University of California Press, 1996).

————, "The Sapphic Strain: English Lesbians in the long Eighteenth Century," in Judith M. Bennett and Amy M. Froide (eds), *Singlewomen in the European Past, 1250–1800* (Philadelphia: University of Pennsylvania Press, 1999).

Jamont, G. "Étude sur le droit des gens mariés d'après les coutumes de Bretagne," Thèse de doctorat, Université de Paris, Faculté de droit (Paris: V. Geard & E. Briere, 1901).

Joyeux, Françoise, *Les corporations à Nantes au XVIIIe siècle*, Thèse de maître (University of Nantes, 1975).

Kaplan, Steven Laurence, *The Bakers of Paris and the Bread Question, 1700–1775* (Durham: Duke University Press, 1996).

Karras, Ruth Mazo, "Sex and the Singlewoman" in Judith M. Bennett and Amy M. Froide (eds), *Singlewomen in the European Past, 1250–1800* (Philadelphia: University of Pennsylvania Press, 1999).

Kelly, Joan, "Did Women Have a Renaissance?" in Renate Bridenthal and Claudia Koonz (eds), *Becoming Visible: Women in European History* (Boston: Houghton-Mifflin, 1997).

Kerbois, Jean-Yves, *Les apprenties Nantais au XVIIIe siècle*, Thèse de maitre (University of Nantes, 1975).

Kerhervé, Jean, "Un accouchement dramatique à la fin du moyen age," *Annales de Bretagne et du Pays d'Ouest* 89 (1982) 3:391–6.

Kerhervé, Jean, François Roudaut, and Jean Tanguy, *La Bretagne en 1665 d'après le rapport de Colbert de Croissy* (Brest: University of Brest, 1978).

Kowaleski, Maryanne and Judith M. Bennett, "Crafts, Guilds, and Women in the Middle Ages: Fifty Years after Marian K. Dale," *Signs*, 14:2 (Winter 1989): 474–501.

Landes, Joan, *Women and the Public Sphere in the Age of the French Revolution* (Ithaca: Cornell University Press, 1988).

Laurent, Jeanne, *Un monde rural en Bretagne au XVe siècle: La Quevaise* (Paris: Ecole Pratique des Hautes Etudes, 1972).

Lebrun, François, "Un charivari à Rennes au XVIIIe siècle," *Annales de Bretagne*, 93:1 (1986): 111–13.

——, "L'evolution de la population de Rennes au XVIIe siècle," *Annales de Bretagne*, 93 (1986): 249–55.

——, "Le mariage et la famille," *Histoire de la population française tome 2, de la Renaissance à 1789* (Paris: Presses Universitaires de France, 1988).

——, "La religion de l'evêque de Saint-Malo et de ses diocesains au début du XVIIe siècle à travers les statuts synodaux de 1619," *Colloques Internationaux du Centre National de la Recharche Scientifique* (Paris: 1977).

——, *La vie conjugale sous l'ancien régime* (Paris: Armand Colin, 1975).

LeMen, Gwenole, "Coutumes et croyances populaires dans trois dictionnaires bretons du début du XVIIIe siècle," *Memoires de la société d'histoire et d'archeologie de Bretagne*, 60 (1983): 69–100.

LeRoy, Florian, *Vieux métiers bretons* (Paris: 1944).

Le Roy Ladurie, Emmanuel, "A System of Customary Law: Family Structure and Inheritance Customs in 16th-Century France," *Family and Society* (Baltimore: Johns Hopkins University Press, 1976).

Lespagnol, André, "Femmes négociantes sous Louis XIV: Les conditions complexes d'une promotion provisoire," *Populations et cultures: études rèunies en l'honneur de François Lebrun* (Rennes: 1989).

——,*Messieurs de Saint-Malo: Une élite négociante au temps de Louis XIV* (Rennes: Presses Universitaires, 1997).

——, "Les Malouins: profil d'une bourgeosie marchande bretonne au XVIIIe siècle," *La Bretagne au XVIIIe Siècle* (Vannes: Conseil Général du Morbihan, 1991).

Lespagnol, André, (ed.), *Histoire de Saint-Malo et du pays malouin* (Toulouse: Privat, 1984).

Lévy, Andre, *Brest et les Brestois (1720–1789): Etude d'une croissance urbaine au XVIIIe siècle*, Thèse de doctorat, 3e cycle. (Université de Lille, 1986).

Liu, Tessie, "The Commercialization of Trousseau Work: Female Homeworkers in the French Lingerie Trade," in Daryl Hafter (ed.), *European Women in Pre-Industrial Crafts* (Bloomington: Indiana University Press, 1995).

———, *The Weaver's Knot: The Contradictions of Class Struggle and Family Solidarity in Western France, 1750–1914* (Ithaca, NY: Cornell University Press, 1994).

Loats, Carol, "Gender and Work in Sixteenth-Century Paris," Doctoral Dissertation (University of Colorado, Boulder, 1993).

———, "Gender, Guilds, and Work Identity: Perspectives from Sixteenth-Century Paris," *French Historical Studies*, 20:1 (Winter 1997).

Locklin, Nancy L., "Women in Early Modern Brittany: Rethinking Work and Identity in a Traditional Economy," Doctoral Dissertation (Emory University, 2000).

Maillard, Brigitte, "Les veuves dans la société rurale au XVIIIe siècle," *Annales de Bretagne et des pays de l'ouest*, 106 (1999): 211–30.

Martin, Gaston, *Nantes et le pays nantais au XVIIIe siècle: L'ere de négriers (1714–1774): D'après des documents inédits* (Paris: Librairie Felix Alcan, 1931).

Martin Saint-Leon, Etienne, *Histoire des corporations de metiers depuis leurs origines jusqu'à leur suppression en 1791* (Paris, 1922).

Maza, Sarah, *Private Lives and Public Affairs: The Causes Célèbres of Prerevolutionary France* (Berkeley: University of California Press, 1993).

———, *Servants and Masters in Eighteenth-Century France: The Uses of Loyalty* (Princeton: Princeton University Press, 1983).

Les Marchands drapiers de Nantes, XVe-XXe siècles (Nantes: Université Inter-Âges de Nantes, 1988).

Medick, Hans, "The Proto-Industrial Family Economy: The Structural Function of Household and Family During the Transition from Peasant Society to Industrial Capitalism," *Social History*, 3 (Oct. 1976): 291–315.

Minois, Georges, "Rupture de fiançaille et divorces dans le Trégor au XVIIIe siècle," *Memoires de la société d'histoire et d'archeologie de Bretagne*, 60 (1983): 125–41.

Moi, Claude Bordeaux. . .Journal d'un bourgeois de Rennes au XVIIe siècle, Bruno Isbled, (ed.) (Rennes: Éditions Apogée, 1992).

Morel, Marie-Christine, *Les femmes et la justice au milieu du XVIIIe siécle à Rennes (1751–1759)*, Memoire de Maîtrise d'Histoire (Université de Haute Bretagne, 1990–1991).

Niéres, Claude, *Les villes de Bretagne au XVIIIe siècle* (Rennes: Presses Universitaires de Rennes, 2004).

Nye, Robert A. *Masculinity and Male Codes of Honor in Modern France* (Berkeley: University of California Press, 1998).

Phillips, Roderick, "Women, Neighborhood, and Family in the Late Eighteenth Century" *French Historical Studies*, 18:1 (1993).

Pied, Edouard, *Les anciens corps d'arts* (Nantes, 1903).

Pinchbeck, Ivy, *Women Workers and the Industrial Revolution, 1750–1850* (London: Virago, 1981).

Poitrineau, Abel, *Ils travaillant la France: métiers et mentalités du XVIe au XIXe siècle* (Paris: Armand Cole, 1992).

Quataert, Jean H, "The Shaping of Women's Work in Manufacturing: Guilds, Households, and the State in Central Europe,1648–1870," *American Historical Review,* 90:5 (December 1985): 1122–48.

———, "Survival Strategies in a Saxon Textile District," in Daryl Hafter (ed.), *European Women in Pre-industrial Crafts* (Bloomington: Indiana University Press, 1995).

"Quimper: Étude de géographie urbaine," *Annales de Bretagne,* 54 (1947): 117–32.

Rébillon, Armand, *Les États de Bretagne, de 1661 á 1789* (Paris, 1932).

———, "Recherches sur les anciennes corporations, ouvriers, et marchands de la ville de Rennes," *Annales de Bretagne,* 18 (1903): 53–98.

Riet, Didier, "Accoucher seule dans l'ancienne France au XVIIIe siècle: motivations et conduites," *Annales de Bretagne et du Pays d'Ouest,* 98:1 (1991): 67.

———, "Les declarations de grossesse dans la région de Dinan à la fin de l'ancien régime," *Annales de Bretagne et des Pays de l'Ouest,* 88:2 (1981): 186.

Roche, Daniel, *The Culture of Clothing,* Jean Birrell (trans.) (New York: Cambridge University Press, 1994).

Rolland, Muriel, "Des femmes séduites face à la justice: le rapt de séduction en Bretagne aux XVIIe et XVIIIe siècles," *Memoires de la société d'histoire et d'archeologie de Bretagne,* 71 (1998): 247–320.

Roper, Lyndal, *The Holy Household: Women and Morals in Reformation Augsburg* (London: Clarendon Press, 1989).

Saint-Sauveur, E. Durtelle de, *Histoire de Bretagne des origines à nos jours,* vols 1 and 2 (Rennes: Librairie J. Plihon, 1936).

Schneider, Jane, "Rumpelstiltskin's Bargain: Folklore and the Merchant Capitalist Intensification of Linen Manufacture in Early Modern Europe," in Annette B. Weiner and Jane Schneider (eds), *Cloth and Human Experience* (Washington, DC: Smithsonian Institute Press, 1989).

Sébillot, Paul-Yves, *La Bretagne et ses traditions* (Paris: Maisonneuve et Larose, 1968; reprint, 1998).

Seé, Henri E., *Le commerce maritime de la Bretagne au xviiie siècle* (Paris, 1925).

Segalen, Martine, *Fifteen Generations of Bretons: Kinship and Society in Lower Brittany 1720–1980* (Cambridge: Cambridge University Press, 1991).

Sewell, William, *Work and Revolution in France: The Language of Labor from the Old Regime to 1848* (Cambridge: Cambridge University Press, 1980).

Sharpe, Pamela, "Gender in the Economy: Female Merchants and Family Businesses in the British Isles, 1600–1850," *Histoire Sociale/Social History,* 34:67 (November 2001): 283–306.

———, "Literally Spinsters: A New Interpretation of Local Economy and Demography in Colyton in the Seventeenth and Eighteenth Centuries," *European History Review,* 44 (1991): 46–65.

Shorter, Edward, "Illegitimacy, Sexual Revolution, and Social Change in Modern Europe," *Journal of Interdisciplinary History,* 2:2 (Autumn 1971): 251.

Sonenscher, Michael, *The Hatters of Eighteenth-Century France* (Berkeley: University of California Press, 1987).

———, "Mythical Work: Workshop Production and the Compagnonnages of Eighteenth-Century France," in Patrick Joyce (ed.), *The Historical Meanings of Work* (Cambridge: Cambridge University Press, 1987).

Steinbrügge, Lieselotte, *The Moral Sex: Women's Nature in the French Enlightenment*, Pamela E. Selwyn (trans.) (New York: Oxford University Press, 1995).

Stofft, Henri, "Utilisation de la langue bretonne pour la formation professionelle des sages-femmes au XVIIIe siècle," *Dalc'homp Sonj*, 9 (1984) 11–17.

Stone, Lawrence, *The Family, Sex and Marriage in England 1500–1800* (New York: Harper & Row, 1977).

Tanguy, Jean, *Le commerce du port de Nantes* (Paris, 1956).

———, "La production et le commerce des toiles 'Bretagnes' du XVIe au XVIIIe siècle: premiers résultats," *Actes du 91e Congrés National des Sociétés Savantes* (1966): 105–41.

———,*Quand la toile va: L'industrie toilière bretonne du 16e au 18e siècle* (Rennes: Éditions Apogée, 1995).

Truant, Cynthia, "The Guildswomen of Paris: Gender, Power, and Sociability in the Old Regime," *Proceedings of the Annual Meeting of the Western Society for French History*, vol. 15 (1988).

———, *Rites of Labor: Brotherhoods of Compagnonnage in Old and New RegimeFrance* (Ithaca: Cornell University Press, 1994).

Touchard, Henri, *Le commerce maritime de la Bretagne* (Paris: 1967).

Viardi, Liana, *The Land and the Loom: Peasants and Profit in Northern France, 1680–1800* (Durham: Duke University Press, 1993).

Vigarello, Georges, *Concepts of Cleanliness: Changing Attitudes in France since the Middle Ages*, Jean Birrell (trans.) (New York: Cambridge University Press, 1988).

Wack, Mary, "Women, Work and Plays in an English Medieval Town," in Susan Frye and Karen Robertson (eds), *Maids and Mistresses, Cousins and Queens: Women's Alliances in Early Modern England* (New York: Oxford University Press, 1999).

Wensky, Margaret, "Women's Guilds in Cologne in the Later Middle Ages," *Journal of European Economic Studies*, 11:3 (1982): 631–50.

Wiener, Annette, *Inalienable Possessions: The Paradox of Keeping-While-Giving* (Berkeley: University of California Press, 1992).

Wiesner, Merry, "Guilds, male bonding, and women's work in early modern Germany," *La Donna Nell'Economica, Sec. XIII-XVIII* (Florence: Le monnier, 1990).

———, "Having Her Own Smoke: Employment and Independence for Singlewomen in Germany, 1400–1750," in Judith M. Bennett and Amy M. Froide (eds), *Singlewomen in the European Past, 1250–1800* (Philadelphia: University of Pennsylvania Press, 1999).

———, "'A Learned Task and Given to Men Alone': The Gendering of Tasks in Early Modern German Cities," *Journal of Medieval and Renaissance Studies*, 25:1(Winter 1995): 89–106.

———, "Paltry Peddlers or Essential Merchants?," *Sixteenth Century Journal*, 12:2 (1981): 3–13.

———, "Spinning Out Capital: Women's Work in the Early Modern Economy," in Renate Bridenthal and Claudia Koonz (eds), *Becoming Visible: Women in European History* (Boston: Houghton-Mifflin, 1997).

Index

abortion 130, *see also* infanticide
adultery 93, 102, 105
age
    of majority 85
    and work 22, 38, 46, 76
Anquetil, Jaquette 7, 27, 37
apothecaries 60, 64
apprenticeship 22, 49
    contracts 28–9, 58
    for girls 28–9, 52
    via poor house 26–7
aubergistes, *see* innkeepers

bakers 62–3
Bennett, Judith 4–6, 16, 41
bequests 98, 100, 101, 103; *see also* wills
blanchisseuses 16; *see also* bleachers;
    laundresses
bleachers 16, 57, 73
Blois, *Ordonnance de* 104, 109
Brest 18, 20, 32, 42, 58, 60–64, 79, 143
Breton language 9
Brittany 8–10
    culture 9, 71, 77, 144
    customary law 8, 10, 52, 84, 91, 95, 96
    Jean I, Duke of 65
brodeuses 117; *see also* embroiderers
butchers 51, 63, 64, 72

candle makers 46, 61, 135
capitation tax rolls 14, 32, 34, 40, 42, 44–5,
    60, 63, 67, 73, 134
capitation des artisans 51–53, 57
carpenters 32–3, 48, 51
children
    abandonment of 24–6, 106
    care of 5, 22–4, 27–8, 46
    establishment of 30–31, 38, 48, 52, 81,
        102, 108
    illegitimate 24, 106, 137, 139
Chojnacka, Monica 2
clergy 14, 16
cloth; *see* textiles

clothing 5, 6, 15, 28, 42–4, 50, 53, 58, 65,
    68–9, 78–9, 140
coiffeuses (hairdressers) 51
collective action 46, 61, 135, 136
competition 3, 50, 60, 68, 129, 131, 135,
    139
contraband 50, 64–5, 134
convent 10, 27
    as punishment 92, 93, 102, 109, 132
cook 48, 117
corporations; *see* guilds
courts 53, 58–9, 85, 121–3, 128–9
couturières (seamstresses) 15, 49n, 51, 59,
    63, 76
Croix, Alain 2–3, 13n, 18n–19n, 38, 42
Crowston, Clare Haru 2, 7, 15n, 49n

debt 86–9, 95, 98; *see also* property
declarations de grossesse 106, 137–8
denunciation 116–17, 122, 130
Desages, Guillemette 30, 107–9
Dinan 19, 26, 42, 46, 73, 77
domaine congeable 9
domestic service, *see* servants
domestic skills 6, 30, 47, 48, 73
donations 94–6, 98, 100–101
dowry 8, 10, 42, 45, 86–7, 89, 90, 92, 95,
    102
drapers 6, 53, 56, 63, 65–7, 76, 135
dyers (*teinturiers*) 57, 76

education 22, 27–8, 48, 80, 132
embroiderers 34, 75, 119
England 2, 10, 24, 43, 133

"family economy" 7–8, 22, 71, 143
"family-state pact" 97, 111
fileuses 1, 16, 77, 123; *see also* spinners
fishwives (*poissonières*) 36, 46, 51, 70, 110,
    135
flax 19, 71, 77, 144
folklore 5, 131, 145
fouâge tax rolls 13–14, 16, 20
foundlings 24–6

DATE DUE

Demco, Inc. 38-293